The Amulet

The Amulet

My childhood and youth
as a nomad in Sudan

HAMID DIRAR

City *of* Words

Published 2022 by City of Words Ltd.
www.cityofwords.net

Text © Hamid Dirar 2003 and 2022
All rights reserved
Glossary, gazetteer & biographical notes © City of Words 2022

Edited by John Ryle
Design and typography by Lindsay Nash

Cover image: Camel rider in the Bayuda Desert © Alistair Taylor Young
Map and genealogical diagram by Jillian Luff / MAPgrafix © City of Words 2022

Print and digital copies of this book may be purchased from Amazon and other online retailers. Trade enquiries to sales@cityofwords.net

Editorial enquiries to editorial@cityofwords.net

A CIP record for this book is available from the British Library

ISBN 978-1-9160783-1-4

To the soul of Sheikh Annour Duman

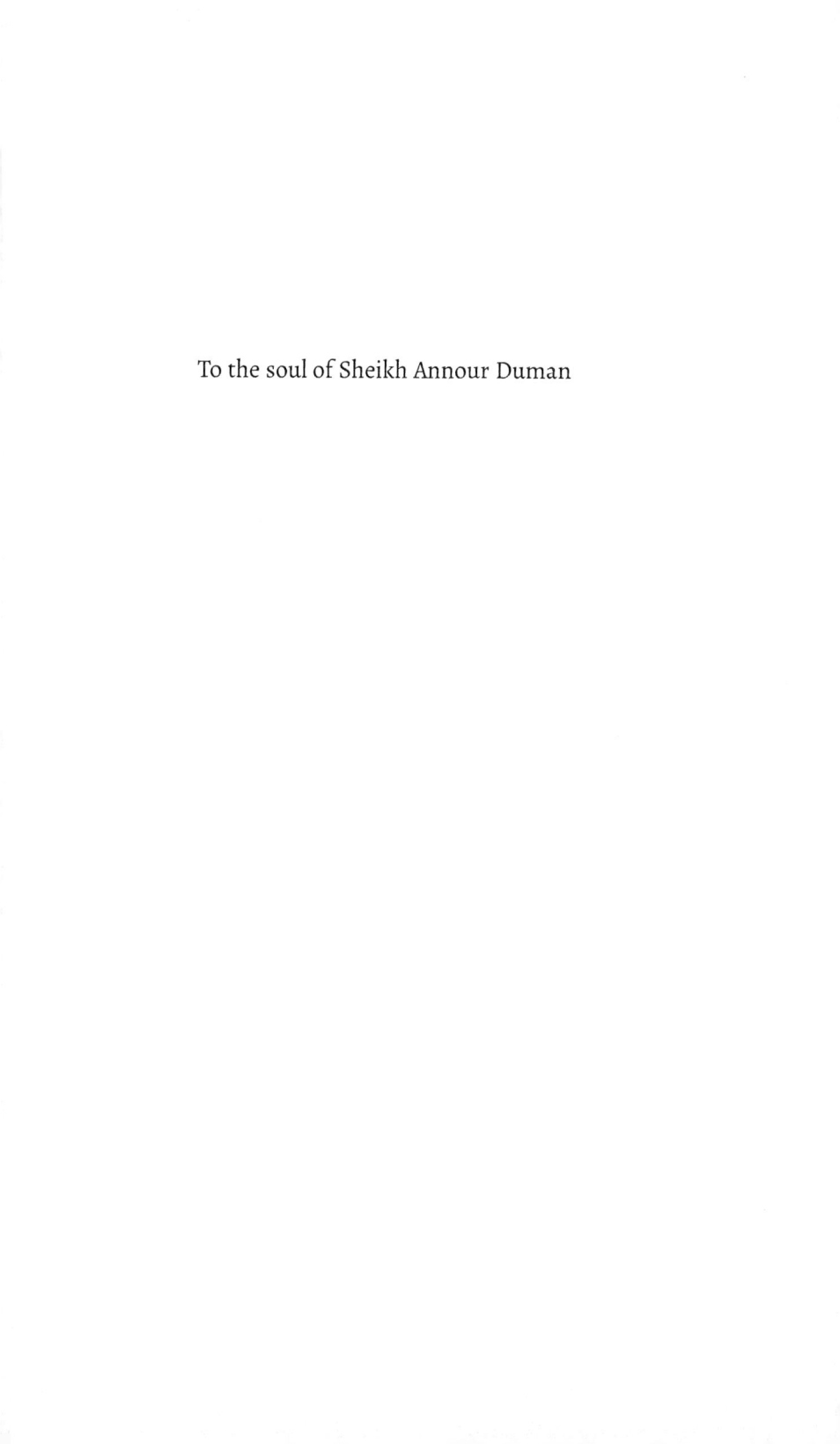

Contents

Map of Central and Eastern Sudan	13
Introduction	15
Acknowledgements	19
Publisher's note	21
Genealogy	22

BEGINNINGS

The Land of Rocks	27
A summons from Mek Nimir	29
The *mek* and the Turks	31
The Mahdists and the Jaaliyin	34
Duman and Diya	38
The death of Duman	41
A waterwheel	42
The funeral of Sheikh Umara Abu Sin	44
The meeting of Feki Umhummad wad Beshir and Feki Ahmed Dirar	46
Feki Umhummad cures Amna's sickness	50
A debt and a death	52
Amna and her suitor	54
Ahmed Dirar's courtship of Amna	56
The *feki*'s revenge	61
The fight of the two *feki*s	65
The last battle	70
Amna's child	75
The Amulet	80
The year of bombs	81
A child with two fathers	83

A blind baby and a rabid dog	85
A famine year	91
A brush with fire	97
A visit from Great-Aunt Medina	99
An acrimonious divorce	102
Childhood afflictions	105
A husband for Asha, a cure for Hamid	107
The death of Asha	111
Amna's new husband	113

CHILDHOOD

The world of warriors	117
My father's dark side	120
I meet my mother again	122
In the rainy season	125
On the move	129
A wedding feast	134
The lost bride	138
What's become of Hamid?	140
A bolt of cloth	141
The cutting	146
Drought	147
The songs of girls	150
A dangerous game and a close encounter	154
A dog dies	157
Lost in the forest	161
Asubri	162

SCHOOLDAYS

Going to school	165
Kidnapped from class	166
Losing Maigulu	168
A flash flood	170
A stolen child?	172

The Year of the Syndicate	174
The road to knowledge	176
Khashm el Girba	178
Limoun	181
Wrestling	185
The river forest	188
Ibrahim's armoury	189
The story of Zahin and Naji	192
A nomad wedding	195
The Blue Bridge Cafés	199
Atalmula and his sons	201
A fight to the death	203
The vast green land	205
The Blue Bridge at noon	208
In the tent of love	213
The interview	216
The Year of Rats	218
Initiation	221
My private parts	225
The shadow of slavery	227
Looking for my father	229
Speaking a new language	232
Problems at school	239
A change of fortune	243
A wrestling match	247
A circumcision party	248
My birth certificate	253
Smugglers	254
How Taha lost his forefinger	259
Sheikh Annour the peacemaker	260
Our private zoo	264
Hunting by moonlight	268
Back to school once more	270

A WIDER WORLD

A lorry journey to Kassala	277
By train to Port Sudan	285
The smell of the sea	287
The locust control campaign	290
The locusts' revenge	294
Change comes to Khashm el Girba	295
Khartoum in a time of revolution	297
A new kind of death	299
Glossary, gazetteer & biographical notes	307

Hamid Dirar

Hamid Dirar is the author of *The Indigenous Fermented Foods of the Sudan: A study in African food and nutrition* (1993) and numerous scientific papers. A biochemist, he has taught at universities in the United States and Northern Ireland. He lives in Khartoum.

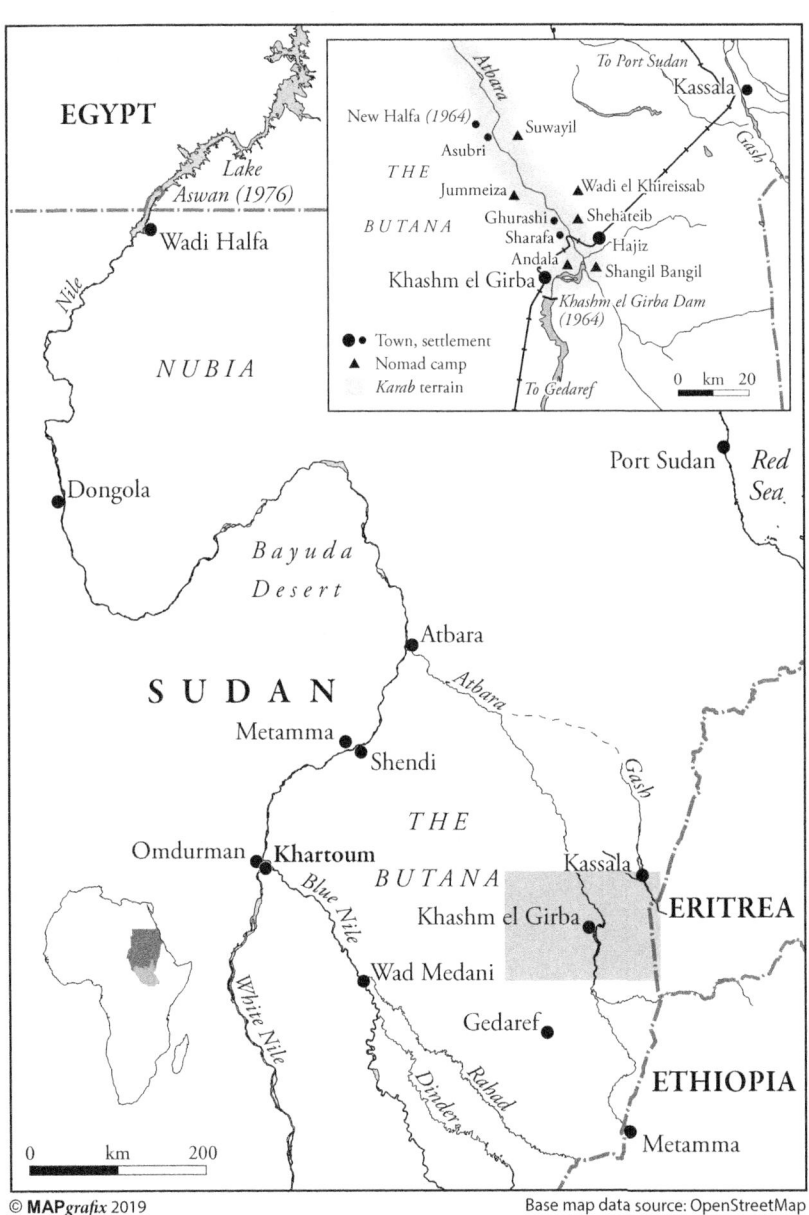

Central and Eastern Sudan

Introduction

I was born sometime in 1940 to a family of nomadic camel herders in Sudan. It was the year we called *Sanat el Ganabil*, the Year of Bombs. The longing for knowledge and understanding that I developed as a boy led me, ultimately, to a life of learning in academic institutions in Europe and America. But it was my early existence as a nomad, harsh and sweet by turns, that made me what I am.

A scar on my left cheek-bone, close to the eye, is all that is visible of the cuts and cudgel wounds I gained in my youth. Under my suit and tie and my laboratory overalls, however, that early life in distant nomad encampments is inscribed on every part of my body. There is the mark of a childhood fire burn on my left shoulder; the imprint of a dog's bite on my arm; a long scar left by the slash of a cutlass on my left leg; and all over my body scores of tiny therapeutic cuts and burns, intended to cure the illnesses of childhood. Growing up in such circumstances could be hard. Not all my contemporaries survived. But the rigours of my youth taught me strength, endurance and patience. And these qualities stood me well in my later journeys in pursuit of knowledge.

To understand a man, you first need to understand his forebears. So this story begins with my great-great-grandfather,

Dirar, the day he left our ancestral home in Nubia. Dirar's story and the other events described in the book are factual; I have reconstructed conversations based on accounts handed down from generation to generation by members of the lineages that converged to produce my brother and myself. Most of those in the book carry their real names; one or two of them have been changed, however. In some cases this is to protect the innocent; the main reason, however, is that so many people in the story have the same name: Muhammad. There are at least nine Muhammads in the story, so I have given some of them alternative names in order to avoid confusion.

I first started to write the book in Arabic, then began again and finished it in English. There remain in the text, however, a number of Arabic terms to which no English translation can do justice. And also some terms from Bedawiyet, or Beja, the language spoken by the Hadendowa people. An earlier version of the book was privately printed in 2003. The present edition, which has been entrusted for editing and publication to Christopher Kidner and John Ryle, is the final version.

Certain things have changed now in the places of my childhood. The dam on the Atbara River at Khashm el Girba, where I first went to school, has created a great reservoir stretching south towards Gedaref, and the agricultural settlement of New Halfa now spreads northwards along the western bank of the river. There is a highway that joins Gedaref to Khashm el Girba and proceeds northeast to Kassala and Port Sudan. Khashm el Girba itself has grown much larger, like other towns in the region. A new concrete bridge carries the road across the River Atbara.

From this point on the river, the last time I visited, you could still see the old Blue Bridge on the right. And beyond the Blue

INTRODUCTION

Bridge, on the east bank, Shangil Bangil, Mirmidayeb and the Timber Bridge – all places redolent of my childhood. Before the new concrete bridge, on the west bank of the Atbara, are other places inscribed in my memory from my early days in nomad encampments and settlements: Sharafa, Jummeiza, Asubri, and on the east bank, towards Eritrea, Wadi el Khireissab, Suwayil and Shehateib. Away from the river, the road now traverses the wasteland of the *karab*, the rough, undulating area that extends from the old eroded banks each side of the river. Then it comes to a flat tableland, and here, on the right hand, is the railway station, Hajiz, which was the site of my first encounter with people from the outside world.

All these places remain recognizable from the days of my youth; and, though the nomadic way of life is on the wane, some aspects of life there remain the same. But the terrain around them has changed drastically. This change is due above all to the destruction of the forests, both by human and natural forces, a process that is robbing so much of the world both of its biodiversity and its long-standing familiarity.

Acknowledgments

Many of the important people in my early life, including those from whom I learned the stories of my ancestors, were still living when I finished writing the first draft of this book in 2003: my mother Amna Duman, Fatima Dirar, Ketira, Ibrahim, *Khali* Ali, *Khalti* Zeinab, Zeena, Hajwa, Khalid Dirar, Beshir Dirar, Rahim, Daw, Hassan Jubar, Aunt Nofal and others. But many of them have died since then. And there are those who had already died. Sheikh Annour died in 1995, my father Ahmed Dirar in 1983, Omar Duman in 1987, Shawish Yousif in 1979, *Habbobti* Halima in 1992, Karim in 1986, Yaru in 1993, Khidir in 1982, Toma in 1989, Rajab in 1998, Zaki in 2002. May they all rest in peace.

Along the road of understanding I have come to know many other good and kind people. In the United States of America, I would particularly like to thank Roald Hoffmann, Nobel-winning chemist and poet, who encouraged me to publish my researches into fermented foodstuffs, published as *The Indigenous Fermented Foods of the Sudan* (1993), and Joshua Lederberg (1925-2008), another Nobel prize winner, who invited me to join the New York Academy of Sciences, though it is too late to thank him in this world. At Cornell, I was lucky also to meet Robert Mortlock and Keith Steinkraus and his wife Maxine, all now passed away. In Davis, California, I am grateful to have known Edwin Collins

THE AMULET

(1921-1991), Robert Hungate (1906-2004), Herman Phaff (1913-2001), Walter Jennings (1922-2012), Hans Riemann (1920-2007), Ralph Kunkee (1927-2012), John Ingraham and Mortimer Starr. This necklace of the good people who have encircled my life would not be complete without Martin Collins and David Harper of Queen's University, Belfast, in Northern Ireland.

The present book was written with all these people in mind, in Sudan and beyond; it is dedicated to those who are still alive, and to the memory of those who have passed away.

Publisher's note

An earlier version of *The Amulet* was privately printed in 2003. The present edition has been extensively revised and rewritten, with the author's agreement. The publisher is grateful to the following: Hamid Dirar's wife, Hanadi Annour; his friends and colleagues, Hassan Beshir Elamin and Ahmed Abu Sin; and Christopher Kidner, to whom Dr Dirar entrusted the text of *The Amulet* for editing and publication. Thanks also, for expert advice and practical assistance, to Mohaned Kaddam, John Hatt, Suliman Baldo, Eddie Thomas, Magdeldin el Gizouli, Andrew Harvey, Joanna Oyediran, Liz Jobey, Peter Fry, Nuruddin Farah, Caroline Walmsley and David Wolton.

Genealogy of Hamid Dirar

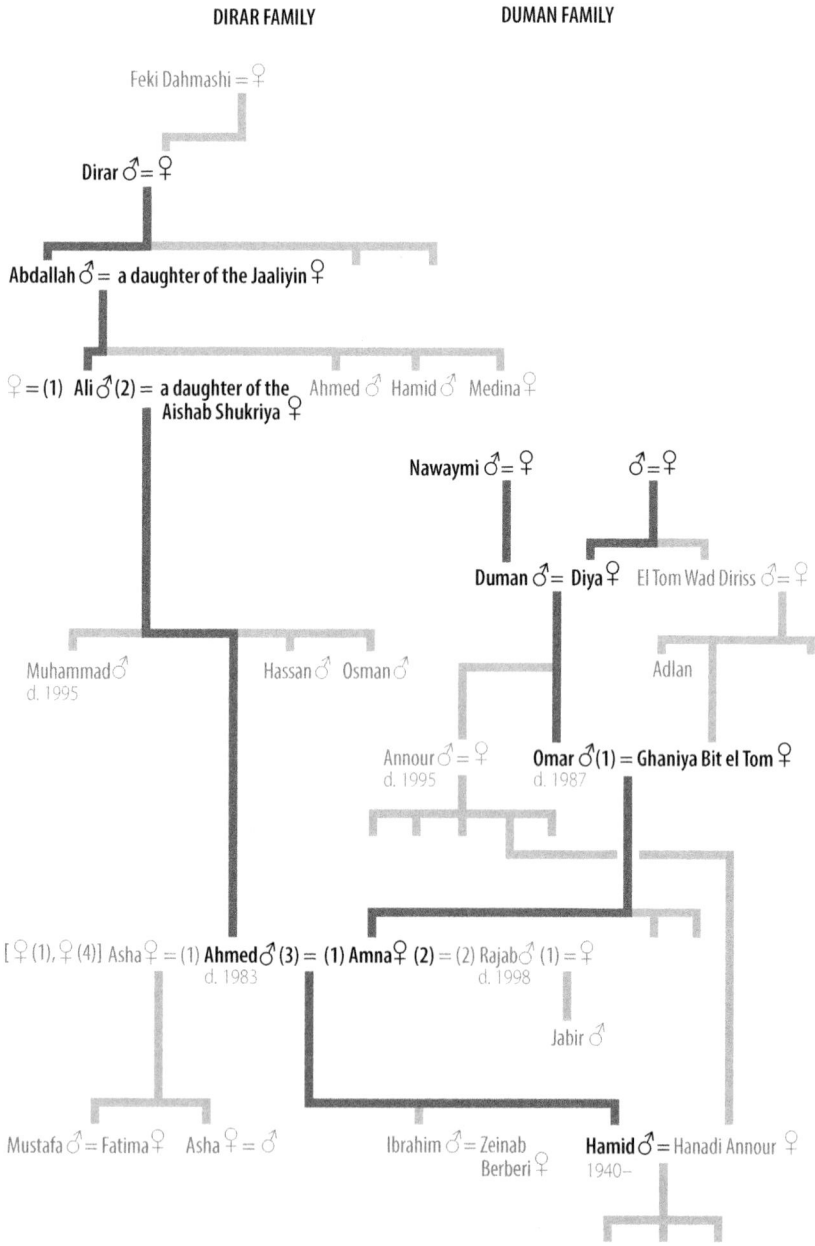

SUMMARY OF HAMID DIRAR'S ANCESTRY

In the early nineteenth century, Dirar – the author's great-great grandfather in the paternal line – is born in Nubia, in the far north of what is now Sudan, on the Nile River, towards the border with Egypt. A carpenter and man of religion, he migrates southwards, to the land of the Jaaliyin people, which lies further south on the Nile, returning to Nubia to marry. His son, Abdallah, moves south again.

Abdallah marries from the Jaaliyin; and his children grow up in the Jaali land, on the Nile near Shendi, in the era of Turko-Egyptian rule. Ali, his first-born, is the author's grandfather. Ali's first wife and children fall victim to Sanat Sitta, the famine of 1889. Later Ali—a maker of waterwheels—settles, with his second wife and their sons, in the East, first in Kassala, then in the Butana, in the land of the mainly pastoralist Shukriya people. His son Ahmed, the author's father, studies in Khartoum, becoming a *feki*, a man of religion, then returns to the Butana. Ahmed's first wife dies after their second daughter is born. His second wife, Amna, from the Shukriya, is the mother of the author, Hamid. Hamid Dirar's paternal lineage is thus as follows: he is the son of Ahmed, who is the son of Ali, who is the son of Abdallah, who is the son of the first Dirar.

On his mother's side, Hamid's great-great grandfather in the paternal line is Nawaymi, from the Nawayma branch of the Shukriya, whose home territory is on the west bank of the Atbara River. Nawaymi's son, Duman, dies young. Duman's widow, known as Diya, becomes the Duman family matriarch.* Diya's eldest son, Omar Duman, marries his cousin Ghaniya, the daughter of Diya's brother, El Tom Wad Diriss (cross-cousin marriage being the norm in many Sudanese societies). Ghaniya gives birth to a daughter, Amna. Amna is cured of sickness in adolescence by a *feki*, Umhummad wad Beshir, and is offered to him in marriage, but he dies before the marriage takes place. Feki Umhammad's first wife, Bit Burbur, puts her son forward to marry Amna in his father's place, but Amna's grandmother Diya refuses. Eventually Amna marries Ahmed Dirar and has two sons by him: Ibrahim, her first-born, and Hamid, the author. Ahmed and Amna divorce; Amna marries Rajab. Hamid is raised by Fatima, his half-sister by another of his father's wives, and by Toshkan, daughter of Hadab, a sheikh of the Hadendowa people. In adulthood, he marries his cousin, Hanadi, one of the daughters of Sheikh Annour Duman, a grand-daughter of Diya and great-grand-daughter of Nawaymi.

Hamid Dirar's background thus includes ancestral strands from the Mahas people of Nubia, from the Jaaliyin of Shendi, and from the Shukriya of the Butana—and, by nurture, from the Hadendowa branch of the Beja people of Eastern Sudan. (See the Glossary, Gazetteer & Biographical Notes for further details of ancestors and kin.)

* As the sister of Hamid's mother's mother's father, Diya, as well as being Hamid's great-grandmother, is also his great-great aunt, Omar Duman, Hamid's maternal grandfather, having married his first cousin.

The Amulet

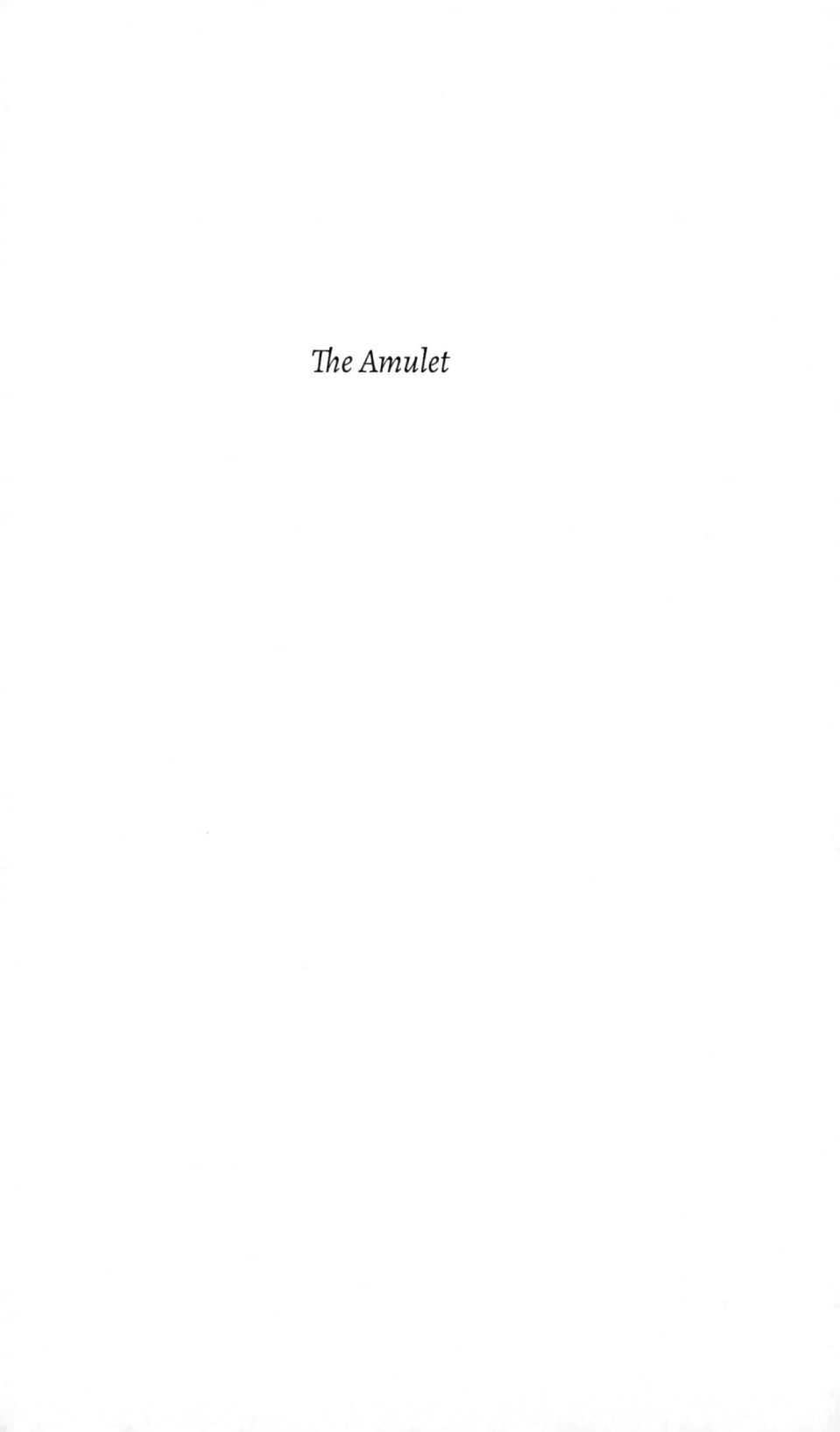

I

Beginnings

THE LAND OF ROCKS

Two centuries ago, my ancestor Dirar left his home in 'Ard el Hajar, the Land of Rocks, never to return.

Here in Nubia, the northernmost part of what is now Sudan, where the Nile meets the Sahara, the desert is constantly seeking to overwhelm the serpentine intruder from the south, and bury it in sand. The year Dirar left it seemed the desert was gaining ground. The river had lost the vigour of youth. Sand dunes piled around the date palms. The narrow strips of fertile land along the banks produced only the bare minimum of crops. In every household in the village where Dirar lived, there were signs of hardship.

Then, as now, the Land of Rocks could only hold so many people. In order for communities to survive some had to leave: for every boy child born an adult male migrated elsewhere. Of those who left, some sought a relatively secure life downriver in Egypt, where they could work as gatemen or cooks; but the more restless souls among them migrated southwards, further into Africa. My ancestor Dirar went south. He had two skills he knew he could use: he was an accomplished carpenter; and he was a teacher of the Holy Qur'an. So he packed a burlap bag with his copy of the Holy Book, his ink-pot and reed pen, his adze, his saw, and his mallet and chisel, then he flung the bag across his shoulder and set out, following the western bank of the Nile until he arrived at the ancient town of Dongola. There he worked for a time in the carpenter's trade before proceeding south, further upriver. This was the start of his great journey – and the later journeys of his many descendants.

On his way south Dirar encountered caravans of slaves, travelling north – men, women and children lashed to each other like cattle, with forked sticks fixed on their necks. Slave convoys like these were a commonplace sight in Nubia. The slaves were well-built, black-skinned captives from the distant Nuba Mountains of South Kordofan. They came ultimately from the same stock as Nubians, like Dirar himself. The Nubians, however, in contrast to the peoples of the Nuba Mountains to the south, had been Muslims for many centuries. In Islamic law this meant they could not be enslaved. The Nubians were themselves slave-owners: their slaves came from the same communities as those Dirar saw being driven north – mountain dwellers from beyond the lands of Islam.

Dirar's people, the Mahas of Nubia – that is to say the people I spring from in the paternal line – are the descendents of indigenous Africans who were Islamised in the middle ages. Together with the other Nubian groups, the Mahas are remnants of the ancient stock that, several thousand years ago, in the first millennium BCE, established some of the most advanced societies of their day. The kings of that time – Piankhi, Shabaka and Taharqa – ruled over much of what is now Sudan and Egypt, forming the twenty-fifth pharaonic dynasty. More than a thousand years later, when nomadic Arabs advanced into the country from Egypt, the Mahas stood in their way.

BEGINNINGS

In the centuries that followed the Arabs swept past the desert lands of Nubia towards the grassy savannah lands to the south. But their brief encounter with the Nubian people left an enduring legacy of Islam and the Arabic of the Qur'an. The Nubians took to Islamic learning so ardently that in later centuries they were credited with spreading the Qur'an throughout the lands to the south of Nubia. In this way the Mahas and other Nubians retained their own indigenous languages, while also acquiring Arab blood and culture. In the style of other Islamised peoples of northern Sudan, they began to assert a genealogical relation to the exalted Prophet Muhammad, claiming to be Khazraj, members of the tribe of the Prophet's maternal uncles, who protected him when he migrated from Mecca to Medina. This history of Islamisation was why a Mahas such as Dirar, although historically kin to the pagan Nuba of the mountains to the south, could not be enslaved.

A SUMMONS FROM MEK NIMIR

Some days of travel on foot from Dongola brought Dirar, the young Nubian, my great-great-grandfather, to the village of Ghureiba, near Korti at the western bend of the Nile. There he was hosted by the Feki Dahmashi, a religious teacher famous for his *khalwa*, a school for teaching the Qur'an. Dirar was offered the post of teacher in the *khalwa*. The *feki* also encouraged him to practice his work as a carpenter, building boats and *sagiya*s, the waterwheels that were crucial to riverain cultivation. (It was customary in those days for a *feki*, a man of religion, to have some other craft, so that he did not depend on the donations of his pupils or their parents.) In addition to being a teacher and a carpenter Dirar acted as *muezzin*, calling the faithful to prayer. He applied himself to his new duties, becoming one of Feki Dahmashi's closest disciples.

Late one afternoon in Ghureiba – it would have been around 1820 – two camel riders entered the village and headed towards Feki Dahmashi's house. They unsaddled the camels and, after the usual salutations, introduced themselves as the emissaries of Mek Nimir. It was a name to be conjured with. Mek Nimir was the most famous person in the region, a celebrated leader of the warlike Jaaliyin tribe, whose heartland was further south on the Nile, at Shendi. The visitors told Feki Dahmashi that the *mek* was in need of men of religion to teach the Qur'an. He was also, it happened, in need of carpenters to build boats and waterwheels.

Feki Dahmashi had taken it upon himself to spread the teachings of Islam wherever they were needed; and the prospect of joining the celebrated Mek Nimir was an opportunity to further his goal, so he decided to answer the call in person, taking Dirar to assist him in the long and harsh journey across the Bayuda Desert to Metamma, a town which lay over the river from Mek Nimir's capital at Shendi. Entrusting the *khalwa* to junior colleagues, the *feki* and Dirar set off from Ghureiba across the desert. Several times en route they were waylaid by bandits, but each time, as Dirar recounted it – and as the story was passed down by his descendants – the great *feki* raised the *Mushaf*, the Holy Book, invoking Allah, and they were left unharmed. Presently the two men arrived at Metamma, on the western bank of the Nile. Here they crossed the river by boat to visit Mek Nimir at Shendi on the eastern bank. The great *mek* greeted them civilly and dispatched them to teach at Hillat al-Fugara, the village of the men of religion, just south of Metamma.

THE *MEK* AND THE TURKS

Not long after Dirar and his Feki Dahmashi had settled there, however, the peace of Metamma, and of Shendi and the whole land of the Jaaliyin, was disrupted by an invasion from the north. It was the early 1820s and the region was being overrun by an army of Ottoman Turks under the command of Khedive Muhammad Ali Pasha, the ruler of Egypt. The invaders annexed much of what is now Sudan, aiming to reap its wealth of human and mineral resources: gold in the Beni Shangul Hills, slaves and ivory from the south. A Turko-Egyptian army under the command of Ismail Kamil Pasha, the pampered son of the Khedive, set off south and east along the Nile. They were to reach as far as Sennar on the Blue Nile. Meanwhile a second army was formed, under the leadership of Muhammad Bey, the Khedive's son-in-law. This force planned to leave the Nile at Metamma and strike westward to suppress the wild tribes of Kordofan.

Starting from the Egyptian border, Ismail Pasha swept up-river, subduing tribe after tribe until he came to the land of the Jaaliyin. Here he met with Mek Nimir at Shendi. It was a fateful meeting; the story is told in Sudan to this day. Ismail Pasha's eyes, it is said, did not fail to note the distinctive beauty of the long-necked Jaaliyin women. And he informed the *mek* that on his way back from Sennar he would like a word with him on an important matter. When he returned, victorious, from Sennar he lost no time in pursuing the issue. With the *mek* surrounded by his entourage, Ismail Pasha, with a huge tobacco pipe jutting from his fat lips, asked him – in public – to supply him with a hundred Jaaliyin virgins, as a gift to his father, the great Khedive in Cairo. Noticing, perhaps, a twitch of the *mek*'s eyebrow, he added that his father would be extremely pleased by such an offering and that it would bring the *mek* great benefits later.

Ismail Pasha, accustomed as he was to power and command, can have understood little of the customs and values of the lands he had conquered. He surely did not realize the full import for a free people of the words he had spoken. Who would dare object, he may have thought, to such a demand from a representative of an empire that extended from Africa to the Middle East – and to Bosnia in the heart of Europe?

But Mek Nimir was the proud leader of the greatest tribe in Sudan, as yet uncolonized. Were his people to be treated as slaves? Apart from the twitch of his brow, he did not reveal his feelings to his guest. Beneath his clothes, however, Mek Nimir's muscles flexed involuntarily, bursting the straps that held the protective leather amulets in place round his biceps. Those close to him hurried to calm him down. "*Mek*, stay big! *Mek*, stay big!" they whispered. "Do not let anger make you small!" This is the way the Jaaliyin today describe the rage of their leader against the Egyptian invader.

The *mek* managed to conceal his feelings. He replied to Ismail Pasha in the following manner.

"Your excellency," he said, "it gives me great pleasure to accede to your request. While my men keep themselves busy gathering the girls together, let me invite you and your company to dine."

The Pasha accepted the invitation. The *mek* explained that his retainers would be building a *zariba*, a thorn enclosure, around them, in order to protect the Pasha's army. The retainers set to work. The victorious Pasha and his men ate their fill. They drank *aragi* – date liquor – without restraint. They feasted till they were drunk as monkeys. And as they did so the thorn fence round them grew higher.

Outside the enclosure, the *mek*'s horsemen were assembling. On a secret signal, he excused himself from the feast. And then, at his command, his men set fire to the thorn enclosure. The dry kindling ignited immediately. The flames soared around the drunken Egyptian soldiers. The mek's men were ordered to kill any who managed to escape. In a few hours the invading army was annihilated.

Mek Nimir and his men immediately retreated towards Ethiopia, on the eastern border. News of the cataclysm very soon reached Kordofan, where the Difterdar, Muhammad Bey, son-in-law of the Khedive of Egypt and brother-in-law of the slain Ismail Pasha, was busy extending Turko-Egyptian control in the west. At first, the great military leader could not believe that a primitive tribe like the Jaaliyin, without modern weapons, would have the capacity to do something like this to a representative of the great empire. Then Muhammad Bey began to rage against the *mek* and his followers. His cry – "Doom and Damnation to the Jaaliyin!" – reverberated across the sands.

Muhammad Bey's army proceeded to ransack Metamma and Shendi, in the Jaali heartland, killing men, women and children. But he did not catch the mek. With the help of the Shukriya people of the Butana and the Humran of Seiteet, Mek Nimir and his retainers escaped eastwards, following the course of the Atbara River into Ethiopia. Here he built a new village that he also called Metamma, in memory of his homeland. For decades to come, Mek Nimir – and his son after him – led raids against the Turko-Egyptian government in Sudan. The Turks continued to rule the country for another sixty years. Their rule was to end only with the rise of the Mahdi in the 1880s.

THE MAHDISTS AND THE JAALIYIN

As news of Muhammad Bey's campaign spread in the region, Feki Dahmashi and Dirar his disciple left the land of the Jaaliyin and returned to Ghureiba in the north, back in Nubia. There in Ghureiba, Dirar married Feki Dahmashi's daughter. One of their sons, Abdallah, returned south again, to the Jaaliyin land, which was by then under Turko-Egyptian rule, like most of the rest of the country. Here, Abdallah married a Jaali woman who gave him three sons – Ali, Ahmed and Hamid – and one daughter, Medina. These were the grandchildren of my Nubian ancestor Dirar; Abdallah's eldest son, Ali, was my grandfather. They all grew up in the Jaaliyin land during the Turkish time.

In these last decades of the nineteenth century the country was beset again by unrest and turmoil. Resistance to the corruption and rapacity of Turkish rule was growing. The government not only took taxes on grain and livestock, but imposed further demands for tribute. These included the notorious *digniya*, the chin-tax, a tax on every human being and every domestic animal big enough to have a chin, excluding monkeys. As a result of these exactions the spirit of revolt gripped the country. A charismatic leader, Muhammad Ahmad, known as the Mahdi, emerged to lead a revolt against foreign domination. In 1885 the last governing representative of the Turko-Egyptian regime, the British General Charles Gordon, was killed by Mahdists in Khartoum, and the city was captured by the Sudanese insurgents. The Mahdi died shortly after the capture of Khartoum and his deputy, Khalifa, took over. The Khalifa ruled with an iron fist, presiding over a religious state. The events of this time drove my paternal ancestor further south, to the area towards

Ethiopia and Eritrea where I was to grow up several generations later.

In 1889 – the year 1306 in the Islamic Hijri calendar – a terrible famine struck the country. Hundreds of thousands of men and women died of hunger. It became known as Sanat Sitta, Year Six. It was at this time that my ancestor Abdallah's eldest son, Ali Dirar – who was not a Mahdist, but an adherent of a rival Islamic sect, the Khatmiya – set out, in desperation, with his family and other relatives, for Gedaref, close to the border with Ethiopia. This area was the granary of the country, as it still is today. On the way Ali buried eighteen of his companions, including his wife and all his children.

Arriving in Gedaref, Ali Dirar stayed with Wad Zayed, a leader of the Dhabanya tribe, and worked under his patronage as a muezzin and a carpenter. He made much use of the abundant sunut acacia trees that grew in the region of the Rahad and Dinder rivers. Soon, however, the people of the area began to complain to Wad Zayed about Ali's conspicuous destruction of the larger trees. That resulted in a restriction of his activities as a carpenter in that region. So he moved on again, this time to a place called Assar, nearer Gedaref, where he married again and had four more sons: Muhammad, Ahmed, Hassan and Osman.

At this time, in the last years of the nineteenth century, the lands that were to become Sudan were the target of another invasion. A British army advanced up the Nile from Egypt. Their mission was to avenge the death of General Gordon, killed by the forces of the Mahdi. Khalifa Abdallah, the Mahdi's successor, sent a huge, but ill-equipped army to meet the British. In 1898, as the British advanced southwards, the Mahdist army began to move north, downstream from Omdurman along the west bank of the Nile, under the command of Mahmoud wad Ahmed.

At the same time as the British invasion war broke out within the country between the Mahdists and the Jaaliyin tribe. As the Mahdists advanced, the leader of the Jaaliyin, Abdallah wad Saad, received a message from Mahmoud wad Ahmed, the Mahdist leader, advising him to evacuate the town of Metamma, on the west bank of the Nile, and move all his people to Shendi on the east bank. But he refused, still feeling the shame of the flight of Mek Nimir from Shendi to Ethiopia after the killing of Ismail Pasha. The Jaaliyin, then and now, are the most widely dispersed of Sudan's tribes, working as merchants and craftsmen throughout the country. Hearing about the imminent confrontation, Jaaliyin from all corners of the land set off for Metamma to help in its defence. Ali, my great-grandfather, grandson of my ancestor Dirar, was among them. He knew that his brother Hamid and his sister Medina were in Metamma. So, with some other Jaaliyiin men, he set off down the Blue Nile northwards to Khartoum. Meanwhile, with just a few thousand soldiers, Abdallah wad Saad waited in their adobe-built town for the tens of thousands of Mahdists to come.

In the end Ali and the other Jaaliyin who had set off to their aid were too late to help Abdallah wad Saad. While they were still on the way they heard news of a cataclysm that had befallen the tribe at Metamma. The Mahdist soldiers had wiped out the defending Jaaliyin. They ravaged the town and its inhabitants. Rather than submit to them, it was said, Jaaliyin women locked their arms together and threw themselves into the Nile. As proud as in the days of Mek Nimir, they preferred to drown than become objects of pleasure for the soldiers of an invading army. Those Jaaliyin who survived – men, women and children and their livestock – were sent back to the Khalifa at Omdurman. Among the captives were Ali's siblings, Hamid and Medina. But

Ali travelled to Omdurman, where he was able to find Medina and obtain her release, and take her with him back to Gedaref.

Soon after the clash between the Mahdists and the Jaaliyin, the Mahdists were confronted by a greater force. The Anglo-Egyptian reinvasion of Sudan led to their defeat at the Battle of Karari, which is known in British colonial history as the Battle of Omdurman. General Kitchener's army went on to subdue the whole country, including the eastern towns of Gedaref and Kassala. British rule was established across Sudan. This meant, among other things, that the leaders of the Khatmiya, the Islamic *tariqa*, or brotherhood, that Dirar and his descendants belonged to, who had gone into exile in Egypt during the Mahdiyya, were now free to return. They settled in Khartoum and in the east, in Kassala, where the Khatmiya had originated.

Since Ali Dirar was a Khatmi, an ardent follower of Sayed Ahmed el Merghani, the leader of the sect, he took his wife, children and sister to Kassala, to the Khatmiya village at the foot of the rocky mountain of Jebel Kassala, with its seven bare peaks that dominate the landscape to this day. The town and its surrroundings, then and now, form a fertile oasis where fruit gardens thrive. Here Ali worked, as his grandfather had done, as a muezzin and maker of waterwheels. Sayed Ahmed el Mirghani was pleased with Ali's loyalty and favoured his voice for the call to prayer. He allotted him an area of residential land where he settled. For a carpenter and builder of waterwheels Kassala was something close to paradise. Yet the wandering spirit of the descendants of Dirar meant that for Ali even Kassala turned out to be a temporary resting place.

DUMAN AND DIYA

Around the same time, in Gedaref, to the south, another wandering ancestor of mine, Duman, son of Nawaymi, from the Nawayma branch of the Shukriya tribe, was engaged in an argument with his father.

It was an old argument, an ancient argument, concerning the virtues of life as a farmer as opposed to those of a herdsman. On a certain day, in the compound in their sorghum farm in Umm Sineibra, Duman cleaned a place to sit near his father under a large thorn tree. He was gazing north towards the horizon. His father's eyes, though, were on the tree.

"My son," said Nawaymi, "this place holds your future and the future of your young brothers. Your mother and I need you here to help us till the land."

"Father," said Duman quietly, "you know that I have no interest in farming. I hate all that crouching in the mud, pulling out weeds like a slave woman. I just can't see how you can do a thing like that."

"In case you forget, son, crouching like a slave and growing crops was the way we fed you until you became what you are now," said his father.

"I don't mean to insult anyone," said Duman, "I just want to say what I feel. And I know farming is not the life I want."

It was not the first time they had discussed the matter. And Nawaymi was beginning to realise that any attempt to dissuade his son was doomed to failure. When he came of age, it was clear, Duman was determined to take his flock and travel north leaving the village and the settled existence of a farmer to lead the nomadic life. He had felt the call of the Butana, the great savannah that formed the principal territory of their tribe, the Shukriya. Here flocks of sheep and herds of camels could graze at will. Where they had settled in Gedaref there was too much rain for this; the muddy terrain was ill-suited for the desert breed of sheep, the hardy animals which his son had begun to raise when he was still a child.

The future loss of Duman's labour was not the only thing that worried the old man. He feared that his son would end up marrying outside their kin-group, the Nawayma sub-tribe. This was the time, he decided, to discuss the matter of marriage.

"If you insist on leaving," he said, "and if you want your father to give you his blessing, then you must listen to what I have to say."

"Yes, father, of course I will." said Duman.

"Son," said Nawaymi, "you need to get married before you leave."

"I beg your pardon, sir?" said Duman.

Again Nawaymi said, "You should get married before you leave,"

"But why now, father?" said Duman hurriedly. "Have I ever given a thought to marriage?"

"I know you have been thinking about it. Your mother told me last year," said his father.

"Well, yes, that's true," said Duman, correcting himself. "I did so. But for only a short time."

"Son, be frank with me; you wanted to marry your cousin Diya. But you thought you could not afford it," said his father. "But I am telling you that you can marry Diya now if you want to."

"Father, that's impossible," said Duman. "You only have to look at her name..."

Diya. It was indeed an unusual name. The word *diya* means blood money, the payment that is made under customary law all over Sudan to settle disputes involving injury or death. Duman's cousin Diya was a beautiful woman: tall, light-skinned and fine-featured, with silken hair down to her ribs. And with her looks went a quick temper and pride to the point of arrogance. After all, was she not the sister of El Tom wad Diriss? And had El Tom not been the owner of over one hundred slaves, and a man whose well-stocked grain stores had saved many Nawayma families from perishing during the Sanat Sitta famine in the time of the Mahdiyya?

Duman looked at his father incredulously. "You know her mother insists that whoever wants her daughter for a wife must pay a huge amount in bridewealth – equal to the *diya* that is paid to the family of a man who has been killed. And, father, you know that *diya* today is one hundred camels. I don't even have a hundred sheep."

"You can leave that to me," said his father. "Since when did we place matters of marriage in the hands of women? Forget what her mother says. It is true that Diya is the most beautiful girl in the village, but she is still your cousin, so you have every right to marry her. I will discuss this matter with her brother El Tom."

It was Diya's remarkable beauty that had led her mother to put such a high price on her head, insisting that her bride-price be equivalent to bloodwealth, to *diya*, the compensation payable for causing a death. Diya's original name had been Fatima, but her new name took over so completely that people forgot what she had once been called. News of the unprecedented bridewealth stipulated for her marriage had spread far and wide among villagers and nomads. The beauty of Diya was compared to that of the legendary Tajuj, the tragic heroine of Sudanese folklore – who Diya claimed to be descended from, and whose love story was known to all. Many young men dreamed of marrying Diya. A woman like that, they thought, would spur them on to achieve their lives' ambition. But others – those who knew they had no chance – muttered that she was a wilful woman who would end up as a nag and a scold.

Then, suddenly, one day, it became known that Diya was now the wedded wife of Duman. Not only that, it was said he had paid only a few head of sheep as bridewealth. No one knew how this had happened. That was his father's secret. But the fame of Diya's beauty stopped there, by convention, at the point that she became the wife of a man.

THE DEATH OF DUMAN

The year drew on and the rains began. And Duman finally left, with his father's blessing, to pursue his dream of the nomadic life, taking Diya, his new wife, with him to the Butana. By the end of the rains his flock had doubled. During the dry summer, he and other nomads of the Butana clustered around local surface wells or travelled with their flocks down to the Atbara River or the Blue Nile. Duman and his wife and his flocks went to the village of Asubri on the banks of the Atbara. Here, according to nomad custom, they stayed under the protection of the local leader of the Shukriya tribe, the well-known Sheikh Umara Abu Sin.

Umara Abu Sin had already gained fame before the coming of the British through his struggle against the Mahdists. After the death of the Mahdi, the Khalifa Abdallah, the Mahdi's successor, had held Sheikh Umara Abu Sin captive at Omdurman for refusing to pay taxes, as he had also held Hamid and Medina, the grandchildren of Dirar. The Khalifa was known to have killed many tribal leaders who resisted him, even his own generals. Umara Abu Sin, it was said, was only saved from death by poetry: by the eloquence of his relative, the great poet Hardalu, who spared neither verse nor prose to appease the Khalifa and free Umara Abu Sin from captivity.

As a stranger in Asubri, Duman built his tent close to that of Sheikh Umara and put himself under his protection. During the next rainy season he took his family and flock again to the meadows of the Butana. The following dry season he returned to Asubri. Thus they followed the annual pattern of the life of nomads in their relation to settled life, the way of life that has endured up to my own lifetime. Through the years the beautiful, wilful Diya, accustomed as she was to a sedentary life, often gave her husband a hard time. She also gave him two sons, Omar and Annour.

Then Duman fell ill. And it turned out that his illness was incurable. On his deathbed he sent a message to Sheikh Umara asking him to take care of his family after he died. And that was what the great sheikh did. Each morning and evening he would inspect Duman's flock, advise his two sons on what to do and ask Diya if she needed anything. But he could not persuade her to accept another husband.

A WATERWHEEL

Sheikh Umara, Duman's patron, had other, more pressing concerns. The British had now occupied the country and quelled all lingering Mahdist resistance. The country that was now called Sudan was enjoying for the first time in years a period of peace, of law and order. The great sheikh now turned to development. He wanted to set an example to his people, the Shukriya, by establishing an orchard of fruit trees and vegetables on the bank of the Atbara at Asubri. Being by tradition a nomadic herdsman however, he knew nothing of this agricultural technology. It was something that belonged to the Jaaliyin, the people of the Nile.

Umara Abu Sin travelled to Kassala to consult Sayed Ahmed el Mirghani, the leader of the Khatmiya, the Islamic sect or brotherhood that he and most Shukriya belonged to. Sayed Ahmed welcomed the idea and praised it. And the man he recommended for the work was Ali Dirar, the Nubian, whose father had dwelt so long among the Jaaliyin before he migrated to Kassala. Sayed Ahmed told Umara Abu Sin that he believed Ali Dirar was the most accomplished carpenter in the business of building waterwheels in the region. He issued instructions for Ali to leave Kassala for Asubri to establish an orchard for Sheikh Abu Sin. So, leaving his family and his sister Medina behind in the Khatmiya village with a cousin, Ali Dirar left for the land of the Shukriya.

At Asubri he set about realizing the Sheikh's project. He started by felling the largest *sunut* trees, as his father had done, to make cogwheels for the first waterwheel, the *sagiya*. Months of diligent work passed before Dirar was finally able to complete the building of the waterwheel and use it to irrigate the land. He then asked Sheikh Umara to provide him with a boy to drive the oxen that turned the waterwheel, tramping round and round from morning to night, and sometimes on into the darkness.

The following morning a handsome Shukriya boy the age of his older son Muhammad stood in front of his hut. The boy introduced himself as Omar wad Duman. He was the older son of Diya and her late husband, Duman, the son of Nawaymi, who had chosen the nomadic life. Under the supervision of Dirar the boy learned how to yoke and drive the pair of oxen. It was in this way that the two sides of my family, the Dirars from Nubia and the Dumans from Gedaref, first came to know each other.

One night Omar was driving the oxen in the dark of night on the riverbank. The oxen circled round and round; the waterwheel moaned and groaned. Omar could see the dim form of a large raft taking men from the east bank to the west. The raft then stopped close to the *sagiya* – the waterwheel – and one of the men on the raft jumped off to moor it to a tree. At that moment the oxen, still not fully tamed, bolted, swinging the waterwheel round so fast that the boy was flung over the steep bank. He would have broken his neck had he not been caught by the thick foliage of a tree.

The incident alarmed Sheikh Umara. He had little confidence in the ability of nomads to run such high-tech contrivances. So when Dirar came to get his permission to return to Kassala, the Sheikh asked him instead to bring his family from Kassala to live under his protection with the Shukriya people and supervise the *sagiya*. The matter was arranged with Sayed Ahmed El Mirghani, the Khatmi leader. Ali Dirar came to Gedaref with his wife, children and goats, leaving his sister, Medina, in Kassala, and entering the world of pastoral nomadic people.

THE FUNERAL OF SHEIKH UMARA ABU SIN

As years passed, the failing health of Sheikh Umara Abu Sin brought the old man to his deathbed and, finally, to the grave. His death cast a pall of grief on the Shukriya. From all corners of the vast Butana plain men trekked to Asubri, walking or riding, to pay their condolences to the family. Those who walked into the camp crouched out in the open sun at a distance from the tent of the sheikh, covering their heads and faces with their *tobs*, the cotton fabric garments that remain the dress of many rural Sudanese to this day. They cried loud in rasping voices in the tradition of the nomadic Shukriya. The camp could be seen strewn with crouching, weeping men.

"*Abouy! Abouy!* Father! Father! No! No! Father! Father!" they cried. Those who arrived on camelback fell off and rolled on the ground while their fully saddled camels, dragging their reins, roamed aimlessly around the camp.

At the tent of the deceased, ululating women danced the death dance, their indigo-dyed calico *tobs* tightly wrapped around their waists and their uncovered hair piled with earth and ashes. They held the sheikh's mare between them, bridled and carrying its saddle up-turned, and pelted it with wood ash and dirt while it neighed and bucked. The death dance continued everywhere. Women of all ages beat the ground rhythmically with their bare feet as they wailed. They screamed and uttered improvised poetry, recounting the merits of the deceased. Other mourners formed circles and swung back and forth with their dangling braided hair waving in the air like streaks of light. Keening slave women beat the *kabbour* drums, half-gourds overturned on pools of water, a spectral sound heard only when an important person passed away.

The Shukriya had every reason to mourn their leader. In the waning years of the rule of Khalifa Abdallah towards the end of the Mahdist era, when there was confusion in the land, Sheikh Umara wad Umhummad wad Hamad wad Abu Sin – to give him his full name – had fought many battles against the Mahdists. He had successfully recovered territory and freed captives drawn from his and other tribes. Many of these chose to live with the sheikh in satellite tents around his camp. But now, with the sheikh gone, some of his long-established Shukriya followers felt that these newcomers were competing with them. They gave them the name *malageet*, the foundlings of Sheikh Umara.

The Duman family were Shukriya. But the Dirars, wanderers from the north via Kassala, were considered among the *malageet*. Following the death of Sheikh Umara, now lacking his protection, *malageet* scattered in various directions along the Atbara River. Among them were the Dumans – Diya and her sons – who moved up-river to lead a fully nomadic life around the village of Ghurashi and the area of the Blue Bridge. Meanwhile the Dirars – Ali and his wife and sons – stayed in Asubri. All except for Ahmed Dirar. My father had inherited the restless soul of his ancestors. And thus began the train of events that led to my own existence.

THE MEETING OF FEKI UMHUMMAD WAD BESHIR AND FEKI AHMED DIRAR

Ahmed, my father, grew up into a young man of great physical strength and difficult temperament. His quick temper, people believed, he inherited from his mother. Over time the fingers on her right hand had become deformed from her habit of biting them when she became angry with her children. (She did this, she said, to stop herself from beating them.) Her son loved adventure, sharp knives, livestock and the nomadic life.

But Ahmed Dirar also had a powerful desire to learn the Qur'an. He enrolled in a *khalwa* in Asubri, and when his teacher discovered his bent for learning, he sent him with the camel caravans to Gedaref to join a larger and more advanced *khalwa* in a village called Abbayo. In two or three years Ahmed became so well-versed in Islamic teaching that his teachers sent him further, this time with the caravans to Khartoum, to the Islamic studies centre at Um Dubban. After years spent there in the pursuit of religious knowledge, Ahmed returned to Asubri as a full-fledged *feki*, a teacher of the Qur'an. He knew the entire Qur'an by heart.

He had become a man of knowledge. But he had not lost his love for the nomadic life. This, with his quick temper, turned him into an eccentric: a learned warrior. Problems flared up as soon as he returned from his educational odyssey. While he was away his brothers Muhammad and Hassan had married two sisters from outside their tribe. To Ahmed Dirar these women were of a lesser race: they were too black to be Arabs. His education had not cured him of the racial discrimination commonplace among the nomads of Sudan. So he severed all connections with his brothers and moved away to the other side of the river, away from the Shukriya communities, to the east bank, to live among another tribe, the Hadendowa.

The River Atbara is the frontier between the Arab tribes on the west bank and the Hadendowa on the east. Among the Hadendowa Ahmed found what he wanted: dogs for hunting, people that he could lead in religious matters, and a wealth of sheep. He became fluent in Bedawiyet, the Hadendowa language. But he did not marry from them. Though he might admire their way of life, the Hadendowa were not Arabs either. Instead, he married a woman from the Arab nomads of the west bank, one from a well-known family, who was pale enough in complexion to satisfy his racial preconceptions. With her he had two fair-skinned daughters: Fatima and Asha. The family continued to live on the east bank, in Suwayil, with the Hadendowa, across the river from Asubri. There Ahmed Dirar pitched his tent close to that of Sheikh Hadab, the leader of the Kalolai branch of the Hadendowa. Soon after giving birth to the second daughter, however, Ahmed's wife Asha passed away, leaving two small girls for Ahmed to care for.

He decided to get married again, to find a wife who could bring up his daughters and give him a son. He became seized by the idea that he should return to the far Jaaliyin land, to Metamma, where he could find a girl among his relatives that he might get married to. He entrusted his daughters and his sheep and dogs to Hadab, the Hadendowa chief, and left on camelback for the long journey to Metamma. There he introduced himself to the members of the extensive Dirar family from which he sprang. Among them his eye fell on Dar Salam Bit Hamid, his first cousin, a beautiful young woman of marriageable age. But when he broached the subject with her family, he was told that she was promised to another man, Ibrahim, a second cousin both to her and to Ahmed Dirar.

This was against tradition: the priority when it came to marriage was always to marry the first, not the second cousin. But because the Dirars of Metamma had been cut off from him and their other relatives far away in Kassala, they told him, the girl had been given to her second cousin Ibrahim. At the time, the fiancé, Ibrahim, was in Khartoum, working as a gardener at the British governor-general's palace. Ahmed Dirar, obstinate and hot-tempered as he was, immediately travelled to Khartoum with his Hadendowa *sodal*, a dagger with a double twist, sheathed at his waist. In Khartoum he put the edge of the dagger to his cousin Ibrahim's throat and invited him to leave the girl for him. Ibrahim had little choice but to agree. The other Dirars, however, back in Metamma, saw Ahmed as a cut-throat ruffian and refused to have anything to do with him. Finally Ahmed came to his senses and realised that the girl, who had been raised in the sedentary life of farmers, was unlikely to accept the way of life he led among nomadic tribes. So one morning he wrote on the ground with his finger outside Ibrahim's hut that he was leaving the girl for him. Then he left and returned to Asubri.

After that time, Ahmed Dirar never returned to the land of the Jaaliyin. And he never again spoke of his relatives there.

Back in the east, the Hadendowa accepted Ahmed Dirar because he was a man of religion, a learned man who could recite the Qur'an by heart. They knew him as a *feki*, one who could cure men and women of diseases by the power of the Holy Book, an exorcist who could drive away demons from the bodies of afflicted people. And they knew that he was commended by Sheikh Hadab, the Hadendowa leader. News of Ahmed Dirar's quarrel with his brothers over their marriages to non-Arab women had spread wide in the region – and this gained him further respect among the Hadendowa. For the Hadendowa, although they were not Arabs, also tended to despise what they saw as African traits, even though, in truth, many of them were themselves at least as dark-skinned as Ahmed Dirar's sisters-in-law.

Ahmed Dirar pitched his tent next to that of the extended family of the Beshirs, one of the Humran Arab families in the settlement. This was not without a reason. The head of the Beshir family, Feki Umhummad wad Beshir, was also a man of religion, He was older than Ahmed and well established as a *feki* among both Arabs and Hadendowa. The two *fekis* would often sit together reciting the Qur'an and disputing matters of the *Sharia*, the body of Islamic law.

The Arabs who lived on this side of the river were as wild as the Hadendowa they lived among. This was what Ahmed Dirar liked. In a few years he was able both to expand his flocks and develop his talents for wrestling and night-hunting, especially the latter, which demanded extra senses in a man. And, each evening and each dawn, he would build his *tuggaba* fire, for reading the Qur'an. In terms of religious learning, though, he was considered a mere apprentice compared to the great Feki Beshir.

FEKI UMHUMMAD CURES AMNA'S SICKNESS

As for the Duman family, in due course, when her two sons came of age, Diya sent the elder of them, Omar Duman, back to Gedaref to get married to his cousin Ghaniya, the daughter of El Tom wad Diriss. They brought the bride to live with them at Shehateib. A year later Ghaniya gave birth to a daughter. She was given the name Amna, the secure one.

Amna grew up in an atmosphere of love and affection provided both by her parents and her grandmother, Diya. She grew up just as Diya wanted: tall, slim and with a complexion that had the right hint of yellow. Her small, well-set teeth, her smooth hair, her long neck, and most important, her fine facial features guaranteed her development into the Arab girl Diya wanted her to be, with no hint of the Africans down south, where slaves came from.

Diya had never seen a black person who was her equal; to her they were all *abeed* – slaves – or freed slaves, or descendants of slaves. For Diya, there was nothing worse for a human being than to be associated with these black Africans. It made no difference whether the person in question had actually been enslaved or not; they were either a slave or a potential slave. Black skin, tight-curled hair, flat noses – these were all things that she could not stand.

At the age of twelve her grand-daughter Amna was afflicted with a recurring nasal bleeding that Diya and her son Omar had never seen the like of. Diya was immediately alarmed. She imputed the strange condition to the evil eye, emanating from the rabble of people of dubious racial origin all around her.

"Omar, we have to take Amna to a *feki*," said Diya.

"What for, mother?" asked Omar. "Should we not try more herbs?"

"Son, I've tried all kinds of herbs, potions and concoctions – all with no success," Diya replied. "There's no use in following that line of medicine. This is a magical disease. Or else it is the work of a demon."

"What makes you entertain these terrible thoughts, mother?" said Omar. "Most people experience nose bleeds, after all."

"Not this badly. It has wrung all the blood out of her. She is so pale. I am worried we might lose her. It's a disease of the book, I'm certain. The cure lies in the verses of the Holy Qur'an. We must take the girl to Feki Umhummad wad Beshir."

Diya had her way, as she generally did. Feki Beshir prescribed treatment, two treatments, in fact: *mihayah* and *bakhrat*. First, he dipped his reed pen into an ink-well containing the fermented *amar* ink, and wrote certain selected verses from the Qur'an on his chalk-covered wooden slate, called *loh*. When the surface of the slate was fully covered with lettering, he washed it with water from his *ibrig* – the clay jug used for ablutions – and poured it into a half-gourd called *garaa*. Then, leaving aside these washings from the slate, *mihaya*, he took a piece of coarse yellow paper from a pile of old books that was placed on a donkey saddle, and tore the paper into four equal parts.

On the first he wrote a chapter of the Qur'an, the chapter called the Oneness, *Qul-huwa-Allahu-Ahad* (" 'Say' He is Allah, the One"). On the second he wrote the first verse of *Surat al-nas*, the chapter of mankind, *Qul-a-uzu-bi-rabbi-nnass* (" 'Say', I seek refugee in the Lord of Mankind"). On the third he wrote the first verse of the chapter of daybreak, *Qul-a-uzu-bi-rabbi-lfalag* (" 'Say', I seek refugee in the Lord of Daybreak") and on the fourth he wrote the verse of the throne, *Ayat-al-kursi*.

These were the four elements of the *bakhrat* treatment. The girl, he said, should drink the *mihaya* early in the morning as well at sunset. And she should be purified with the smoke from a burning *bakhra* at dawn and at dusk, when skies were crimson. The treatment was to continue without interruption until she was cured.

A DEBT AND A DEATH

Amna recovered. She was well for a few weeks. But the affliction kept recurring and the treatment had to be repeated. This continued month by month for four long years. The payment the family owed to the *feki* grew and grew. By the time Amna reached the age of sixteen she had recovered her health fully, but the family was saddled with a huge debt to Feki Umhummad wad Beshir. Then the Dumans, knowing that outstanding dues owed to a *feki* could develop into a curse, came up with an idea. They offered him the girl as his wife.

This put Feki Beshir in an awkward position. He was an old man with a wife of long standing, equally old, and their sons were grown; he had never thought of getting married again. But nomad custom meant he could not turn down the offer. Here was a respectable family who offered him their daughter to marry; to say that he did not want her would be an insult. And the idea began to grow on him. So he accepted. His wife, Bit Burbur, was infuriated. Although Islam allows a man up to four wives, she felt betrayed. She was so angry she took a stick to her husband, cursing Satan. And she imputed it all, not incorrectly, to the machinations of Amna's grandmother, the once-beautiful Diya.

While all parties planned and connived and quarrelled, however, Heaven's own plan overruled them all: one night Feki Beshir died suddenly, in his sleep.

This event brought a long train of problems in its wake, the brunt of which fell on the bereaved Amna. Who would dare to marry the betrothed wife of the late *feki*? He was not just a man but a holy person with powers beyond the grave. Amna could read fear and suspicion on people's faces when they met her. She wondered if she would ever get married. Would she have to follow her promised husband to the other world? Why did he go away leaving her to face this world alone? She felt that the great *feki* had betrayed her by dying. She wondered if he was now aware of her isolation, her loneliness and her misery. It was a cause of shame among her people to show sorrow for such a loss. Amna cried, but secretly. And she prayed.

Only he – only the *feki* himself – could be on her side, she felt. He would support her, even from the world of the dead. In her sorrow, she conceived the thought that the *feki* had not abandoned her of his own volition. Surely he could not have just left her like that? She had heard it said that he might have misdiagnosed her disease, that instead of performing an exorcism of a demon he had given her medicine for the evil eye, that it was the demon that had been the real cause of her affliction. And it was the demon, it became clear to her, that had also killed the *feki*, and had gone with him to the grave.

So Feki Beshir had not meant to leave her. Yes! That was it. He would always be with her in the afterlife. He would be on her side. Did he not have supernatural powers that Allah gave him because of his devotion to the Holy Book? With this new confidence in continued protection from the late *feki*, Amna entrusted Allah with her future and went about her daily life again.

AMNA AND HER SUITOR

When the rains came that year, the camp moved from Shehateib, the dry season site on the river, to Wadi el Khireissab, directly away from the river on the tableland, where the dark soil was. Here a green carpet of pasture covered the narrow plain and *kitir* trees – leafy acacias – were scattered across the land.

Bit Burbur, the *feki*'s widow, Amna's would-have-been co-wife, was sitting in front of her tent, watching her elder son, Zaki, who sat on the ground, nearby, plaiting a rope.

"Zaki, my son," said Bit Burbur, "when am I going to witness your wedding day?"

"You know I have no money or sheep, mother," said Zaki, speaking carefully. "And besides, I have no girl in mind."

"I have got the girl for you, son," said his mother.

"And the *mal*? The bridewealth?"

"The girl I have in mind does not require any *mal*, not in your case," said Bit Burbur. "It is Amna I am proposing as your wife. Amna Duman."

Zaki resumed his work, plaiting the rope.

"The Dumans will not ask for money, you know," Bit Burbur added, coaxingly.

"But mother," said Zaki, "you know that whoever touches the *feki*'s bride is going to be harmed by him."

"Not you, Zaki. You are his son. He won't hurt you."

Bit Burbur was convinced that the Duman family would agree. Her son was the heir to his father's rights and possessions. Those possessions included Amna. No other man would be interested in the girl now. Anyone who even dared think of her as a wife risked punishment from beyond the grave. And no nomad family would want an unmarried young woman on their hands beyond the age of eighteen.

But when she went to Diya's tent to offer her son in marriage to Diya's grand-daughter, Diya turned her offer down.

Bit-Burber was astonished. "I am shocked that you should refuse my son," she said.

"Woman, I am not refusing your son," said Diya. "I am saying that he has to pay the *mal*." And Diya named a price as great as the bridewealth that had once been demanded for her.

"But you gave the girl to Zaki's father with no payment," said Bit Burbur. "We have every right to have her on the same terms."

"We gave her to Feki Beshir," said Diya. "But Zaki is hardly the same man as his father. Just pay us the sheep required and the girl is his. Give me the sheep, Bit Burbur; and you can have the girl."

"She had an illness of the Book," said Bit Burbur. "Everyone knows that."

"She was ill before, but now she is fully recovered," said Diya.

"Believe me, Diya," said Bit Burbur, with anger in her voice, "nobody is going to marry that child of yours. Whoever touches her puts his life in danger from the *feki*."

"And then," she added, "there is your debt to us."

"The day I get the *mal* of Amna I will repay you what I owe," said Diya.

That day, however, was to be long in coming.

AHMED DIRAR'S COURTSHIP OF AMNA

Following the death of Feki Beshir, Ahmed Dirar moved to fill the void created by the loss of the great *feki*. He had strengthened his social position in the small community of Arab families in Shehateib and Khireissab. His flocks had grown. He was the only carpenter in the area; Arabs and Hadendowa both bought the articles he made. His tent was close to that of the Beshirs. His daughters were still young, but he lodged them alone in that tent where older women, notably Bit Burbur, visited them daily.

Ahmed Dirar also travelled to Kassala. Here he met Sidi al Hassan, the man who had taken over the leadership of the Khatmiya sect after the death of his father Sidi Ahmed el Mirghani. Sidi al Hassan made Ahmed Dirar his *khalifa* – his deputy in the Shehateib region. In this way Ahmed Dirar, the son of my grandfather, secured for himself a social position as a holy man among the nomads of the area. His love for sheep, dogs, daggers, hunting and the Qur'an occupied his life.

A year or so after the Beshirs had been rebuffed by Diya, an idea occurred to Ahmed Dirar. Why not seek Amna for himself? The idea fermented in his mind. He saw not only a beautiful young woman, but also someone calm and pious who would best suit his purpose in helping him bring up his two little daughters. He was not blind to the problems he would face, problems far greater than those the Beshirs had encountered. But Ahmed Dirar was a man who liked challenges, and even feuds. He planned carefully, weighing all facts and taking into account the psychology of every important person to be encountered.

Soon Bit Burbur began to notice that Ahmed Dirar was behaving somewhat obsequiously towards her. At first she dismissed the notion. Then she became sure that there was something new in Ahmed Dirar's behaviour. Not only did he milk his sheep for her; he even offered her a young ewe as a gift, saying that he appreciated the unflinching support and help she gave his daughters. What was it that had suddenly prompted that appreciation, Bit Burbur wondered. It was not long before Ahmed Dirar broached the subject of his intention to marry Amna Duman. At first Bit Burbur was taken aback at the suggestion, but after considering for some time she thought: why not? It was not such a bad idea after all. Ahmed Dirar also discussed the matter with Zaki, the rebuffed suitor. Zaki showed a feeble initial objection, but in the evening, mother and son deliberated over the subject and decided to give Dirar the go ahead for his plan to try his luck with Diya. Since the Dumans had refused them – the well-reputed Humran family of Feki Beshir – then let them give their daughter to this stranger of unknown roots – and most likely of negroid ancestry, to judge by the shape of his nose.

Still going about his business cautiously, Ahmed Dirar reminded those who warned him of the wrath of the deceased *feki* that he too was a *feki*, a bearer of the Qur'an, a man of religious descent and upbringing. He went further and spread the idea that the fiancée of a *feki* could only be betrothed to another *feki* of equal standing. This part of the plan was meant to forestall any attempt from another party to compete for the girl.

Thus it was that Ahmed Dirar set the stage for approaching the

Dumans. But he realized that bringing them round to the idea would need a totally different technique. Their interest centred on riches, on sheep, of which he had plenty. This was clear. But which of the three Dumans should he first approach? The person to speak to first was probably Annour, the younger son of Diya, who was the girl's paternal uncle, and, unlike his brother Omar, a man who could express his own opinions, rather than repeating Diya's. He was the least racially prejudiced of the Dumans, a born diplomat. He had developed his talents by working as a *muhafiz*, an askari or guard, for the ruling tribal leaders, the family of Abu Sin. This had given him the opportunity to listen to meetings held to resolve disputes, and learn much in the way of sorting out problems in peaceful ways.

Annour, Ahmed Dirar believed, was a civil person. If he could win Annour to his side then the latter could easily convince his brother and mother to agree to the marriage. Unfortunately Annour was away in Asubri with the Abu Sins. Ahmed Dirar had to wait. Meanwhile, he resorted to a ploy that was in line with his plans. He changed the area where he took his flock for pastures, such that each morning he drove the animals by Diya's tent, repeating the same thing in the evening when returning home. Diya took a good look at the sheep and the three or four camels that accompanied them. That she liked. Looking at Ahmed Dirar, though, she saw something she did not like: not so much his strong, well-built figure, but his large nose and lips. These were features she had always disliked. She remembered Ahmed's father Ali back in Asubri, a truly black man whose nose was huge and flat and whose Jaali accent sounded quite foreign to her.

At length, her son Annour arrived and saw for himself the parade of sheep by his mother's compound. He, too, was impressed. When Ahmed Dirar opened the subject of marriage with him, Annour accepted the idea readily. Annour knew that his brother Omar had five daughters, four of whom had attained marriageable age by nomad standards. He knew that his brother was worried that the delay in Amna's marriage would jeopardize the future of her younger sisters. Amna had to get married soon if her sisters were to get married in their turn. Annour was also aware that the chances of Amna gaining a husband more acceptable than Ahmed Dirar were slim. People were afraid of the spirit of the deceased *feki*. And although Annour Duman did not believe in *fekis* and their alleged powers, he understood the beliefs of others.

Meanwhile, Bit Burbur discussed the subject with Ghaniya Bit el Tom, Amna's mother. The old woman was aware that Ghaniya and her daughters had all been subjected to the stick of Omar Duman and the sharp tongue of his mother Diya, who was Ghaniya's father's sister, and her mother-in-law. She also knew that a wife could influence her husband by raising the subject repeatedly in moments of intimacy. Ghaniya was happy to hear the news that a Jaali man was interested in marrying her daughter. A Jaali was sure to give her daughter a good life, particularly in material things such as clothing, perfumes and household wares. That he was was a *feki* commended him further. For this reason Ghaniya began to prepare her daughter mentally, trying systematically to erase the prejudices instilled in her by Diya, and refill her brain with new ideas.

But Ghaniya did not have the last word. Ultimately she had no say in the matter at all. The final decision, she knew, was in the hands of the matriarch, Diya, her mother-in-law and paternal aunt. When Annour broke the news of Ahmed Dirar's intentions to Diya, she contemptuously rejected the idea. For Diya, it was out of question to give her granddaughter to a man of such doubtful family roots – one of those Jaaliyin who roamed the Shukriya land with no one knowing where they came from. It was always a question of roots for Diya: ancestry and pedigree were what mattered. *Al iriq dassas*, she would say: lineage conceals surprises. She had a fear of the return of inheritable characteristics. Who could guarantee that some day, due to a mistake – such as the one that would be in the making, were Dirar to wed Amna – a child of negroid appearance might not pop up in the Duman family? And further, she wondered, why had this man, Dirar, objected to the marriages of his own brothers? Why did he object to their marrying black women to the extent that he severed all relationships with them for life? And why was he so hot-tempered, like red pepper, if he himself had African blood? It must be a trick. The man was feigning noble behaviour to deceive them.

On the other hand, she wondered, if he did have negroid ancestry, why had the Bawadra Arabs of Asubri given him a wife, although they were the cousins of the Shukriya? His two daughters looked Arab all right – apart from Fatima's protruding teeth. But no, no – look again at Ahmed Dirar's nose. His lips. No, there was no way for him to marry Amna. And his father, so dark! No way. There were hundreds of proper Shukriya men who could ask for Amna's hand.

But the Shukriya men did not show up. And Ahmed Dirar kept sending mediator after mediator to convince Diya. They came from all walks of life. The pressure became too much to bear, especially after her two sons lost any desire to support her point of view. Amna was growing older every day. In a rare moment of relaxation Diya gave a faint indication of possible willingness for Dirar to marry her. Mediators and go-betweens immediately pounced on the opportunity. In a single day Ahmed Dirar journeyed to and from Kassala to bring the palm-leaf mats for the tent, the perfumes, the dates and most importantly, the *zihba*, the clothes for the bride, as specified by Bit Burbur. He gave these to Bit Burbur in her role as the groom's guardian and declared that the wedding rites would all be observed at her house.

But Ahmed Dirar had to contend with another foe, one who dwelt not in this world, but in the realm of the spirits.

THE FEKI'S REVENGE

Away in the other world, nothing stirred up the wrath of Feki Beshir's soul as did the new articles brought from Kassala. These, he saw, were now stored in his own former tent, and in the care of whom? Of his own wife. And for whom? For his Amna! He had been displaced. The *feki*'s spirit, baleful and vengeful, stormed out of the grave that night to deliver its first blow.

Bit Burbur checked the items brought by Ahmed Dirar from Kassala, but to her surprise she discovered that the man apparently had no idea of the kind of clothes he was supposed to have bought.

"Ahmed!" she shouted. And when he came to her she demanded: "What is this that you went all the way to Kassala to fetch?"

Surprised, he asked her what she was referring to.

"The clothes you brought are all the wrong ones," she said.

"This is strange, Bit Burbur," said Ahmed Dirar. "I am surprised to hear this. You checked these pieces one item after the other when I arrived from Kassala."

"But this cloth is the one the girls nowadays call *habboba-booli*, the "Grandma, urinate" cloth!" said Bit Burbur. "I would never have let you bring that. And this one here they nickname, *alsheett wajaa algananeett,* "Alas! Pain in the ass!" And there are important ones that are missing, Ahmed. You haven't brought the *tob* called *surrati*, nor the *gurbab*, the wrap-around, or the *algarmassis*, or the one called *alkhumri*. And you also seem to have forgotten to buy the *firka* – the red bridal wrapper. For heavens sake, what have you done?"

Ahmed was astounded, having gone to great pains to get the right cloths, leaving his sheep unattended and borrowing another man's camel to bring them from Kassala.

"Bit Burbur, as far as I know, I brought all these clothes as checked by you," he said.

But Bit Burbur told him that if he wanted to marry Amna he would have to go back to Kassala and get more. Diya, she said, was already hinting that she might change her mind. Neither spoke of who or what might have caused the confusion. But soon rumours went around that the Spirit of Feki Beshir was behind all this swapping of clothes. A quarrel, they said, had developed between Bit Burbur and Ahmed Dirar, and this was surely the work of the spirit of the *feki*.

When Dirar went back to Kassala, he made sure to pay a visit to the Mirghanis, leaders of the Khatmiya, the Islamic movement that the Dirars belonged to, with the intention of rallying their help in the spirit battle waged by Feki Beshir against him. And he bought a new set of bridal clothes. When he returned to Shehateib he was pleased to find that Bit Burbur was adding the last touches to preparations for the wedding day. At last he felt able to relax.

But the Spirit of Feki Beshir was far from relaxed. The Spirit tautened at the hard-headedness of Bit Burbur. She had to learn that Amna was his, and his alone.

Just one day before the appointed day for the wedding, Bit

Burbur's first cousin Adam died suddenly. He was a man of repute, a tribal leader of some weight among the Humran, upriver at Wad el Hileiw. His death created new difficulties. Not only did it oblige people to postpone the wedding ceremony, but it was linked by many to the wrath of the Spirit of Feki Beshir at the prospect of the match. Bit Burbur dismissed the rumours and insisted on going ahead with the preparations for the ceremony when the appropriate mourning period had passed.

But once more the Spirit of Feki Beshir hovered overhead. If the death of a first cousin was too remote in kinship terms, perhaps the death of a brother would clinch it.

Ijeil, Bit Burbur's younger brother, was a strapping young man, a playboy given to debauchery. Every evening he slipped away from the camp at Shehateib to the village of Sharafa across the river on the west bank where a number of freed slave women lived. Since the ford across the river and the Blue Bridge were both at some distance from the camp, Ijeil normally crossed the river by swimming. After spending the night at the village he would swim back in the late morning to Shehateib.

It was early on one of those mornings that the Spirit of Feki Beshir left the grave and headed for the river. There it turned itself into a crocodile that lurked in the deep waters, and waited for a rendezvous with Ijeil. The crocodile hid itself beneath a rocky outcrop that overhung the water on the east bank. Once in a while it would move up and down in the water to keep its muscles in shape and its body limber. And now and then it would pop up its nostrils to get some air. At the same time the eyes would come up to scan the west bank to see if the prey had shown up.

The spirit-crocodile paid little attention to the boisterous activities of the girls who came down to the river to fetch water. And the girls did not notice it. They spread out along the water edge, some filling up their water skins and singing, others washing clothes by beating them on rocks and jumping on them with their feet, sliding one foot after another. The donkeys that carried the water were left to graze on the grass festooning the edge of the water.

Close by, the crocodile could see some fat goats watering themselves. But it had no appetite for the goats. It was waiting for the dish it could truly savour: Ijeil! It would not be long now.

And here came Ijiel rambling down the bank, his long *tob* trailing behind him. Young, strong and brave, a man who scared most people: the dust bolted from his footfalls as he strode down the path. As was his habit, he went through a routine when he came to the river. The girls on the other side knew it well. At the edge of the water he stripped naked, divesting himself of his clothes – his *tob*, *surwal* and *gemiss* – and his shoes and a number of leather-bound amulets that he wore around his upper arms. He then waded into the water with one hand covering the rift between his buttocks and the other hiding his private parts. He was aware of the adolescent girls across the river, a hundred metres away, each looking furtively at his magnificent figure. Secretly, one suspects, he enjoyed it, but he pretended he was unaware. When the water came to his waist he dived deep into it and came out splashing water around. He swam for a few moments and then retired to a shallower nook where he scrubbed himself, without soap. Now he came out covering himself in the same manner as before, in the custom of nomad men. He crouched down and wrapped all his clothes in a ball, the amulets in the pockets of the *gemiss*, and fixed the bundle on his head with the drawstring of his *surwal*. Then he entered the water to swim across the river, clothes above his head to keep them dry.

In its hiding place beneath the rock the crocodile stirred. Ijiel was oblivious of any danger. He was worried only about getting his clothes wet. The girls on the bank saw the crocodile appear above the surface of the water surface and head for the man. They shrieked in chorus, but before they could draw breath again the monster seized Ijiel and dived deep, leaving only a bundle of clothes bobbing up and down on the surface of the river. Some girls fainted; others ran to the camp to break the news. Their water-skins floated away with the current. The girls who stayed at the river said they heard the crocodile crunch Ijiel's bones right there under the great rock. The donkeys continued their grazing.

THE FIGHT OF THE TWO FEKIS

After Ijiel's death Ahmed Dirar began to feel that he really was in a feud with the deceased *feki*. But he had confidence in his own spiritual powers. This was a fair fight, he thought, one between equals, *feki* against *feki*, one bearer of the Holy Book against another. Being dead or alive made no difference in the world of spirits. Ahmed Dirar opened the Book and read Yassin, his favorite *sura*. Throughout the mourning months he read it day and night in solitude.

Many of those who once acted in good faith as go-betweens and mediators now withdrew. Ahmed Dirar and Bit Burbur found themselves alone, the spirit of the *feki* hovered over their lives. Some tried to convince Dirar to slaughter a ram to propitiate the soul of the *feki*, which he refused to do. His whole future as a *feki* rested on the outcome of this battle. He told the go-betweens he was not about to fall for women's talk.

Bit Burbur passed through a period of fear and trepidation.

She felt that she had unnecessarily put herself in a dangerous position, in the line of fire between the two holy men. But as a widow of a *feki* herself she felt she should show fortitude. She declared that once the mourning period was over she was going to proceed with the wedding preparations if and when Ahmed Dirar deemed it appropriate, notwithstanding the warning signals sent by her late husband from the world beyond. Meanwhile Diya adopted a strategy of wait-and-see. She was hopeful that the battle would end with the defeat of Ahmed Dirar.

Amna was almost completely forgotten during all those events. But everything that happened strengthened her belief in the soul of her late betrothed. The events were proof enough for her that the great *feki* was not going to abandon her. He would always be at her side, to protect her against those who meant her harm.

The rainy season began and the camp moved from the river at Shehateib to the high land of Wadi Khireissab to grow sorghum. That year was a good year, and harvest time was the time for weddings. There was an uneasy lull in the tug of war over Amna. Diya was waiting for Ahmed Dirar to be defeated by the Spirit of Feki Beshir. But she also wondered whether Ahmed Dirar might have won the battle. Perhaps she should stir things up again? Any mishap that took place would be imputed to the soul of the dead *feki* and she could make use of that. Meanwhile Bit Burbur sent her young daughter, Ketira, to Ahmed Dirar to suggest a date for the wedding. He sent the girl back with the suggestion that Bit Burbur set the date with Diya. But when Bit Burbur went to see her, Diya announced that she was completely against the whole marriage. She had changed her mind, she said, because Feki Beshir visited her in a dream and warned her against the wedding.

"Diya", said Bit Burbur, "you can't do this now. You know the man has spent his money in buying the wedding articles already."

"But," retorted Diya, "you also know, Bit Burbur, that my granddaughter could get caught up in this fight between the two *fekis* and get hurt."

"They both love Amna and that is why they are fighting," said Bit Burbur. "You know that. Neither of them is going to hurt Amna at all,"

"Well, Feki Beshir didn't exactly hate your brother Ijeil – may Allah rest his soul – but look what he did to him, devouring him like that in broad daylight."

"None the less, Feki Beshir is not going to hurt that girl, Diya," said Bit Burbur, though now she felt less assured.

"Even if he isn't, he may kill her husband if this man of yours were to get married to her. I don't want my granddaughter to become a widow while she is so young, Bit Burbur. I am sure you understand that, don't you? We are dealing here with a spirit; we are not dealing with a physical being."

She continued: "Why doesn't this man, Dirar, look for another woman? There's nothing more abundant in these parts than women looking for husbands. Why Amna?"

"I told you. He loves her and won't even look at another woman," said Bit Burbur quietly.

"Nonsense! Don't give me that love thing, The man was married before and had children and he is much older than Amna anyway, so what love are you talking about? I think he is only enjoying the challenge he is facing and the publicity he is getting. He has always been in love with adventure, hasn't he? I have known him since we were all together at Asubri. He is a trouble-maker, a wild man. Look at him now: spears, daggers and dogs. These things don't sit well with the Qur'an that he is carrying around," said Diya.

"Diya, let's be honest," said Bit Burbur. "You do not want the man because you suspect that he has a slave ancestry. Isn't that the truth?"

"Suspect it? Well, you were the one who said it, not me. You and I have seen his father Ali Dirar, the *muezzin*. Would you give that man your granddaughter, Bit Burbur?" Diya asked, with a sly look at her interlocutor.

"It's true Ali Dirar was dark and had a large nose," said Bit Burbur. "The Jaaliyin all look like that. Yet they are not of slave origin. Their hair is not frizzy. Ahmed's mother, whom you have seen back in Asubri, is half-Shukriya from the Aishab sub-tribe."

Diya looked at her.

"Bit Burbur," she said, "you know that saying about our brothers the Aishab – may Allah forgive them – don't you? 'He who has no tribe should join the Aishab'? We all know the Aishab accept people indiscriminately. I suggest you go back to the man and tell him in a nice way that Amna adamantly refused to accept him. And concerning that Aishab connection, remember that a man is his father's child, not his mother's."

Bit Burbur returned home and broke the news to Ahmed Dirar.

The hot-tempered Ahmed cried out in rage, "That old hag, Diya! She is nothing but a whetstone for arguments and quarrels. Is she asking for trouble? Then trouble is what she will get. Who does she think she is, playing with other people's destinies like this? In case she does not know, tell her she is out to meet the devil himself. We shall see who wins!"

With those impetuous remarks, Ahmed Dirar declared open war on Diya, whom he had hitherto treated with prudence and tact. Now he had two enemies, the Spirit of Feki Beshir and the flesh-and-blood Diya. Both would be against him in a protracted war for Amna.

Straightaway Ahmed Dirar reactivated the earlier marriage mediators, moving back and forth from household to household with fiery determination. He talked personally to Omar and Annour Duman, reminding them that by nomad standards the girl was getting old for marriage and that Allah would not accept this complacency and reticence from their side; they should speak out loud, he said, and tell their mother that she should not play games in serious matters like this. Besides, he told them, their reputation as men of their word would be harmed among the nomads if it was known that decisions were taken for them by their mother. He told them that it was not right that they should leave the future of the poor girl in her grandmother's hands. When did women ever know about life? When did men ever place matters of marriage in the hands of women?

Omar Duman, Amna's father, was easily influenced. He was wound up by Ahmed Dirar's rhetoric and declared himself in favour of the marriage. So now hopes rose once more. Bit Burbur began preparing for the wedding again, though she had a lingering suspicion that Diya would soon reassert herself. Ahmed Dirar was happy as things took a turn his way. He took his flock to pastures in the cool evenings. His sheep, he knew, were fattened best by taking them for *serba*, the night-grazing.

The Dumans changed their minds back and forth, one way and another, sometimes convinced by Ahmed Dirar and sometimes by Diya.

And away in the other world, Feki Beshir tossed and turned uneasy in his grave.

Then he decided on a knock-out blow, one that would send his enemy into oblivion.

He turned himself into a snake.

THE LAST BATTLE

One moonlit night, Ahmed Dirar was tending his sheep in an area of thick savannah grass. He had nothing on his mind but to fatten his sheep, his fine flock busy grazing in front of his eyes. He was one of the richest men in the region; his flock had multiplied over this last *kherif*, the rainy season just ended. Daydreaming thus, he entered a thick growth of elephant grass. He heard a faint hissing sound, the rattling sound of a *washasha* snake, rubbing its scales against one another. With the instinct of the hunter, he broke stride to investigate. He felt the snake close to him. He caught the whiff of its breath on his leg. The *washasha*, the rattlesnake, he knew, was even deadlier than *abdaraga*, the cobra.

Ahmed Dirar carefully looked around in the thick grass, his heavy stick at the ready, but he could spot nothing in the dim light of the gibbous moon and the shadow of the grass. The snake was hidden behind one of the many small saplings in the tall grass. It was very close to Dirar, waiting to discharge its mission from the land of the dead. It waited, flicking its tongue.

Though Ahmed could not see it he knew that if he moved it would strike. He watched and listened for the faintest signs of its whereabouts. His flocks and sheepdogs came towards the grass in which he was standing. He raised his stick to scare the animals. Then the snake struck, sinking its fangs into his left calf muscle. Ahmed swerved and brought his heavy curved stick down on the ground, jumping away as he did so. When he looked back he saw that he had broken the huge snake's backbone. The snake tried to slither away but could not. Frantically, Ahmed hit at the reptile until it died. He tied a tourniquet round his leg and hurriedly rounded up his flock and began moving it towards the camp. The camp was just behind a nearby coppice of *kitir* trees, but he felt the poison rising up in his body and an excrutiating pain took hold of him. He left the flock behind and, dragging his leg with great effort, he limped towards the camp as fast as he could. He knew he had to get back to the camp before the poison reached his heart. He was certain that the snake he saw and killed was the Spirit of Feki Beshir, and that the only cure lay in the Book, the Holy Qur'an. He had to reach the camp as quickly as possible before the venom took him, too, to the place where Feki Bashir was. He must get hold of the Book.

At home, his little daughters, Fatima and Asha, were playing with Ketira, when their father broke into the tent, seized his *jurab*, a leather container, and began groping inside it. The girls screamed and Ketira ran to Bit Burbur. Soon all the camp dwellers were at his tent. Ahmed Dirar opened the Book with difficulty and began to read the *sura* Yassin. Every now and then he would rub spittle on the bite. Bit Burbur brought him roots. He refused, saying that they were useless for that kind of snake. When he finished reading the *sura*, he rummaged into the *jurab* once more to fish out a reed pen and a well-stoppered ink bottle. He ordered Fatima to bring him a wooden slate and began writing snippets of verses from the Qur'an. When the surface of the slate was full of the large letters he quickly washed it with water from the *ibrig* and drank the water.

That night Ahmed Dirar lay in a grievous condition, in terrible pain. He could not sleep; nor could he move. People in the camp began to murmur that Feki Beshir had finally won the battle. The news of his condition reached Karim, a Jaali friend of his – another of the fiery-tempered group. Tall, thin, gaunt, with a slight hunch on his back, Karim was often told that he was never going to gain weight because of his hot temper. Hearing the news of Ahmed Dirar's state, Karim left his village, Sharafa, at daybreak. In a few hours he was sitting on the edge of Ahmed Dirar's bed. He found him delirious, writhing, flecked with foam, his leg tied with cloth strips of sundry colors, torn out of women's *tobs*, raised high and tied to one of the rafters of the tent to try and minimise the spread of the poison.

Karim was the closest to kin that Ahmed Dirar had. As such he took it upon himself to try and save Ahmed's life by persuading him to admit defeat, apologize to Feki Beshir and abandon the idea of marrying Amna Duman. Karim offered to go on Ahmed Dirar's behalf and slaughter a ram on Feki Beshir's tomb as an offering, to appease the holy man and ask forgiveness. For a long time Karim tried to get a response from his friend to his suggestion.

But Ahmed Dirar refused, point blank.

Ahmed Dirar survived his first night. But it did not look as if he would survive a second. The onlookers were expecting him to die. His weeping daughters gathered around his bed.

At that moment Diya came up with something that once again, stunned the whole camp. Suddenly she declared that she was fully for wedding her granddaughter, Amna, to Ahmed Dirar and that she would not change her mind again. She said this was needed to help the man get off his deathbed.

"Poor man," said Diya, "I believe he is dying more of love than of snake-bite."

She followed this opinion with an announcement that the marriage was to be registered now and immediately and all the formalities and legal and religious aspects be completed on the wings of haste.

When this news reached Karim in Ahmed Dirar's tent he rushed to the Dumans' tent overflowing with bitterness.

"This is a trick that is not going to see light," he said to Diya. "Now that you see him dying you want to inherit the man's wealth."

Karim returned to Ahmed Dirar's tent and explained that Diya was trying to play a trick on him.

"I need not tell you about the devilish wiles of that old woman," he said. "You know her better than I. We are dealing here with the devil incarnate, in case you forgot, Ahmed," said Karim.

Ahmed Dirar gave no sign.

"This is not a matter to keep silent about," said Karim. "Will you just say something to stop those people, to keep them from harming you and your own, your daughters and your wealth?"

Finally, with great difficulty, Ahmed beckoned Karim to approach. Through pain and delirium he asked him clearly to go to the Dumans and convey to them his acceptance of the offer. He deputized him, Karim, to represent him in all the legal matters of the marriage. By that evening, he said, Amna should be his.

Karim told Ahmed that he was in no state to deputise anyone. Did he not realize a plot had been staged against him? But Ahmed assured him that he understood the whole thing very well. This could be his dying wish, he told Karim. And he asked him to see that it was fulfilled so he could die in peace.

Karim had no choice. He went to the Dumans, this time with a lowered head, and conveyed to the grinning Diya the consent of Ahmed Dirar.

That day the legal aspects were observed in the presence of a few dignitaries and a man of religion from Sharafa village. Amna Omar Duman became the wife of Ahmed Ali Dirar.

From his sick bed Ahmed Dirar insisted that the marriage be consummated right away. The idea drew ridicule from the people round Diya, yet Diya herself welcomed it. There would be witnesses that all the steps of marriage had been completed before the man's demise. According to the custom of the nomads, the perfumed bride was to be taken to the groom's tent in the cool breezes of the very early hours of morning. Half-way to the tent the groom was supposed to come out and carry his bride, circle the tent with her seven times and then take her inside.

The bridesmaids taking the bride to her groom knew that he would not be able to come for his bride. In case he did not come out, as expected of him, should they take the bride back? But in the small hours a man came out of the groom's tent whose face they could not see. He seized the bride and carried her off into the groom's tent without making the customary seven rounds of the tent. Too late, they realized that the man was Karim, the best man, instructed by Dirar to bring him his bride.

At this point Amna saw for the first time the state of her bridegroom. A carcass of a man! She could hardly make out what he strove to say to her. Her tears rolled down. She spent the two or three hours before sunrise, sobbing, then sneaked back to her mother's tent. Diya asked her about her groom's condition. Amna told her grandmother that the man was going to die any moment. Diya calmed her down, while she calculated the fortune that would soon accrue to them.

Nomads do not sleep beyond dawn. They sleep early and wake early, witnessing the sunrise. Every day reports would come of the state of Ahmed Dirar. Three days after Amna's first night with her groom, he was still alive. Diya became apprehensive. Early one morning, she walked out of her tent and thought she saw something moving in front of Ahmed Dirar's tent, bent over like a monkey. She summoned her granddaughter, Nofal, Amna's sister, and asked her what it could be.

"Grandma," said Nofal. "That is Ahmed Dirar himself, carrying out ablution for his morning prayer."

So Ahmed Dirar survived the snake bite. He emerged from the battle a more powerful *feki*, particularly among the Hadendowa tribes of the eastern bank of the Atbara, and now with a new wife. He finally took the place of Feki Beshir.

For Diya, however, a new war had just begun. *Feki* or no *feki*, Amna was not going to stay with that man! The fires of the hatred that burnt into her could only be doused with divorce. The dispute between them continued. Ahmed Dirar swore he would never again eat or drink in his mother-in-law's house. At least that was what Diya claimed.

AMNA'S CHILD

A year after Diya saw Ahmed Dirar at his prayers in front of his tent when he should have been dead, Amna gave birth to her first child – a boy.

Ahmed Dirar was happy because after two daughters he now had his first son. Even Diya was happy because the baby was her first great grandson, from her first grand-daughter, from her first son. And her happiness was for a special reason. She had been half-expecting a monster. She was relieved and exhilarated that the baby turned out to be a pure Arab-looking child, with no sign of Africa in its looks.

The first hour following the delivery of the baby, Diya hastened to slaughter the *hurrara* goat, thus proclaiming the child *hur*, a free person, not a slave. A week later she slaughtered the *simaya* goat, whereby Ahmed Dirar gave the child the name of Ibrahim, after the relative who had married his first cousin, Dar-Salam, back in the Jaali land. After one more month, Diya asked her son, Omar, to *arrib* – arabise – the boy, that is, to circumcise him. She took it for granted that circumcision was an Arab custom, one which distinguished that Semitic race from the Hamitic blacks of Africa. Diya claimed that the Prophet Muhammad – peace be upon him – was born circumcised, just like his great grandfathers, the prophets Ibrahim and Ismail.

Later the child was marked as member of the Shukriya tribe with three parallel vertical cuts on each cheek. Such ritual scarring is an African practice if ever there was one, but Diya was not aware of this. For her, the Shukriya tribe was an Arab tribe going back in ancestry to Gaafar al-Tayyar (Gaafar Ibn Abi Talib), the first cousin of Prophet Muhammad, and the brother of Ali Ibn Abi Talib, the famous caliph of the Prophet.

The arrival of the baby Ibrahim calmed things only temporarily. Diya never for a moment forgot her grudge against Ahmed Dirar. She decided that the child had nothing to do with him. He showed not a single physical trait in common with his father, she decided. The child was all Duman. But ancestry concealed surprises, she reminded herself. And another child would very likely reveal some of those unpleasant surprises. When his child came out apparently pure Arab some of the women in her family reproached her for her suspicion of Dirar.

"Not quite," she would reply, "*al-iriq dassas!*"

At length Diya began weaving the intricacies of a plan to divorce Amna from Ahmed Dirar. She intended to accomplish this during the two breast-feeding years, before Amna picked up the seed for the second child. One blazing summer noon she found the opportunity she was waiting for when Ahmed Dirar was offered a calabash of water at her tent. As Ahmed was holding the calabash in the act of drinking, crouched on the ground, Diya came and stood right there over him. Hands akimbo, she loudly asked the men in the gathering to bear witness that "this man has taken water in my tent. He has perhaps forgotten, but some time ago he had pledged on the divorce of his wife not to eat or drink anything in my house."

Having finished what she wanted to say, she proceeded immediately to point out three men among those present to take the witness stand as and when they were asked to do so. The accusation had the corollary that, as of that moment, Amna could not stay with her husband in the same tent. According to tradition, to renege on such a pledge was tantamount to divorce. Diya took immediate measures to see to it that Amna and her son moved from Dirar's tent to her own. She took no notice of Ahmed Dirar's remonstrance, saying simply that he had every right to take his case to court, that was if he had a case. And, in order to secure the separation of Amna from her husband she convinced her sons to move the family from Shehateib to Jummeiza across the river.

For his part, Ahmed Dirar thought he did not lose much. He had always been a loner. As far as his disputes with Diya were concerned, he had already won the most important one and gained Amna for wife. Besides, he already had children from his first wife, including a male child for that matter. It did not matter much if he did not marry again. Now, he thought, he could have a break from the obligations and fetters of married life and all the social vexations it entailed. He would go back to the care-free life of a bachelor, back to his sheepdogs and daggers.

So Ahmed Dirar crossed the river again. However, after two full years of that kind of life, he decided that he had enough of it. Besides, the idea that Diya was happy thinking that she had finally won the battle began to cross his mind over and over again. He was now full of steam, ready to wage a new round of war against Diya.

"She said I should take my case to court," he reminded himself. "Well, why not? She has taken away my wife and son for two years now. I could beat her in court."

So one morning Ahmed Dirar left Shehateib to Almarkaz village, a place that is now called Khashm el Girba, and took his case to the court of Sheikh Awad el Karim Abu Sin, the *nazir* himself, where he recounted his grievances against the Dumans.

An askari was dispatched to Omar Duman with a court order to present himself before the Sheikh at a specified date. At that date the Dumans, Diya, Omar, Amna and the child arrived at Almarkaz and stayed with Shawish Yousif and his wife Halima Bit el Tom, Diya's niece and Amna's aunt. Presently they all went to court.

The court proceeding did not take long. Dirar's witnesses were called upon to take the stand first; his friend Karim was the most important of them.

"What's your name?" asked Sheikh Abu Sin.

"Abdal Karim wad Taha," replied Karim.

"What tribe you belong to?" asked the sheikh.

"Jaaliyin," answered Karim.

"How long have you been living with the Shukriya?"

"For quite some time now."

Sheikh Abu Sin looked straight into the man's eyes. When he

stared like that men shook and their knees buckled.

"How old are you?" asked Abu Sin.

"About forty," said Karim.

"Wasn't your mother, the widow, married to Umara wad el Ayess when you were a young child?"

Karim had not thought that the *sheikh* who ruled over the whole vast Butana land would have such information on a single family – and a non-Shukriya family too.

"Yes, Sheikh al Arab," came the faltering voice of Karim.

"Then how long have you been with the Shukriya?" followed up the sheikh.

"Almost forty years, Sheikh al Arab," quavered Karim.

"Now you have forty years among the Skukriya and you call yourself Jaali?" said Abu Sin. "You are no longer a Jaali; you are a Shukriya."

"Yes, Sheikh al Arab." For who would disagree with the Sheikh Awad al Karim Abu Sin?

"You are invalidated as a witness. Now leave the stand; you probably have some grudge against Shukriya such as the Dumans," concluded Abu Sin.

Ahmed Dirar, whose main witness had now been dismissed, broke out in wild words.

"Take him away too," the sheikh ordered. "And call the witnesses of the Dumans."

Three Shukriya nomads, clad in *tobs* stained from the work of the camp, entered the court.

"Did you see Ahmed Dirar drink water at Diya's tent two years ago?" asked Abu Sin.

"Yes, Sheikh al Arab."

Diya was sure she had won the case now.

Then the Skeikh stared at each of them in turn.

"What do you three know of a pledge taken by Ahmed Dirar not to eat or drink at Diya's tent?" asked the Sheikh.

The three men exchanged nervous glances.

The Sheikh said, "You heard my question. Do not let me hear a lie."

"We knew nothing of a pledge, Sheikh al Arab," one of the men replied. And the other two nodded assent.

Omar Duman jumped to his feet fuming and gnashing his teeth. Like Ahmed Dirar he was a man who harboured anger.

"Take him away, too!" came the order. The *muhafizin* threw Omar Duman down at his mother's feet.

The sheikh took coffee and gave his verdict. Dirar was given back his wife and child, but Amna was instructed to wait with her people at Jummeiza until Ahmed Dirar bought her the offerings of clothes, perfumes and housewares.

This is how justice was done in the old days at the court of Sheikh Abu Sin.

THE AMULET

It was there at Jummeiza, while waiting for Ahmed Dirar to bring the offerings, that Amna Duman had a vivid dream, a vision.

She saw herself under a white canopy, a *khulla*, the mosquito net used to protect a new mother and her infant. While she was lying there she saw Feki Beshir in very white clothes by her bedside. Amna looked at the holy man and found a sympathetic look on his face. She lost no time to plead with him that she be divorced from Ahmed Dirar.

In her dream Feki Beshir tucked his right hand into his pocket and drew out an amulet, a *hijab*, a piece of white paper, folded, that carried writings of selected verses from the Qur'an. The holy man gave the amulet to Amna. She accepted it without question. Then the *feki* disappeared and Amna woke. For many hours she tried to understand what had happened. This was surely not just a dream but a vision with a meaning. What could be the link between a canopy of birth, an amulet, and the white cloth? She did not tell anyone for fear of being reproached for her enduring attachment to Feki Beshir.

A few days later, Ahmed Dirar arrived at Jummeiza with the required clothes, perfumes and household paraphernalia and took Amna and Ibrahim, their son, who was now four years old, back to Shehateib. The family was together once more. They spent the winter and dry summer months near the river with the rest of the small community of Arabs among the Hadendowa. Amna even forgot the idea of getting divorced from her husband; at that point, she felt, the man was good to her.

THE YEAR OF BOMBS

That year the *kherif* came early and heavy rains fell. When the camp moved to Khireissab, the rainy season site, Amna was six months pregnant. Members of the community kept themselves busy tending their flocks or growing sorghum. It was 1940. In Europe war had begun. But the people of the camp were oblivious of events in the outside world – a remote place that affected them little.

The little they knew of what was happening in the wider world that year was brought to them by Annour Duman, riding on his white donkey. He told them that the British rulers of the country were involved in a war with another European power, the Italians. The Italians had colonized Eritrea and invaded neighbouring Ethiopia. When khaki-clad soldiers began to appear in the creeks round the Blue Bridge the people of Khireissab began to believe Annour's news of the war that they were not part of.

Benito Mussolini, the Italian dictator, was doubtless as unaware of their existence as they of his. But he was intent on dealing a blow to the British – and their allies the Americans. So on 4 July 1940 Italian war planes took off from Eritrea with orders to cut the route that led from Eritea to Sudan and across the Atbara River over the Blue Bridge near our camp. Few people in Khireissab had ever seen a plane, let alone one that rained fire on the land below. At the first explosion every living thing in the camp bolted in chaos: donkeys, camels and sheep, dogs, goats and people. The dogs ran away barking, the goats ran bleating, men and women ran screaming. Everyone fled: the old carried the young, the blind carried the lame. They fled from the open tableland and took cover in the creeks and among the *karab*, the rough area of hillocks and knolls beyond.

Only one man did not run. The elder Jubar, a man of seventy years of age, wrapped his *tob* round his waist and took his sword and shield in order to patrol the camp to guard it against any invader. Jubar had a family reputation for bravery to uphold. It had come down to him from his grandfather Abu Makna. He was not about to run from death. But this Don Quixote was rescued forcibly by two young men who wrestled him to the ground and dragged him down the creek. And the Blue Bridge remained intact. When the Italian planes had left and things became quiet once more, people resumed their normal activities. The sorghum harvest came, the stalks left standing in the fields where the sheep and goats stripped them of their leaves. That year was later dubbed *Sanat el Ganabil*, the Year of Bombs.

A CHILD WITH TWO FATHERS

The rains ended. The green land turned straw-coloured as the pastures dried up. The dark soil of the tableland began to crack. Still the camp had not yet moved to the summer site at Shehateib creek.

Ahmed Dirar was away at Suwayil. He left his pregnant wife at Khireissab and asked his neighbour Taha, in the event that the child was a boy, to call him Hamid, after his uncle, father of the beautiful Dar Salam, back in the Jaaliyin land. Late one night, as it was recounted to me later, Amna felt the child coming. She woke her mother-in-law who went to wake their neighbor Atalmula to ask him to fetch the midwife.

Atalmula's daughter emerged from the tent.

"Girl, would you please tell your father that I want to see him urgently?" asked the old woman. There was no reply from the girl.

"Girl! Do you hear me or are you still asleep?" said the old woman sharply.

"I heard you grandma, but I can't wake him up," the girl replied shyly.

"What do you mean you can't?" asked the old woman.

Embarrassed, the girl explained, "Father is lying too close to mother to be aroused from his sleep."

"That kind of sleep can wait," said the old lady. "If you are not going to wake him, I'll rouse him myself."

At this point, though, Atalmula came out of his own accord. On learning of Amna's state he ran across the sorghum fields to the midwife's tent.

Back at Ahmed Dirar's tent Amna's labour pains were starting. The midwife asked the women who had gathered there to light a fire and tie a rope to the middle rafter. The labour pains came at ever shortening intervals. Amna was told to crouch on a mat on the floor of the tent and hold tightly to the dangling rope as the baby was being delivered. Thus it was that she gave birth to me, Hamid, her second child. Moments later the midwife exclaimed "*Mabruk!* Congratulations! It's a boy." Fatima and Asha gave the customary shriek, the *zaghruta*, that proclaims a male child. Amna took a close look at the infant, the shape of its nose, the colour of its skin. She looked at it with the eyes of her grandmother, Diya, who abhorred the dark skin of those with African ancestry.

"It is green! It is blue!" she whispered in dismay. These are the words used in Sudan for those with a dark skin colour. The nose of the infant was flat. *Ancestry hides surprises.* Diya's words rang in her head. She knew her grandmother would not be happy. And Diya was bound to arrive sometime soon.

Then, later, when Amna was nursing her baby, she suddenly had a thought. The Amulet! This was the meaning of the night vision she had, the vision of Feki Beshir. This was his gift to her. The canopy was a symbol of birth. And the amulet, the *hijab*, the fold of paper, was the child himself. He was the Amulet of Feki Beshir! The child was named Hamid, as his father wished. But to his mother he was the Amulet. Did that mean that she was going to be divorced after giving birth to the Amulet? Yes!

This was how I, Hamid Dirar, came into the world, the son both of a living man, and of a ghost.

A BLIND BABY AND A RABID DOG

Two weeks later Diya arrived from Jummeiza. Amna was still under the birth canopy when Diya cast a mute look at the... the... *thing* that her granddaughter was cradling. Bereft of speech she just stood there, until Amna gave her the opportunity to vent some of the steam imprisoned in her chest.

"It is good to see you, grandma," said Amna.

"It is good to see you too, child," replied Diya. "My, my, what do we have here?" She was trying to play with the infant with her fingers, but looking at the flat nose.

"Grandma, the baby needs Arabization," said Amna.

"That is not so important, my dear," retorted Diya, wondering whether Amna really imagined that that child she begot from Ahmed Dirar this time was actually an Arab. "Boys can get circumcised anytime later, you know."

"Well, how about the marks, the cicatricization? Will you be here when the time comes?" asked Amna pleadingly.

"Amna, what has got into you? You know that marks are not an obligation for men," replied Diya.

"It won't help anyway," she murmured to herself as she turned to go out of the tent on her way to visit other families. "Today a baboon," she murmured, "tomorrow an ape."

Amna followed her with her eyes, reading correctly what was in the mind of her grandmother – she was not happy with the child. The family was now adulterated with African blood as far as Diya was concerned. But Amna had already convinced herself that her child – blue or green or whatever colour – was the Amulet of Feki Umhummad wad Beshir and that the *feki*'s spirit would be the child's guardian angel throughout its life. The *feki*, she was certain, would have a plan for the child's future, a good future, otherwise he would not have given it to her.

One week after my birth, before the arrival of Diya, Ahmed Dirar took his mother and the two girls to Suwayil where he had a sorghum farm that needed urgent harvesting. He asked Bit Burbur to take care of his wife and the baby. Amna according to custom, would be staying in the canopy for forty days before doing any household work or travelling anywhere.

When Diya arrived she was now still more intent on divorcing Amna from Ahmed Dirar before she begot a whole drove of slaves in the Duman family. The pure line of the Dumans should not be adulterated with the murky blood of these pagan tribes of the Nile.

"Amna, I have always warned you against this unholy marriage. Take a good look at this new-born, Amna. Do you like what you see?" asked Diya, her eyes bulging.

"Grandma, you are very cruel. What is wrong with my baby? Oh I know what you're thinking," said Amna with tears welling in her eyes.

"You like its colour and its flat nose? Tell me!" shouted Diya.

"Yes I do. And you only see these two features? Why don't you see his large head, his large ears, his thin neck; didn't you always say that those were the signs of the free Arab race?" said Amna.

"Yes, but a pure Arab should have all attributes of purity together. Your baby is *mawallad* at best – a hybrid, a mulatto," said Diya. "You should not hazard another offspring with this man, Amna. Get rid of him and his children. You are still young and you can marry the best of the Arab men and a rich one, too," said Diya, cajolingly.

"I will not leave my children," Amna said. "Besides, my baby here is a gift; he is the Amulet that Feki Beshir gave me in a vision."

"I beg your pardon? What are you talking about?" asked Diya.

Amna told her grandmother about the vision and the amulet she was offered by Feki Beshir.

Diya thought for a moment. "So the *feki* gave you only one *hijab* – one amulet? Well, well then. All the more reason to get rid of the father and child. For one thing, the *feki* did not want you to bear another child from Ahmed Dirar. Second, the *feki* as the guardian spirit, will take good care of your child."

"It's all been done for you, you see?" Diya added, baring one of her rare smiles to help the words register in Amna's mind.

"But, mother, the man has not done anything wrong to me since the court," said Amna.

"What could he do worse than what he is doing right now? He has taken the old woman, the girls and the sheep away and abandoned you here like a leftover to be thrown to stray dogs. I warn you, child, he will show you more abuse yet."

"But it's your life, not mine," Diya added. "I am leaving tomorrow and you are on your own. Just think about what I have told you,"

Left for the most time alone in her tent, Amna fell victim to a dismal state of mind, augmented by a number of misgivings that made her think that the signs for the baby's future did not augur well. Its chances of success in life seemed bleak. Sign after sign attested to this.

Just one week after the birth of the Amulet, Zaki's wife, a deaf-mute beauty of the Humran, gave birth to a blind female child with rolling green eyes. People were horrified. Whoever cast an eye on those unseeing green eyes rushed to Amna's tent to have a look at the beautiful eyes of her baby in order to wipe out the image of the cursed blind child. Everybody except for Diya thought that Amna's baby was a cute thing, nothing African about its features, not even the nose. Most non-negroid Sudanese were of dark colour, anyway, they all knew.

Zaki himself came. "I came to have a look at your baby, Amna. They told me it's a beautiful boy – not like the thing that my wife has begotten," he said. It was unusual for a man to enter the tent of a new mother, but when Zaki saw the green blind eyes of his newborn daughter he had been so shaken by the sight, so afraid something would happen to his own eyes, that a visit to Amna was a remedial necessity.

Zaki called his daughter Zahara – Venus – in the hope that some day her eyes would flare up like the luminous planet. The name was also a blessed one because it was the name of Prophet Muhammad's daughter Fatima-al-Zahraa.

Amna did not like what was happening around her: first, bombs and now a blind baby. The Amulet of Feki Beshir certainly did not seem to carry a halo of sanctity over its little head. A number of mishaps had accompanied my birth. And then something even more eerie happened. Late one evening with clouds hanging overhead – it was the end of the rainy season and the night was dark – when people in the camp were preparing to sleep, a barrage of stones hit the camp, sending people scrambling out of their tents, screaming in confusion. The sky was raining rocks, they thought. But they soon discovered that the stones were not coming from the sky. So they must be thrown at them by someone here on earth. Who could that be if not the Hadendowa across the creek? The Kinjir Hadendowa were in conflict with them over agricultural land. It must be them who had instigated the present surprise attack.

Amna felt the stones and pebbles pelt her tent and at first she thought that perhaps some children were playing by throwing the stones. But then the stones were too many and the attack continued unchecked. She wanted to call for someone to see what was happening, but before she could do that she heard voices emanating from the other tents complaining about the stones too.

The dim night left no chance of discerning the source of the stones. The thick mimosa forest, the *waara*, in front of the camp was calm and gave away no sign of moving objects. Behind the camp, nothing could be heard moving in the *karab* areas and creeks of Shehateib. The people were becoming more and more frustrated each minute as the phenomenon continued with no signs of abating. Now, exasperated, men in the camp took their swords and shields, girded themselves with their daggers and set off for the Hadendowa camp across the creek. But before they were out of earshot they heard the women calling after them that the stones were still falling on them. It could not be the Hadendowa!

Then they realized that the phenomenon could not be of human origin, but must be the work of a demon, of *Haddafa*, the thrower. Bit Burbur told them she remembered long ago, when she was a bride, that her husband, Feki Beshir, had stopped *Haddafa* by reading verses from the Holy Book. But Ahmed Dirar, the only *feki* in the area now, was not there to chase the demons away. Little children nestled close to their mothers that night of wrath until the phenomenon stopped of its own accord.

In the following days the idea of attack by a demon gave place to another hypothesis: it was the work of the spirits of the dead. It was thought that the souls of ancient great-grandmothers were outraged because last year members of the camp had not observed the *rahmatat*, the annual festival to appease the spirits. So it was decided to carry out the *rahmatat* right away, although it had a specified day of the year. Goats and sheep were slaughtered and the meat was given to the children. They were to eat it only at sunset and then only behind the tents, not in front of them as with other meals. That night, too, the girls and women who did the wet milling of sorghum dough did not clean up the querns and saddle stones used for milling. They were left for the spirits and ghosts of the dead grandmothers to lick clean when they visited the tents late in the night after everyone was asleep.

Once the ordeal of the stones was over and people began to live their normal lives once more, Amna began to wonder why it had all happened at the time of the birth of her child. Before long, her suspicions were reinforced by an incident of yet another kind.

She and her baby, my young self, were sleeping peacefully in the dark of the night inside her tent on the palm-leaf-frond sleeping platform, the *serir*, when she heard a faint sound beneath the bed. She started and piled more rags under her child on the hard rib-like fronds. She listened more intently. Something was hacking at the underside of the bed, an animal. It was breathing heavily and tearing at the fronds and the rawhide strips that bound them together. It was Ahmed Dirar's dog, she realised. And it was rabid. The deadly disease had now reached its furious stage. The animal could break the bed any time now and bite her baby. Or bite both of them. That would mean death!

There was nothing more feared by nomads than a rabid dog or a mad hyena. Ahmed Dirar had been warned that his dog was rabid, but his love for the animal made him dismiss the idea altogether saying he knew dogs better than anyone in the camp and that the dog was simply ill with some other disease. In Amna's tent the animal continued tearing at the bedstead. Her new-born child was lying on the bed unaware of the lethal threat just one inch below. She was panicking. The dog would not go away on its own accord, and she herself, as a a new mother, was not supposed to move. She groped for something to use as a stick but could find nothing. Meanwhile, the dog succeeded in cutting away some rawhide strips and the fronds began to drift apart. Amna tried to call Taha, whose tent was not far, but she was so scared she could not find her voice.

Finally Taha heard the commotion. He came with a stick, lured the dog out from beneath the bed and killed it with one fatal blow. Nomads do not use swords to kill rabid dogs as their blood and saliva is to be avoided.

Still Amna could not sleep. Far out in the valley, night owls were hooting. She kept her child tightly pressed against her bosom for fear of owls sneaking in the tent and feeding the baby their own milk and carrying it away. And not only owls but devils, demons – and a host of other Satanic invisibles. Hadn't a Hadendowa woman stepped on a demon's imp in the ashes of one of those abandoned campsites? And hadn't the baby devil screamed under her foot? And didn't the devils take Kaltoum's white baby and swap it for a black-skinned child? They were real and present, these changelings and elf-children.

A FAMINE YEAR

The day Amna completed the customary forty days in the *khulla* birth canopy, Ahmed Dirar arrived to take her and her children to Suwayil.

Amna and the children – myself the latest addition – were put into an *utfa*, a small cabinet secured to the back of a camel, and then we were off to Suwayil with Dirar leading the camel. As a forty-day-old infant I was sick and vomited most of the time. No potion helped. Amna carried with her fenugreek seed soaked in water in a small bottle gourd, with which she tried to feed the baby now and then. Because it was the end of the rainy season, the party did not travel along the tableland where there was no more water, but took the ups and downs of the *karab*, keeping close to the river.

As Ahmed Dirar was leading the camel with its passengers, he noticed two woolly-haired Hadendowa warriors stalking him, one on each side, at a distance. His little party was being waylaid. His right hand tightened around his spear and his whole body readied for action. Then it occurred to him that the Hadendowa bandits might be mistakenly thinking they were Lahawin. The Hadendowa had killed a Hibushi Lahawin man some years back and the Lahawin had recently taken their revenge. The Hadendowa, he guessed, were now trying to kill a Lahawin.

Ahmed Dirar called out, in the Beja language, that he and his party were Shukriya and were on their way to Sheikh Hadab, leader of the Hadendowa of Suwayil. And he mentioned his own name, Feki Dirar, in the hope that the men had heard of it. The brigands who had been shadowing them withdrew without a word, and the little party then proceeded in peace to Suwayil, where they found the two girls and their grandmother in their tent, pitched close to that of the leader Hadab, the Lion.

Life went on as usual for three or four months. But pastures at Suwayil dwindled and Ahmed Dirar was forced to take his flock to Asubri, where he camped not far from his relatives. He lived there by himself with his sheep, dogs and daggers, away from people. He returned once more to the kind of life he loved the most, a life alone. Once every so often, he would send provisions such as grain, coffee beans and salt to his family at Suwayil. He sent those materials with the Hadendowa men who came to the small market of Asubri. When they returned to Suwayil their wives would run up to Amna to give her the good news that her husband sent her food or clothes. On one occasion, Ahmed Dirar bought a she-donkey and sent it back to Amna. The jenny was bought without its new-born offspring, so it brayed very often, missing its young. Later the Hadendowa women told Amna that the frequent braying of the donkey did not augur well. She should pray to Allah that things did not turn bad for her family.

Amna, in fact, had already noticed that things were getting worse. The intervals of time between the batches of food her husband sent began to grow longer and longer. Soon the family supplies reached alarmingly low levels, amounting to almost nothing at times. The donkey continued to let out its sinister cries. Food became scarce. Suwayil, the land of hardship and famine, began to show its ugly face as the year plunged into the lean days of late summer.

As the vice of hunger continued to tighten Ahmed Dirar ceased sending food to the family at all. The land turned brown and barren. Not a blade of grass was to be seen. The donkey continued to bray. Goats stood on their hind legs, but the trees they tried to browse had no leaves, only thorns. Thorns were plentiful. There were the hooked thorns of *kitir* – the wait-a-bit thorn – the short stout thorns of *laot*, the long, thick, dark thorns of *hijlij*, the white thorns of *sayal*, the shorter thorns of *samur*, the yellow thorns of *sarob*, the tiny, malicious thorns of *sidir*, the jujube tree. All thorns; no leaves, no pods, no fruits of any kind, no tender twigs, nothing edible to animal or man. Noontime crickets screeched in the *laot* trees, heralding the arrival of the scorching, dry heat of the simoom, the wind from the Sahara Desert. The simoom skimmed the last traces of moisture from the barks of the bony trees and turned the skins of men and women into something like those of the mummies in ancient

Egyptian burials. Men and women, survivors of thousands of years of this, moved about like living spectres.

As if all that was not misery enough for Amna, her two children, Ibrahim and the baby Hamid – myself – contracted *um-oo-oo*, the whooping cough. Now the serenade at Amna's door was complete: a braying donkey, growling dogs, howling hyenas, squealing wind, hooting owls and oo-oo-ing children. Hadendowa women came to the rescue, with a time-honoured treatment for whooping cough: donkey milk. We children accepted it readily because we were hungry. There was no sign of our father.

We pulled through. So now we were all immune to whooping cough. But the number one killer, hunger, was still on the prowl. Suwayil was becoming a less and less hospitable place each passing day. There came a point when people had to flee the land. That was what Fatima did. She went back to her folks on the west bank at Asubri. Now Amna and her sons, Ibrahim and myself, were left alone among the Hadendowa, immune to whooping cough maybe, but still vulnerable to measles, cowpox, diphtheria, poliomyelitis – and hunger. As things got worse young Hadendowa warriors took to livestock theft, supplying the camp with meat they had stolen and slaughtered in the bush. Ibrahim, my brother, Amna's older son, got meat and tallow from them. Amna could not stop him. She told him to keep it secret from our father. As a *feki*, he had warned her before not to feed his sons stolen meat. But Amna thought the children should not die of hunger because their father did not provide for them. On the west bank, she knew, he had a large flock of sheep which he wanted to keep and save from the bad year, while seemingly paying no attention to the fate of his own children.

Amna neither spoke nor understood the language of the Hadendowa. When Fatima had been with her, it was she who did all the communication with the tribal women, as she spoke their language, Bedawiyet, fluently. Once Fatima left, Amna found difficulty in talking to her neighbours. She could only communicate with the help of two sisters who were of Maghreb origin, who looked like Egyptians and who spoke both Arabic and Bedawiyet. The turmoil of the Mahdist era had brought these two women here to Suwayil; now they were married to Hadendowa men. One of them, Sekina, was mother of Mustafa, the leader of the livestock thieves. Thanks to his mother Mustafa had a pale complexion and silky hair, rather than a canopy of tight-curled hair like the rest of the warriors.

One afternoon Amna found a man standing at her doorway. It was Osman, the younger brother of Ahmed Dirar, my father. Like a stork he stood there on one leg, leaning on a staff. One of his arms was useless, the fingers lumped together like a witch's broom. His right leg was bent at the knee so that the knee jutted out with the toes pointed permanently downwards. His right eye was half shut. Osman Dirar was a victim of polio, a reminder of what could happen to Amna's children. He had become an itinerant *feki* who roamed the land along the Atbara River. With the ends of his thin *tob* trailing behind him, he hopped his way through the wilderness from one nomad camp to another. With his books in a burlap bag slung over his shoulder, like his ancestor Dirar, he went about writing amulets, washing *mihayas*, writing *bakhrat* and performing exorcism among the nomad Arabs. They saw him as a more religious and pious man than his elder brother Ahmed Dirar. They called him El Feki, a title they rarely gave to his brother. He taught the Qur'an to their children, though Islam barely interested them.

When Osman learned that his brother was on the west bank with his sheep, he decided to spend the night in Suwayil and leave in the morning. Amna, though, thought that Allah had sent Osman to help her. She held to him by the hem of this *tob* and implored him to take her and her children to the west bank. Osman at first refused saying that his brother was a difficult man and he would not like his family to move without his prior consent. But Amna insisted and the man, seeing the miserable condition of the children and the plight of the woman, yielded at last.

In the morning they struck our tent and secured a camel from Sheikh Hadab. It was almost noontime when we moved towards the river. The camel which carried the rolled mats of the tent and various paraphernalia was led by Osman, who walked ahead while Amna with her sons rode the donkey and followed behind. The party duly arrived at the edge of the river at a point Osman said was the ford. There, Amna dismounted, put Ibrahim on the saddle of the donkey and carried me in the crook of her arm. Osman entered the water first, leaning on his staff, leading the camel by the reins. Amna followed urging the donkey to brave the water in front of her at the heels of the camel.

The progress was slow as Osman moved ahead, holding to the camel reins and to his staff with his other hand. Amna, behind him, found herself plunging deeper and deeper into the water. She saw Osman up to his neck. Then the donkey tripped, flinging Ibrahim off the saddle. She scooped him up from the water and gave a death shriek, the *sekali*, hoping some one would hear her, she could see Osman trapped struggling between the front legs of the camel.

Amna's screams were heard by a group of shepherds who were spending the hot noon hour under the trees on the west bank.

Seeing the wailing woman and flailing arm of a drowning man, they came to the rescue. Osman's staff, slipping on the stones of the riverbed, fell from the *feki*'s hand and floated away. Osman continued his ungainly struggle with one arm and one leg, taking now and then a gulp of choking water through his nostrils and mouth. Death hovered over them. But the shepherds arrived just in time. They pulled Osman from the water and laid him out on the hot sands sputtering water and vomit.

"Woman,' they asked, "are you crazy, carrying an infant and following a cripple through this deep water?"

"How could I know this would happen," said Amna. "People cross the river every day. And Osman has always fared well before."

After that, Amna feared the river her whole life.

A BRUSH WITH FIRE

Our party finally reached Amna's tent, close to the tent of Ahmed Dirar's parents. Ahmed Dirar arrived from the river forest and helped her settle down. He brought with him new timbers for the tent and *serir*. When he discovered that a few more outer pegs and the bent rafters of the domed tent were not good enough he went back to the forest to get new ones – and ropes for lashing together the frame of the tent.

But there was no grain, Amna asked Ahmed repeatedly to get grain for the family, but he could not find it in him to sell one of his sheep. He waited for money to come from his carpentry work or from his religious medicaments. But that money did not arrive, and antagonism grew once more between him and his wife. Amna began to ask some Shukriya families for grain.

On one occasion she came back to her tent carrying sorghum from Bit-Umara, daughter of the late Sheikh Umara Abu Sin to hear Ahmed Dirar pounding coffee beans. She worked herself up into great rage. This was a man who could find money for his coffee but could not provide food for his children, so that she was forced to beg for it when every one in the camp knew that her husband possessed one of the biggest flocks of sheep in the region. She decided to give that man a lecture in responsibility.

She left me, baby Hamid, on the bed in her tent and, swathed in her *tob*, took her rage to Ahmed Dirar. She rebuked the man harshly for enjoying his coffee while she ran from tent to tent among strangers begging for grain to feed his children. She held him by the *tob* and asked for immediate divorce. But Ahmed refused adamantly saying that the stars were nearer to her than divorce. Prophet Muhammad, he told her, said that divorce was to Allah the most abominable of all the impermissibles, the *halals*.

Demented by Ahmed's crushing reply, Amna started screaming hysterically and rubbing the end of Dirar's *tob* into the fire. Meanwhile, back at her tent the forgotten child – myself, Hamid – fidgeted and stirred. There was no one around to keep him company. The child began to cry and roll. He rolled over towards the end of the *serir*, closer and closer to the glowing coals of the fire in the brazier.

Amna continued her quarrel with her husband, her ears deaf to sounds from the outside world. She spoke passionately and demanded a divorce with vehemence. Ahmed Dirar refused to yield.

Back at the tent, the child rolled over once more, placing itself at the verge of the bed. Then it rolled a final time and fell into the glowing coals of the brazier. *Tushshsh!* The child's silky skin began to crinkle with heat. Screams turned to gasping shrieks as the smell of burning flesh began to pervade the tent.

Only then did Amna register the cries of distress. She dashed back to her tent to find the child's left shoulder part-consumed by the fire. Immediately she applied a poultice of sour sorghum dough to the burnt shoulder. She tried to stop me screaming by breast feeding and lulling me. But I was in agony and could not stop. That made Amna herself join me, crying in great bitterness. It seemed to her that everything in life turned against her. She cried and cried together with her child in her lap. Women gathered round her trying to comfort her but she felt herself a stranger among strangers. Her problems had been compounded; not only did she have a stubborn husband, but now there was an injured child as well.

A VISIT FROM GREAT-AUNT MEDINA

At that time Amna had no idea of yet another problem that was on its way from Kassala town. Two days later the problem arrived: Medina, Ali Dirar's sister, whom he had rescued from the Mahdists in Khartoum. Medina arrived one afternoon from Kassala, and entered Amna's tent. She announced that she had come to stay. Amna, was shocked at first by her appearance, by her blue-black colour and large nose. Later, she would put her fist on her nose to mimic it. Medina settled with Amna in the tent, the tent of her nephew, Ahmed Dirar. Amna thanked Allah that they were far away from her family, particularly her grandmother, with her well-known views on African facial features.

Medina was close in age to Diya. She was a quiet person who talked in whispers but very articulately. As the days passed by, Amna found she was not such a problem after all. Medina was decent and helpful and assisted her with the children and household chores. Her personality began to erase the initial impression of her black colour and large nose. Amna began to thank Allah that this pious and patient woman had arrived. A mutual love and respect grew between the two women.

Then, with no warning, Diya arrived for a visit, accompanied by her son Annour.

"*Salam aleikum*," she greeted Amna as she entered the tent.

"Grandma!" Amna exclaimed.

"What is it child? You don't look exactly happy to see me," Diya said, looking suspicious.

"Of course I'm happy to see you, Grandma," Amna said quickly.

At that moment Medina was out socializing with the neighbours.

Diya examined the burned child. By this time I was recovering fast. And my accident was not the reason that brought Diya from the Blue Bridge. In Amna's tent that day what concerned Diya was her campaign against Ahmed Dirar.

"So I heard that your husband has been treating you badly," said Diya looking askance at Amna, approaching the matter carefully.

For a moment, Amna did not talk.

"He did not get grain for his children," she said quietly.

"Well, if he wants them to die of hunger, they are his children," said Diya. "You have to save yourself. You have a strong and prosperous family in us, so what's your problem? Just give the man his sons and come back home where you belong."

In fact Amna had already decided once again to leave Ahmed Dirar – and leave him for good. She was only waiting for her baby to get over his burns.

BEGINNINGS

But at this moment Annour Duman interrupted. He had a different view.

"Amna, my daughter," he said, "I heard of your problems with the father of your children. But remember that these things always flare up between man and wife. I suggest you treat the man in a nice way until you convince him to take you to us at the Blue Bridge."

"Think of your sons," he added. "You are lucky you have boys not girls. They are your future. Try to solve your problems gently. The proverb says 'don't undo with your teeth what you can undo with your hands'".

Diya gave no attention to her son's talk. She could not care less about Ahmed Dirar's sons. She wanted their line to stop before something more disastrous appeared in her family.

And now Medina entered the tent. She extended her hand to Diya who took it without a word. Amna replied on her behalf.

"Grandma Diya, this is Medina Dirar, my husband's aunt. She arrived from Kassala a few weeks ago,"

"Yes. I figured she would be a relative of your husband's, Amna," said Diya, staring at the dark-skinned woman now sitting on the *serir*.

"It is good to meet you, Diya. I have often heard of you and I am glad to see you today," said Medina gently.

"I never heard of you," said Diya. "Though I knew that you must exist somewhere in this world. I guess nobody cared to tell me."

"Grandma!" Amna hastened to interrupt, to forestall disaster

Medina sensed that Diya meant an insult of a kind, but herself being a pious person, gave her the benefit of the doubt and tried to cool things down.

"Diya, it is really good to see you and I am happy that you

have arrived in good health from that long journey from the Blue Bridge," she said.

"In a way I am glad to see you too," said Diya.

Then turning to Amna she said "Are you coming home with me child, or do you still want to grovel about in the stench of things here?"

Diya thought that she had found her trump card in Medina. Allah had sent her the living proof of what she had been fearing: the Dirars were black Africans! Those who had been blaming her for picking on the Dirars would no longer oppose her. Now she had the best chance to bring about the divorce of Amna from Ahmed Dirar.

"For years I have been telling you and your father that these people are of doubtful origins," she continued. "But you wouldn't heed what I said. Now the facts are here staring you in the face, in your own house. The day I saw that second child of yours with its flattish nose and greenish colour I knew that those were signs that did not bode well. From what I can see, Amna, you have only one way to redeem yourself: disconnect yourself from these people. I am telling you straight: divorce the man by any means available."

With that, Diya left Amna's tent and returned to the Blue Bridge with her son Annour. He was unaware of the seeds of disruption that his mother had sown in Amna's fertile heart.

AN ACRIMONIOUS DIVORCE

When the child Hamid, my younger self, now ten months old, had recovered from his burns and was crawling about the tent again Amna felt free to go ahead with her plans to seek a divorce from Dirar.

She carried the baby pressed against her left side in the cavity of her arm and dragged the other boy, my brother Ibrahim, by her right hand as she left for the village of Asubri, two or three kilometres away, where the ruling Abu Sin family held their tribal court. She explained her ordeal in detail. She cried and blew her nose. The problem was not new to the members of the court, many of whom had been present at the earlier hearing held at Al Markaz. A date was set for the hearing and the *muhafizin*, the sheikh's policemen, subpoenas in hand, were asked to gather the adversaries and their respective witnesses on the set day.

The court was composed of an august body of sheikhs of distinguished lineage. There was the patriarch, Sheikh al Hassan wad Ahmed wad Abu Sin, and his son, Sheikh Umhummad wad al Hassan wad Ahmed wad Abu Sin. There were two other sheikhs from the Abu Sin line, Sheik Umhummad wad Adlan wad Darraj um Assighayir wad Abu Sin and Sheikh Yousif wad Umara wad Umhummad wad Hamad wad Abu Sin. The court also had a scribe, who was a man of religion and a representative of the Nawayma Shukriya sub-tribe, whose name was Umhummad wad Dakin wad el Fahal.

They convened on the prescribed date with Ahmed Dirar and Amna Duman and their supporters. Amna was accompanied by Fatima, and my brother Ibrahim and myself, a crawling baby. The children and their mother were awed to see the members of the court sitting in their white *tobs* in a half-circle on deckchairs, a kind of furniture that had been introduced by the British. The court should have been presided over by Sheikh Umhummad wad al Hassan, the *umda*, but he was setting off on another mission appointing Sheikh Yousif to take his place. As he was mounting his horse, the *umda* turned to Sheikh Yousif to remind him that the court had been very patient with Ahmed Dirar in the previous hearing at Al Markaz.

"This time," he added. "Take good care of Amna and see to it that she gets what she wants." Having said that, he nudged his horse and left.

So the sheikh's vote against Dirar had been cast. The decision had effectively already been taken. The hearing became just a formality to legalize the decision. Nevertheless the court began listening to the arguments advanced by Dirar and Amna. Amna put her child on the ground at her side as she talked and gesticulated. The child crawled around, attracted by the patina of the wooden chairs on which honourable members of the court sat. Finally, the court asked Ahmed Dirar to divorce Amna Duman. He agreed to do so on the proviso that she gave him his children. Amna vacillated, but the members of the court cried "*Deffigi! Deffigi!*" Pour! Pour! they said, meaning that she should agree to give away the children. So she agreed.

She was standing up with me, Hamid, in her arms. She took two steps towards the seated *sheikhs* and flung me to the ground in front of them, in a cloud of dust and dirt. Then she turned away and walked in the direction of the Blue Bridge. The cries of the child behind her did not cause her to turn, or cry out, or slow her pace. The court dispatched two askaris on camelback to ride after her and take her to her family.

The court had given no consideration to how the baby was going to fare. Neither the parents nor the court members attended to the words of the Holy Qur'an which specifies that mothers shall give suck to their offspring for two whole years, if the father desires to complete the term. The Dirars were now faced with the immediate problem of feeding a baby ten months old who was, just moments before, being happily being suckled by his mother. The task fell to my half-sister, Fatima. At the age of eleven or twelve she found herself suddenly with the responsibility of bringing up a child. In accordance with the nomad belief that a young human being could best be nurtured with the milk of a goat, Ahmed Dirar brought a nanny goat from his herd and tethered it to a tree near the tent where his daughters and the boys lived. This was to be the new mother of Hamid, source of the milk that would keep me alive.

The goat turned out to be a hard-headed one. She was called the Sharrada, the escaper, the recalcitrant. Both her horns had been snapped off by Ahmed Dirar to restrain her. Between a recalcitrant father and a recalcitrant goat, the child – I, Hamid, the Amulet – now had to make my way in an equally recalcitrant world.

CHILDHOOD AFFLICTIONS

Only a few days after the court's decision Ahmed Dirar took his children, Fatima, Asha, Ibrahim and myself, and his mother, and left for Suwayil. Here early rains brought good green pastures. The little child was left for Fatima to care for. Her beautiful younger sister, Asha, a hard-headed and rebellious girl, never cared about such things. All household activities were carried out by the docile Fatima. The grandmother was now too old to help.

Fatima tied Sharrada, the escaping goat, to a tree and daily brought her straw and grass and water. She milked the goat four or five times a day. The most challenging of her new responsibilities was to ensure that the baby slept. I was accustomed to being breast-fed. I would not fall asleep unless given the breast. Fatima's problem was solved when Toshkan came to the rescue.

She was the spoiled daughter of Sheikh Hadab himself. At the age of seventeen, she was the most beautiful girl on the camp, the only daughter of the tribal leader, well-fed and pampered. Now, each time the infant wanted to sleep, the young lady would give him her breasts to suck on, albeit without the reward of drawing nourishment. But I went to sleep peacefully nestled tightly against her warm body. Toshkan developed an attachment to me. Many times she would take me to her father and ask him to milk a goat for me. And although the great leader never milked goats under normal circumstances, for Toshkan he did it readily.

Yet I suffered diarrhoea, vomiting and nausea, loss of appetite and fever. The time-honoured cure for these childhood illnesses known to the nomads was *dukhan*, a smoke bath for the mother. The mother would dig a pit in the ground, place acacia wood in it and set it on fire to generate smoke. She would then spread a palm leaf mat with a central hole over the pit and sit naked on the contrivance, wrapped in a *shamla*, a plaid blanket made of goat hair. The smoke would deposit helpful chemicals on the sweat beads on the woman's skin, which she would scrape off to treat the teeth and gum of the child. And the child would also suck the smoke-impregnated milk of his mother. The treatment would be repeated over several days.

But the child in Fatima's hands had no mother; and it was strictly forbidden for a young unmarried girl to smoke herself. Seeing the deteriorating condition of her baby brother Fatima decided to break the rules.

She told her grandmother of what she intended to do. The old woman was horrified. It would be a blow to the girl's chances of getting married. What would people say when they saw an unmarried girl take a smoke bath? So she asked Fatima to anoint a large smooth stone with sesame oil and smoke that instead. But Fatima knew that that treatment was not the best and went on with her original plans.

She smoked herself until the heat of the pit had her dripping sweat and the smoke choked her. She coughed and coughed, although her head was outside the *shamla*. Smoke penetrated the thin blanket and found its way to her throat. She kept turning her face left and right to avoid the wisps of smoke bellowing out of the woollen wrap. Her eyes watered and her nose ran while she endured the burning fire underneath. Finally, when she was ready, she asked the old woman to hand her the child with the unhealthy-looking body. With cries of *bismillahi* – in the name of Allah – she applied the medicament to the child under the supervision of her grandmother.

That night, it seems, I slept well for the first time. And in the days that followed, I recovered completely.

A HUSBAND FOR ASHA, A CURE FOR HAMID

Soon Ahmed Dirar found a husband for Asha, his younger daughter by his first wife. Asha was preoccupied with her own beauty; she had often given him a hard time due to her stubbornness and individuality. It was a common practice among the nomads to wed such a girl to some man as quickly as possible, even at eleven or twelve years old. The man whom Ahmed found for Asha was a Jaali dervish. He took her to the west side of the river, to Asubri. Her grandmother decided to accompany her to help her settle in her new home. Fatima was now left alone with her little brothers and her father. She dealt with all the women's duties in the home.

For some time now she had noticed a change in the child Hamid's behavior. There was a sluggishness in my movements and an enlargement in my belly. I was sick again. A week later the sickness had laid me low and it seemed to Fatima that I was on the verge of dying. My belly became distended like a fruit. It was a strange disease, Fatima thought, one that probably afflicted only a – a motherless baby fed on goats' milk. She had never seen or heard of anything like it before. She sat on the bed beside me, sobbing in a low tone. In a few days time, she believed, her baby brother would surely pass away.

She was struck, she recollected later, by my patience and endurance, as if nothing alarming was happening to me. When I tried to raise my head, my thin neck would not bear its weight, and I slowly fell back on the sleeping platform. I would roll my eyes in their sockets from side to side. I never cried, and there was a flicker of hope in my eyes that never faded. Ahmed Dirar, who came to the tent only in the evening, knew that children often died at that age unless Allah decided otherwise. He was of the view that the nursing, diagnosis and cure of Hamid's sickness was strictly women's business.

One morning Fatima saw that my condition had reached a critical stage. Nothing was moving except for the heaving and falling of my rib-cage and my eyes that rolled pitifully from side to side. She ran to her neighbour, Nakashot, an old woman.

"Nakashot, please come and see Hamid, he is dying," she cried.

"You need to consult Rayhot," said Nakshot immediately. "Take your donkey and move fast until you reach Rayhot's camp. Do not even drink water at her house. She is the best medicine-woman to be found. And don't do anything to irritate her because you need her help."

Rayhot was a strongly-built Hadendowa woman of about fifty

years of age. She had four children, two sons and two daughters, all of them married. Their father was a man chosen for her by her own father when she was thirteen years old. Later she divorced him. She said things that women usually did not say, even in the presence of men. She raised her own sheep and goats and was adept in tanning leather and making water-skins.

"Stop crying," she told Fatima, when Fatima arrived at her house, "Your baby brother will not be the first or the last child to die. What did you feed him during the last months?"

"Sorghum porridge and goats' milk, mostly," replied Fatima.

"Was the milk boiled or raw?" said Rayhot.

"Raw," answered Fatima.

"At what time do you normally give the child the milk?"

"Fresh warm milk in the morning and the evening, but cold milk in the day time."

"I would say it was the cold milk that caused the child's distress," said Rayhot. "Go home and I will be with you shortly."

Two hours later, while Fatima was sitting at the side of her sick brother, Rayhot and another woman, her assistant, approached the camp. Fatima heard a clatter of metal tools coming from underneath the assistant's clothes – knives and daggers and a whetstone.

Rayhot seated herself on the edge of the palm-frond *serir* and prodded the baby's belly. "You Arabs call it *abu-shreisheef*, this disease. It needs immediate surgery."

Then turning to her assistant, she said "Timinnit, give me the dagger and the whetstone."

She ran the edge of the blade a number of times against the stone and then pulled at a small leather purse hanging from her neck, and finished the sharpening process by rubbing the blade on its leather strap.

"Both of you girls climb up the *serir*. Timinnit, you hold the child's arms firmly down on the bed. Fatima, you hold the child's legs. You press the knees down. Sit on them if need be."

Rayhot gave these orders with a fierce look that could not be disobeyed.

The two girls took their positions, holding the motionless child down on the bed.

"I am now going to start bleeding the child's belly," said Rayhot as she held the dagger, a sharp-pointed twisted weapon, at the ready. "Any kick from that child could drive that metal blade right into his innards," she warned.

The first cut released a dark and ever enlarging morbid drop of blood. They noted a twitch, but the pain did not seem to have registered.

Three more cuts followed rapidly. Then I released a shriek so powerful that Fatima could not believe it had issued from her baby brother's throat. Where did all that vocal power come from? She thought of demons. The child was possessed! What if those forces of the unknown grabbed the dagger?

Rayhot raised the dagger and waited until my spasm had waned away. But when she was about to make another round of cuts, I freed my leg from Fatima's grip and knocked Rayhot's face with my knee. She shouted furiously at Fatima.

"I knew that you would let that happen! You want that child dead? I still have twenty cuts to make before I'm through!"

She continued to cut into the child's belly, making small cuts in three rows on either side of the navel, murmuring in a low, incomprehensible voice as she stooped over the tiny, naked body. Fatima and Timinnit, intimidated, tightened their grip. As she worked Rayhot glanced at the child's tiny penis and testicles.

"If this child has any talent at all," she said, "It must be in that large head of his. That is, if he lives to realize his potential."

Now dark blood pulsed from thirty cuts. Rayhot rose to her feet, I was sobbing. Fatima cleaned the blood from the wounds with a thin strip of palm leaf. Rayhot instructed her to apply warm molten suet to the wounds when the bleeding had stopped.

Outside the tent, Fatima asked, "Is my brother going to live?"

"Didn't you say your father was a man of religion as well as a carpenter?" said Rayhot. "Let him pray for his son instead of running about from tree to tree like a woodpecker."

"If my brother regains his good health, Rayhot, I promise to give you a goat," said Fatima.

"You are sweet, child, but your father would not approve, even if I bring his child back from the grave – like that prophet did, what's his name? Yes, Isaa Ibn Mariam."

In less than two weeks I regained my health, with a lifetime of tiny scars to show for it, visible to this day. But I am sorry to say that Rayhot never got her goat.

THE DEATH OF ASHA

Following the divorce, Amna lived the wandering life of a nomad with her Duman kin. They were sometimes in Jummeiza, sometimes in Shehateib and at other times near the Blue Bridge in Shangil Bangil, on the east bank of the river.

When she had cooled down and her hatred for Ahmed Dirar had subsided she began to think about her children. The yearning to see them filled her mind so much that one day she asked her brother Umhummad wad Duman to take her to Suwayil. Arriving at Suwayil Amna found her two sons well. But she was shocked to see Asha. She looked like a bag of bones unable to move from the *serir*. Soon she learned what had brought her niece so low. She knew that Asha had divorced her first husband. Now, of all men, her father had found her another itinerant Jaali dervish, a bearded, wandering fool, as Asha described him. She had refused him completely and threatened to kill herself if her father forced her to marry him. Ahmed Dirar insisted. She refused. The dervish, seeing the escalating fury developing between father and daughter, wisely withdrew.

So, thought Ahmed Dirar, if the woman does not want a man of religion then why not bring her a young Hadendowa warrior? But when the young Hadendowa man came to ask her, she rejected him too. Asha did not like people choosing her husbands for her.

In his anger our father Ahmed Dirar resorted to blows, beating Asha with the heavy shepherd's stick he carried. The young woman's robust body was able to take the blows until one last one fell on her kidney. She never got up from that final blow. This was the condition Amna found her in when she arrived at Suwayil. Fatima told Amna that the Hadendowa women had prescribed a cure for her sister. She told her they said that Asha must be given a blood bath and that the cure must be applied without delay. Amna asked her to ask her father to donate a goat for the purpose. The goat was slaughtered and the blood collected in a large wooden bowl. She carried the container with the blood in it still warm and entered the tent where Asha lay.

Amna stripped the young woman of all her clothing. She could not believe that what she was looking at was the Asha she used to know. When she was about to apply the blood to Asha's naked body, her niece looked at her and whispered, "Aunt Amna, I am beyond repair. Don't waste your time."

"You will be all right," said Amna. "Now let me apply this medicine in the name of Allah, most compassionate, most beneficent."

She daubed the whole body with blood, muttering Islamic incantations, in the hope that a miracle would happen, and wrapped Asha in a *tob*. But in a few days Asha passed away. The news spread wide that she had died from a blow on the kidney from our father's shepherd's club.

AMNA'S NEW HUSBAND

After the death of Asha, Ahmed Dirar packed up, took his children and sheep, and left Suwayil for the Blue Bridge. In Shangil Bangil he found himself again with the families of the Jubars, the Atalmulas, the Beshirs and the Dumans. Here some of his friends took the opportunity of the presence of Ahmed Dirar and Amna Duman in the same camp to try and bring husband and wife together once more. It was for the sake of the children, they said. These go-betweens talked mostly to Ahmed Dirar and Omar Duman. Both of them refused the idea at first, but Ahmed Dirar finally agreed to take his wife back.

Then Amna's grandmother Diya called her son Omar and said to him, "I see old women have been talking to Amna of late and I am afraid, Omar, that she is now thinking more and more emotionally about her two children. She told me yesterday that she noticed that all women in our family, including her sisters, are begetting female babies, while she is the only woman who has male children."

"I don't like this at all," Diya continued. "I want you to tell Amna clearly that if she ever agrees to go back to Ahmed Dirar, she should never call you father again."

Omar Duman took the message to his daughter. For Amna that meant she now had to choose between a father and a husband. As a nomad woman, though, she did not really have an option: she had to choose her father. In the circumstances in which she found herself, if she chose her own husband she would be considered something close to a prostitute. Nomad tradition stipulated that a divorced woman, especially a young and beautiful one like Amna, should not stay long in that status. She should be given to a husband – any husband – as soon as possible. This was in case she did something shameful in a moment of weakness. A divorced woman in a nomad camp was considered a liability. Islam also prescribes a smaller bridewealth for a divorced woman than for a virgin wife. So Amna's suitors included widowers and already married men, old men and poor men, cripples, deaf, blind and lame men, and ugly, cross-eyed and mentally retarded ones.

Despite these pressures, tradition and Islamic law both ordain that a divorced woman cannot be forced to get married. The first man who asked for Amna was cross-eyed. She refused him. The man complained, "What's wrong with me that Amna didn't like?"

Diya was quick to answer, "Nothing is wrong with you. A camel is not aware of the bend in his neck." Most people thought Diya rejected the man because he was poor, though.

Shortly after, a new suitor appeared. His name was Rajab. He was a widower and had a conspicuously projecting narrow forehead. Some people insisted that they could still see the imprints of the midwife's fingers on the sides of the forehead. He came from a small tribe that people in the area believed to have its origin in Kordofan or the White Nile, that was therefore likely to be part of the Baggara, the cattle-keeping Arabs from the West. Baggara people were perceived to be more African in appearance than other tribes. So people were surprised that Diya accepted the man heartily. Later they discovered that he was rich in cattle, not just goats and sheep like other people. His tribe, the Diweihin, were the only cattle-raising Arabs in the Shukriya land, supporting the notion that they were indeed Baggara, a word that means men of cattle.

Although the Dumans had agreed to give Amna to Rajab, the latter knew that the woman was a divorcee of a *feki*, a man of religion, and he did not want any problems. He therefore decided to go to Ahmed Dirar and ask his permission to marry Amna. Ahmed Dirar replied with affected surprise, "What do you want with a crazy woman like that? I certainly do not want her, if you want to marry her, just go ahead, I give you full permission." But when the man left, Ahmed Dirar began reminding people that in spite of Diya's objection to his own African roots, she now wanted to give the same woman to a Baggara.

Rajab had lost his first wife to the river, but she left him a small child, a boy. He had been deeply affected by the death of his young wife. And he came to Amna to help him raise the child, as he heard about her pious character. By nature he was a compassionate man. He shared with his son all the sorrows that surrounded a breast-fed child that was suddenly separated from the bosom of his mother.

The wedding day arrived. But Ahmed Dirar, angry now, forbade the members of his household to attend the festivities, which were held only a hundred yards away. And to make sure they could not, he resorted to a measure not known in the tradition of the nomads: he fettered his two sons, Ibrahim and myself, to the central post of the tent. Fatima managed to sneak out and Diya gave her meat and dates to take to her brothers before her father discovered her absence. So at least we enjoyed food from the wedding party of our mother. What we did not know was that we would never have the chance to live with her again.

II

Childhood

THE WORLD OF WARRIORS

The world I was born into was far from centres of government. It was a world with its own sources of authority, a world lit by fire, where the old ways endured. We kept time by the seasons and by the rising and setting of the sun. Morning was called *sabah*, late morning was *dhiha*, noon was *nihar*, afternoon was *dhuhur*, late afternoon *assur*, sunset was *mughrib*. A person was either young or old; years hardly mattered. Distances were measured in man-days, donkey-days, and – the longest – camel-days. Events in the wider world were recorded in the names of years: Sannat-Sitta, Year Six, the famine year of 1889. Or the year I was born, 1940, *Sanat el Ganabil*, the Year of Bombs.

It was at night in Wadi el Khireissab that the old world was most present. A group of youths might gather by the light of a wood fire and watch a religious elder reading the ground for signs of the unknown, Beyond them womenfolk would be watching, bare-breasted in the Hadendowa manner, a *foda* covering their lower limbs, one corner tucked at the waist, the other half seeking – but failing – to cover the rest of the body. The quiet of the camp would be broken from time to time by the howl of a distant hyena or the shriek of a lamb accidentally trodden on by its mother in the *zariba*, the thorny acacia enclosure where domestic animals were kept at night.

The young men in the camp had woolly manes of hair in the Hadendowa style, plaited at the back into short braids weighed down with a mixture of animal fat and clay from ground-up potsherds. Each of them carried a single-toothed comb, the *khulal*, carved from acacia wood. But the elder they were watching in this case had, by contrast, short-cropped hair, covered by a white skull-cap, and sported a stubbly, white-streaked beard. And he was visibly Nubian, not Hadendowa.

The young men were warriors, like their fathers and grandfathers before them. They were raised to kill when need arose. Valour, magnanimity and support to women and the weak came at the top of their moral code. These were the kind of men who fought for Osman Digna, the Hadendowa commander of the forces of the Mahdi. They had been noted on account of their courage by Winston Churchill in *The River War*, his book about the British invasion of Sudan. They were Rudyard Kipling's "fuzzy-wuzzies", famous as the only adversaries the British came across who were capable of breaking the British square, the key formation of imperial military might. They were the ancient Beja of the time of the pharaohs, as African as the soil they trod.

Lean, black, brown or bronze-coloured, at night in the camp, they watched the fingers of the old man making signs on the earth. Their broadswords, sheathed in cured cowhide scabbards, lay across their laps or their shoulders, the hilts of their swords they kept close to their right hand. These were complemented by the *sodal*, a double-twisted throwing-dagger and the *bilbil*, a throwing stick. On the ground lay their shields, disks of impenetrable hippopotamus hide. When the men stood up they revealed their dirt-coloured *tobs* and black unbuttoned *sideiris* – waistcoats – and their huge *surwals*, loose cotton trousers. Across their bare chests leather-bound amulets dangled from their necks on plaited leather thongs; more amulets hugged the biceps of their upper arms. The old man was armed too. Although I could not see it, his spear lay on the ground on his right hand side. Above his hip-bone, on a broad leather belt you could glimpse the ebony handle of the *khanjar*, a single-twist dagger.

The old man would reach into a bag lying on the ground nearby, rummaging for a moment then producing an object from another realm, from the realm of literacy that lay far beyond the camp in Wadi el Khireissab. It was a book, the Holy Qur'an. He would beckon one of the women to put her finger anywhere she wished on the open book, then murmur something I could not hear. Perhaps it was a description of the person who had stolen her *zumam*, her gold nose stud. Later, to a young man, he might reveal the location of a missing camel, and inform him that in a short time he could expect to get it back, unless, of course, Allah willed the contrary.

I saw all this many times – the swords, the daggers, the amulets and the Book – for the elder who conducted these rituals and stayed behind to tousle my head was my father, Feki Ahmed Dirar. He barely noticed me, though, boiling milk on my own small cooking fire, a child just pulling out of a bout of kwashiorkor, with a massive head on a slender neck, a belly of unholy size, and legs as thin as sticks.

Milk was my ally. I could use any amount of milk. But I did not forget to leave some to feed my leveret, the *dagoy*, nestling close to me. I had taught her to hide herself in the daytime from the eyes of humans and dogs, concealing herself in the sheepfold. And then to come rushing to me in the evening when I kindled the fire to boil up milk to drink. My brother, Ibrahim, had helped me catch the *dagoy*. He was nine years old now, already an accomplished shepherd and hunter. Fatima, my half-sister, remained my surrogate mother. Of our father, though, we could never be quite certain.

MY FATHER'S DARK SIDE

The pride of a nomad is in the wandering. At the end of the rainy season father decided that we should leave Khireissab for Suwayil. But a month or two later he decided that we should move, once more, back to the area of the Blue Bridge, to Shangil Bangil, not far from Khireissab. As usual, whenever we moved, father, girding his *khanjar* dagger and carrying his spear and heavy stick, drove the flock ahead of us. I never saw my father with a sword, but he had a fine shield of hippo hide.

Ibrahim was riding an ass while I was riding behind Fatima on a she-donkey, holding to the rear pommel of the saddle. The donkeys were also carrying our tent and our household wares. Father had stopped using camels some time before, when one was gored by a pointed stump on which it fell. Close to sunset time, when shadows merged into each other and the landscape dimmed, we plunged down a deep ravine fringed with tall trees. The ravine was called Um Jadad, Guinea Fowl Creek. As we descended into the valley deeper darkness fell. I lost sight of the sheep but could hear their bells jangling ahead of us. When we ascended the opposite bank and were almost out of the tree area, my father decided that we should spend the night there.

Because we were to move again early the following dawn, we did not pitch our tent. Father banked the fire close to the flock and he and Ibrahim milked a few goats for our supper. I had no idea why we were always on the move, nor why it seemed that we always came across such fearful valleys as Um Jadad. It was a dreadful night, out in the open, in the pitch dark, listening to the eerie hootings of night owls down in the valley. Owls were creatures of ill omen; everything I was told about them by the older folks was bad. All I could do was remain as close as possible to Fatima.

Sunrise found us already on the road and in the afternoon we were at our destination, the small Arab community at Shangil Bangil. The camp lay in the lee of a high bank at the bend of Shangil Bangil creek close to Kibeirizzan, the Timber Bridge that carried the railroad across the Atbara River. Our tent was on the edge of the camp. Those of the Jubars, the Beshirs and the Atalmulas straggled up the *khor*, the creek. They were protected there from the north wind by the high bank of the creek and the knolls of the *karab*, the eroded land along the banks of the river. At the new site Ibrahim found his fellow shepherd Hassan Jubar, and Fatima found her old friend Ketira. Each evening I went to Bit Burbur or Bit-Annour to listen to their stories. Sometimes during the day I would follow Ibrahim and Hassan when they took the flocks for grazing.

One night I was awakened by a great noise and angry wrangling. My father had come into the tent wielding a club with which he was hitting Fatima. Why, I did not know. As Fatima jumped here and there avoiding the blows, the heavy stick fell on articles in the tent reducing them to fragments. Fatima was standing on the *serir*, pleading with him. But father just went on hitting her. First Asha, now Fatima had fallen victim to my father's rage. I cringed in the farthest corner of the bedstead close to the grain stand. Father was surely going to kill her. My body shuddered with each blow. I cried out at the top of my voice.

Then the neighbours, men and women, broke into our tent. Atalmula wrested the stick away from my father's hand shouting at him, "Are you going to kill this one too, Ahmed?"

That single question brought a sudden end to my father's fury. His energy flagged as two men, Atalmula and Taha, hauled him away. Silence took over, punctuated by the sobbing of Fatima. My sister and I spent the following hours in misery, aware more than ever of the menace that was our own father.

I MEET MY MOTHER AGAIN

At the end of the rainy season that followed, our camp moved from the tableland down to the *karab* of Shangil Bangil. The new site was at the grand meander of Um Gamiess *khor* which formed a high bank at the edge of a plateau called Goz Wad el Kakar. The bend in the watercourse embraced a large plain of alluvial soil which supported the growth of a forest of tall *sayal* trees. The river was very close, perhaps one kilometre away. The *khor* carved steep banks as it grazed the cliff at the edge of Goz Wad el Kakar. The camp was on the low ground at the edge of the plain. Beyond the *goz* to the south-east, were other important *khors*, Mirmidayeb and Hadab Hadab. A few kilometres downriver, the other side of the railroad to the north, lay Shehateib.

The river forest was untouched by animals during the rainy season. In that time the plants regenerated. By the time we came down to Shangil Bangil, the lush undergrowth of the river forest was impenetrable. Soon the goats would open passages and trails into it for man and sheep to follow. The large trees of the river forest and the tall *sayal* acacia trees on the alluvial plain of the creek would be garnished with foliage and fruits. A strict law prohibited the shaking of trees to make their fruit fall. Animals could consume only windfalls. And the sheikhs of the tribes prohibited the felling of trees. It was the only one of the British colonial laws that they respected with any consistency, because of its obvious benefits. The river forest and the dry grasses that covered the rough terrain were normally enough to support the lives of both man and animal till the rains came.

Sheep, unlike goats, were not fully supported by the forest and grazing in the *karab*. Those shepherds who had large flocks and wanted their sheep to keep their weight during the summer months took them to graze on the clay plain, one day's march away from the river. They spent two or three days in the pasture land without water; then they were brought to the river on the third or fourth day.

Goz Wad el Kakar had been, in decades gone by, the site of a huge Mahdist camp where a great number of families dwelt. In the waning years of the Mahdiyya the camp was ransacked by hostile tribes, including the Nawayma Shukriya, my mother's people. The massacre of the Mahdists at that time was so complete that the only remains were women's beads that had fallen to the earth. Women and children spent hours there collecting beads of all colours, shapes and sizes. Many went to the *goz*, an area of sandy soil, in the hope of finding some buried treasure or a piece of gold. Looking for beads at Wad el Kakar was one of my favourite activities.

That and pursuing young birds of various kinds with long poles. Ibrahim and I were fond of chasing the young of the owl and the red-billed hornbill, which we called *ab-koo-koo*. I feared the owls because of the myths woven around them and because of their swivel-heads, that turned round almost a complete circle, tracking you with their gigantic eyes. Furthermore, unlike other birds, the owl had horns, or horn-like feathers, like a goat or a cow.

Ibrahim and I were chasing a fledgling hornbill when I heard the voices of women calling my name. Fatima and Ketira were among those waiting for me at the tent, It was full of women. I was always afraid of groups of people, especially women, but Fatima and Ketira ushered me in.

"Come to your mother," they said.

As far as I was concerned I already had a mother in Fatima. Who was this woman? She was a stranger. She sat there, tall and slim, with a long slender neck. She was wearing, like most women then, a *tirga*, an indigo-dyed blue stole, the indigo staining part of her shoulder. Like Ibrahim, she was yellowish in complexion. Like him she had well-set tiny teeth, which I saw as she smiled at me. Her face, round and lean, seemed to radiate compassion and endurance.

She took me in her arms and embraced me tightly, showering my face and head with kisses. I wanted to free myself from her arms, but I waited. She was crying. Tears pearled down her eyes, wetting my shoulder and my neck. As a boy raised among the war-like Hadendowa, I found the situation shameful. The other women mimicked her maternal feelings, murmuring "Poor child", "Poor Amna", or "a mother's heartbreak".

My mother asked me to sit beside her on the palm leaf mat. She gave me a small shiny, reddish fruit, which she called *banadora*. It was a tomato, the first I ever tasted. The fruits I was used to were wild fruits gathered in the forest. There was the fruit of the *dom* palm. There was *lalob*, the desert date, *Balanites aegyptiaca*. And there were others – the cherry-like *nabak* or *sidir*, *mukheit* (or *aizen*), *meikah*, *humbuk*, *sha-w* and *tamr-el-abeed*, the "the date of slaves". But the tomato was delicious.

I found I liked my mother. The time I spent with her was a new kind of pleasure. But soon my father spoiled things again, contriving as usual to roil the placid waters of life whenever he could.

While out with the flock one afternoon my brother Ibrahim contracted a fever. He came back to the camp leaving the sheep. Father came to punish him. I ran out and hid behind the tent. I saw Father enter the tent and begin hitting Ibrahim and shouting at him. Ibrahim took off to the forest, staggering aimlessly, feverish, delirious, to recover the sheep. His fever lasted for days. I wondered why my father was so cruel and so displeased with us, his children. The answer I never really discovered. But I learned from those incidents and others that he was not a man to love. I did not know that Islam taught that thoughts like that towards a parent were forbidden. Why had he caused Asha's death? I asked myself. Why would he beat Fatima, the sweetest and most compassionate young girl in all the camp? And why would he not see that Ibrahim was sick and could die of fever?

IN THE RAINY SEASON

It was a good rainy season. The tents of our little camp were scattered over a large area of Khireissab. Our tent was the closest to Hajiz railway station. The camp was inside a grove of *kitir* trees. Just a short walk from the camp was the station. Father always had this inclination to live just on the verge of civilization, close either to the railway station, or the Blue Bridge or Kibeirizzan. Being a Jaali, he made acquaintances among the Jaaliyin who ran the railway business. Contact with the civilized world seemed to be the respite he needed when he had had enough of the adventurous life he led among the wild tribes of the area. It was as if he never did fully trust those tribes, including the small community of Arabs he attached himself to.

The station buildings were grouped into two complexes, each consisting of five round, white rooms with conical roofs. Each room was surrounded by a small, high stone wall fence. As with all railway stations in Sudan, one complex of buildings was situated at each end of the station precinct. The track at the station had a double line. One led to a siding which carried special carriages which held drinking water for the personnel of the station. In addition to the station-master there were the *derissa* workers, the maintenance crew. They took daily excursions on a handcar, a rolling trolley manually propelled by a hand-operated lever. Two men would stand on the rear end while another pair would stand in front. To operate the machine, two men would push the lever down, then the other pair would do the same, alternately standing upright and bending down. It was because of this that we called the machine *fengiss-dengir* – stoop-and-bend.

The trolley car boss, the *ostah*, sat with his feet dangling in the air only a few inches above the ground, sporting, as his sign of office, one of those British tropical pith helmets, with khaki shorts and knee-high white socks. His job was to spot faults in the rails and in the telegraph line that ran parallel to it. Whenever there was a damaged part of the railway, the maintenance workers would haul their trolley off the rails and set about repairing the track. Heavy rains would often take away sections of track, or clog the culverts, or wash away the ballast, or demolish the telegraph line. All these were dealt with by the maintenance crew, Their skins were jet black; only their *ostah* had a different complexion. He was paler-skinned, a Jaali like my father. As the *derissa* workers travelled on their trolley cart their dogs ran alongside. The dogs were used to catch wild game to supplement the workers' sorghum porridge.

Our camp had very little connection with the life of the railway, in spite of its close proximity. But we made use of it during the rains. The steam engines were fuelled with coal and the coke – spent coal – was shovelled off the train and piled at the station. We took some of it, reduced it to powder and used it to cure the foot rot that afflicted the sheep during the rains. The station was also of use to us because it had a shop. In the evenings, father would sometimes give us, Ibrahim and I, a piaster or two to buy *ajwa*, soft dates. The shop was in the southern building complex while the shopkeeper lived some way away in the northern section, so we used to go to him at his house and then follow him as he led us to the shop. He carried with him a kerosene lamp with the burning wick enclosed in a glass casing. I wondered why the shopkeeper had to carry light in that clean place, while we roamed the wilderness in darkness without ever thinking of a light source. The shopkeeper carried the lantern by a long handle swinging by his side. I could make my shadow shorter by coming closer to the lantern and longer as I moved away. In all cases the shadow of my head was disproportionately large. Ibrahim always made fun of this, calling me by the nickname *dejja*, hank of wool. I played all the way to the shop with my shadow and his.

The rainy season that year was excellent. Our sheep all produced lambs and gave plenty of milk. Most of this was soured and churned to make butter and ghee for the dry summer. Each evening I carried the *omra*, the round milking pail, to the flock, where my father would milk a sheep for me. The *omra* was made, remarkably, from *dom* palm leaves, cunningly processed to make them watertight in the following manner. The palm leaf has a thin woody part in the centre that runs the length of the leaf. On either side of this runs a softer part. The woody streak is called the *hangoog* and the soft part the *saaf*. An *omra* is woven by wrapping bundles of the *hangoog* with the *saaf* to build the container in the same way one builds a clay pot, layer by layer. Then a small seat is built in the same manner and attached to the bottom of the container, so the *omra* looks like a large wine glass, lacking a stem. To make it leak-proof, the inner surface is rubbed with milk and then inverted over a smoke pit for an hour or so. The process is repeated several times the chemicals in the smoke and the heated milk proteins react to give a dark plastic layer that covers the whole interior of the container, making it impervious. Nomads believe that milk in the hot *omra* keeps longer and is healthier for children than milk in other kinds of container.

Each night I would climb onto the family bedstead to sleep. Fatima and Ibrahim did the same. Father, like all adult men without wives, slept out in the vicinity of the animal enclosure, on the ground. One dark, rainy night a hyena broke into the Jubars' *zariba* and killed a goat. I woke up to the noise of shouting men and baying dogs. We depended on guard dogs at such times.

And I depended for all kinds of things on my own dog, my beloved Maigulu. One night I was woken up to a strange touch on my head. A sweaty nose! Then a warm tongue. It licked my head. Aagh! A hyena! Or was it a lion? The lion of Yoya, maybe, which pulled children by their tiny feet out of the tent into the night. Or a leopard, which would break your neck before dragging you to its lair? I was terrified. My head turned numb. I was unable to move. The tongue continued to caress my head. Fatima and Ibrahim were fast asleep, or perhaps they were no longer there, already killed and eaten by the beast that was licking my head. In the pitch darkness I could see nothing.

The tongue moved to my ear. Could it be a boa constrictor? Zaki said the boa swallowed its victim whole, starting with the head.

Finally I managed to let forth a shriek, the loudest of my life. Every one in the camp came running to the tent.

"It's a lion!" I cried. "A leopard! A hyena! A boa! A wart-hog!" Fatima held me to her bosom saying, "Hamid, *gool bismilahi!* Hamid, *gool bismillahi!* Hamid, speak! Say *bismillah!*"

Then she said gently, "Hamid that was not a lion. That was Maigulu, your beloved dog."

Maigulu! I remembered that the previous afternoon my father had shaved my head and, in the custom of the nomads, covered it in sesame seed oil to prevent sun-stroke. Maigulu, sniffing for food during the night, had taken the liberty of helping herself. My pulse slowed down. I loved Maigulu the more for delivering me from my night fears. I have loved dogs ever since. Where is the happiness in a world without dogs?

ON THE MOVE

It was time to move once again. Father had decided that we should leave the Blue Bridge and go to Suwayil downriver. So Fatima dismantled the tent, assisted by her friend Ketira, and we packed all our luggage on two donkeys and left, following the flock driven by Father before us. It was the beginning of the rains. When we arrived at Suwayil, we found that the pastures were already lush and the animals there had made up their body weight. The Kalolai Hadendowa of the region enjoyed plenty of milk. The Hadab camp had already moved up to the rainy season site on the clay plain. It was because of these early rains, the *kherif*, that my father had decided that we move to Suwayil. The rest of the Arab community at the Blue Bridge never went there. At Suwayil we were received by old friends. One of these, a boy named Osheik, a friend of Ibrahim, recognized our flock at a distance and came running to meet us. He was joined by his younger brother, my friend Idriss. Osheik was so happy to see Ibrahim that he walked backward facing Ibrahim as we drove into the camp. This sent him capering into a short, thick *kitir* bush that fixed its talon-like thorns into his body, staining his *tob* with blood.

Osheik and Idriss were the sons of a religious Beni Amer man whom we called Seidna. Their mother was the daughter of the leader of the tribe, Sheikh Hadab. When the rainy season was over and the camp was moved down to the *karab* and the river forest, Seidna decided to teach Osheik and Ibrahim how to read and write. Idriss and I were too young, but I accompanied my brother as he went for lessons and when they went to gather wood for the *tuggaba*, the evening fire for study of the Qur'an. In this way I picked up the Arabic alphabet, which they sang to memorise it. But I could not write it.

When the boys completed a certain level of learning the Qur'an they made beautiful designs on their wood slates and went round the camp from house to house singing songs of praise for Prophet Muhammad. For a *feki* in those remote areas, *Seidna* had an unusually creative mind. He came from Eritrea, where most of the Beni Amer resided then. He was not just a religious teacher. He would take his pupils to the forest on the riverbank, where he showed them how to swing from tree to tree using the long rope-like vines. It was said you could travel from Suwayil to Shehateib and the Blue Bridge by swinging from one vine to another.

New developments in our family, however, disrupted Ibrahim's education and marked a turning point in all our lives. Fatima was to get married to Mustafa, the leader of the Kalolai band of young livestock raiders. Like Fatima, Mustafa was considered white of skin, a colour he inherited from his Moroccan mother. Apart from this he was a typical Hadendowa warrior, sporting a heavy shock of greased hair into which he stuck his *khulal*, with his neck and upper arms clad in leather-bound amulets, and his shield, sword, stick and dagger strapped around his waist. Beyond this, his long *shirwal*, *sideiri* and *tob* showed that he was a man who had money.

The wedding day came. A caravan of camels arrived at our house late one afternoon, each tied by its bridle to the tail of the one in front of it. They were carrying goods including the *burush* for a new tent and clothes and perfumes for Fatima, the bride, and food items including sorghum grain, groundnuts, dates, sugar, coffee beans, onions and salt. According to custom the young boys from each family pelted each other with dry camel dung as the camels proceeded.

Women danced and sang, swaying to the drums, their long arms slapping their hips. They had golden brooches in their noses, on the left side; gold earrings on their ears; and chokers of gold around their necks. They wore bracelets on their wrists – silver *suwars* and ivory *kims* – and silver bangles on their feet. There were coloured beads in their hair and wound round their upper arms. After sunset, men and women holding naked swords upright in front of them began the sword dance. Then came the *heeb-heeb* dance in which young warriors leapt in the air with broadswords unsheathed. The young warriors staged a mock-fight, clashing their swords and shields together. Women beat their thighs and stamped on the ground. The clashing swords, the drums, the singing voices travelled through the night drawing others from neighbouring camps. But our Dirar relatives across the river at Asubri boycotted the festivities.

Despite his change in status Mustafa did not desist from livestock theft. My life was a paradise of protein. Each morning I woke up to find the large wooden *gadah* full to the brim with meat in solidified animal fat. Farewell to marasma! Farewell to kwashiorkor! The Hadendowa called that kind of meat *inglet*. Preserved in suet it could remain a long time without spoiling. But Father was not happy with the new state of affairs. He kept telling Fatima not to feed his children stolen meat, meat that was *haram* – forbidden. The Hadendowa, though, did not look on that meat as taboo. It was a long-standing tribal tradition that young men must practice livestock theft, as a test of bravery.

Finally father decided to leave Suwayil for good and take us to the Arab community in the Blue Bridge area, leaving Fatima behind to lead her new life with her husband and her Hadendowa in-laws. I knew nothing of the matter, but the day of the departure, early in the morning, I noticed unusual activities going on in the tent and the corral, the *zariba*. Father was packing his carpenter's tools in a saddle bag and he had his spear in his hand, when it would ordinarily have been stuck into the thorn hedge of the *zariba*. The donkey stood there saddled up, Ibrahim was taking the flock out of the *zariba* accompanied by the lambs and kids when normally these would have been separated from their mothers. These were all signs of decampment; yet Fatima did not pull down the tent. And she was crying.

Finally Ibrahim explained what was happening. And now, at the age of four, I had to decide whether to stay with Fatima or leave with him and Fatima. I received no help in this decision from any member of the family, not even from Ibrahim. I thought he must have connived with the others to keep me in the dark. Maybe my destiny had been drawn up already, written on the Preserved Slate in Heaven, so that whatever decision I might take would not be any different from what had been written for me up there. Still I had either to stay or leave.

Father and Ibrahim just took off. Neither of them looked back. Fatima and her husband, Mustafa, stood silently by their tent. Even Fatima, my step-sister, my surrogate mother, would not help me. I took a few quick steps towards the departing party. Then stopped. I looked over my shoulder at Fatima, standing there expressionless. I dashed again towards Ibrahim and father, only to stop midway between them and Fatima. I began to cry, torn by the agony of not being able to take a definite step in either direction.

Fatima broke down, and started to run towards me, gesturing for me to come back. I sat down and cried. At that moment I took my decision: Ibrahim had left, the dogs and the sheep and goats had left. Fatima had her husband. But I had no one here. Fatima was not a playmate. She did not go out to graze the sheep in the beautiful meadows or capture pet rabbits for me. She had to stay at home. And I had to catch up with Ibrahim. A tiny, naked, frail figure, I ran until I caught up with Ibrahim and he pulled me onto his donkey. Despite my earlier sense of abandonment I knew that he was happy with my decision. Father drove the sheep hard and my brother and I lagged behind as our jenny was weak and became tired. Father never looked back, as was his wont whenever we moved. He soon disappeared from our sight.

Now we were alone in the wilderness, travelling east, parallel to the river forest. We came down the steep bank of a gully. In the centre of the sandy bed of the watercourse our donkey tripped and collapsed. We took the luggage off its back and managed to make it stand up once more. Some passing shepherds laughed at us and Ibrahim got mad at them and began yelling and shouting, while reloading the donkey with the luggage. He failed to notice father's expensive saw lying on the sand at a distance from us. When we caught up with father and he discovered that we had lost the saw he beat us.

So at the age of four, I was separated from my sister Fatima, my surrogate mother. I did not see her again for another twelve years. At that moment, between Suwayil amd the Blue Bridge, I had been standing on the brink of time, deciding between her and my brother, looking over my shoulder towards the past, then forward towards the future.

A WEDDING FEAST

Father was invited to a wedding occasion in an Arab camp on the west bank close to the river forest so we stopped there on the way. The camp was situated at the bend of a wide *khor*. Camps at this season were located in such places because the high bank protected the camp both from the winter winds and then the dry wind from the Sahara. The silt that accumulated in such places supported the growth of *sayal* trees, which provided legume pods for young lambs and kids kept in the camp, and shade and firewood for its human inhabitants. The *khor* had dense growth of the tough slender grass called *tumam*. This was used to make rugs and pallets.

I was happy waiting for the wedding day because at the ford just before we crossed the river, father had carved me a spear out of the stem of a *juweir* tree that grew on the banks of the river. Apparently, he wanted me to be a spearsman like himself. Perhaps he was happy I chose to come with him. It was the only occasion he ever gave me a gift. He had removed from the stem small cylinders of bark, creating an alternating pattern of bark and bare wood. He had whittled the tip to a point that did away with the need for an iron tip. I loved my spear so much that I could not wait to show it off at the wedding. As the day wore on, though, the pangs of hunger drew my attention to the fact that they had left me no milk or food of any kind. Fatima would never have done that. I wondered what she was doing now.

I tried to dismiss that feeling of hunger but only succeeded for so long. I could not just go on like that. Something must be done. Older people said, "Hunger is an infidel: kill it!" I had no idea what exactly an infidel was or why he should be put to death. I walked to a nearby tent to ask for some food, but I was surprised to find no one there. I entered it and made myself at home, setting about the business of looking for food. I saw a wooden bowl overturned beneath the *serir* with the dried out remnants of porridge and milk. But the vessel in which the porridge was cooked did not even contain the *sheitt*, the dry thin flakes of cooked dough. Likewise, the container for *mulah*, sauce, had nothing in it. There were no containers hanging from the rafters. I was about to leave when I saw a *butta*, the squat container for *samin* – butteroil or ghee. It was dark and well-wrapped in a ghee-soaked net of rawhide straps. It definitely contained food.

Sluggishly, weak with hunger now, I clambered up the *serir*. The *butta* looked like a large earthenware pot. The uninitiated might think it was made of clay. But the *butta* is in fact made of the stomach lining of a camel, sealed with a mix of roasted sorghum grain and *kadaba*, black gum, plus old pounded rags. After drying, the container is wrapped in rawhide strips. The *butta* is the heaviest container in the nomad household, the container of choice for storing *samin*.

I plunged my right arm down the neck and into the container and touched a cool mass of solidified, granular *samin*. This was butteroil kept for the lean months of the late summer and the early days of the *kherif* rains. I filled my hand and my mouth. To a nomad, ghee is dream food. I ate till my face was smudged with fat, and my right arm, from finger tip to armpit, was fully greased and my chest and belly were covered with runnels of melting ghee. Then I decided to anoint my whole body with fat. I drenched every inch of my body with ghee, adding an extra quantity to my feet, remembering that nomads believed that *samin* would force out the thorns most deeply buried in the flesh of the foot. (My feet lodged many thorns. Like all nomad children my age, I rarely wore shoes.) Satisfied with my foray, I climbed down from the bed and made my way back to headquarters, a paradox, an emaciated creature who was dripping fat. There, in the sand under the tree, I fell asleep. But the smell of ghee travels, sending pheromonic messages far and wide. Among the recipients were thousands of *shen-shen* ants. They were soon *en route* for this new source of nutrition.

In the meantime Righaya, the younger daughter of Albigiet, arrived from the river with two waterskins on her donkey. As she entered the tent, carrying one of the *girbas*, she noticed that the house was not as tidy as she left it two hours before. She placed the water skin on the *seidab*, the wooden ledge made to hold the waterskins. Now free to inspect the house, she saw the oily mess on the *serir* and checked the *butta*, to find that almost half of the *samin* was missing. At about the same time the ants arrived at the source of food, my ghee-soaked body. And I woke from my doze suddenly, screaming and rolling out onto the hot sands.

"Chaaaaak! Waaaaay!" I rolled and rolled back and forth, rubbing my skin against the sand, the *shen-shen* clinging fast to me. At Albigiet's tent, they heard my shrieks. Finding me soaked with ghee and attacked by ants the women realised what had happened. Laughing, they drove the ants away. Some of their mandibles lodged in my skin and had to be picked out one by one. The story of the *shen shen* and the butteroil thief was briefly the talk of the camp.

The day that followed was the day of the wedding feast, the night when the bride would be handed over to the groom. As usual, Ibrahim took the flock out to graze while my father went to the river forest to find some timber to make a bed of wood and rope – an *angareib* – for sale. The tents around the wedding house were mostly empty. Men were served lunch under the large trees at the bend of the creek. We children moved from one empty tent to the other. Everything seemed normal until we reached the most remote tent. It was not empty. Inside a young woman and a man were in the act of sex. They were half-naked, We boys sat at the entrance of the tent watching. The woman was young and her breasts were still standing, her skin pale and honey-coloured. She was on all fours, facing the doorway of the tent, less than two metres from where we sat. Her braided hair fell down the sides of her face, almost touching the bed. The thrusts of the man riding her made the braids swing back and forth.

The woman signaled to us desperately to go away, but she could do no more than gesture at us. The man seemed unaware of our presence and continued as if we were not there. And we continued sitting there, a row of naked boys watching and listening to the squeaking *serir*. One child bent low and peeped between the woman's breasts trying to see if penetration was complete, though it seemed to me that it would be more proper just to sit and watch like the rest of us.

THE LOST BRIDE

In the days leading up to the wedding, the bride, Nefisa, just fifteen years old, had been subjected to the standard process of beautification: anointed, massaged with a *dilka*, an abrasive material made of sorghum, her feet and hands embellished with henna, perfumed, pomaded, her hair plaited into long thin braids, and any hair on her forehead, arms, legs, armpits and sexual organs removed with ash and twisted threads. Her body had been smoked each day with sandalwood. Sandalwood chewing sticks were placed at her side. She was kept away from sunlight to foster the paleness in her complexion, and fed fine food to make her plump for her bridegroom to enjoy. She was as smooth as silk and clean as a mirror, as fragrant as a flower.

But Nefisa had a dark secret in her heart she did not divulge even to her closest of kin or to her *wezira*, her bridesmaid. It was to turn the wedding into a tragedy.

The groom was ready for the night. In the darkness he would, in traditional fashion, seize her from the women who brought her to his tent. He was expected to take his bride by force. Young men would be in hiding behind his tent to register the bride's reaction. He had to make her scream in pain. And in the morning the evidence of her virginity and his virility would be displayed: bloodstains on a white bedsheet. Bayaki, the bridesmaid, noticed that the bride seemed to have no anxiety about these events to come. Could Nefisa have gone through the experience before? Impossible. She dismissed the idea. And indeed that was not Nefisa's secret. Her intent was darker.

When Bayaki went to Nefisa's tent that evening she found her gone. The women waited for a while thinking that Nefisa went to the *khor* for the call of nature, although it was something women usually did in groups, for safety. When she did not return, her mother was informed. Not finding her daughter among the women at the tent, she rushed into the darkness towards the *khor*, but she could find no sign of the bride there. Nefisa's mother knew something about her daughter that nobody else knew: Nefisa had been forced into the marriage and had resisted. The groom was rich, but she did not want him. Her refusal was ignored. Her mother thought his riches would soon prove to the girl that she was wrong. But Nefisa was not waiting for that. Rather than take him as her husband Nefisa had resolved to give her life to the river. And in the darkness she drowned.

I began to see that women had special problems. I did not yet know there would be greater tragedies concerning women later in my life.

Two days later we were on the road again. We crossed the river at a point just east of the Blue Bridge. The ford was a very tricky one. It was like a low waterfall with currents running swiftly between slimy, moss-covered rocks. People and animals crossing the river often slipped on the rocks. This was the reason the ford was called Shangil Bangil – Jumble Tumble. We managed to cross safely; and returned to our small Arab community, this time without Fatima, I was entrusted to Ketira, Fatima's dearest friend. She was the one girl in the camp who resembled my sister in piety, sweetness and compassion. She was dark and Fatima was pale, but that made little difference to me. The first problem I faced in the community of Arabs was one concerning the Arabic language. I spoke better Hadendowa – Bedawiyet – than Arabic and I was mocked when I inadvertently introduced Hadendowa words in Arabic sentences. I began to shrink away whenever I had to speak Arabic in a group of Arabs.

WHAT'S BECOME OF HAMID?

In Jummeiza my mother Amna had come to her folks to give birth to her second child from her second husband.

"Father, have you heard the news of Fatima Dirar's marriage?" she asked her uncle Sheikh Annour.

"Yes, I heard," said Sheikh Annour, as he saddled his fast white Egyptian donkey, the *Rifawi*.

"I wonder what has become of Hamid," said Amna, as though talking to herself.

"I would imagine that the child has been left with his sister for the time being," said Sheikh Annour Duman. "He is still young."

"I don't know," whispered Amna, looking far into the eastern horizon.

"Don't worry, daughter, the child will be all right," said her uncle.

"If he remained with Fatima, I would have no fears at all. But if his father took him with his brother I cannot see how he could survive following that wild man from one Hadendowa tribe to another," said Amna.

"You have a suggestion?" asked Sheikh Annour, tightening the donkey's saddle and turning his face towards Amna.

"Yes I do, father," she said, addressing her uncle respectfully, as though he were her father. "I'll be grateful if you were able to travel to the Blue Bridge and see if the wild man has the child with him. And if you find the child bring him to me," She referred to Ahmed Dirar as "wild man" because among the nomads one would never say the name of a husband, still less an ex-husband.

"Amna, you know that, by court order, the boys belong with their father," said Sheikh Annour.

"Yes, father, but I am sure you could coax him into giving me the young child for the coming months. Or if not to me then to you. You need a boy anyway," said Amna.

Sheikh Annour, the father then of four girls, contemplated the latter idea for some time. "Well, what can I say? I will try, but not in the coming few days. Are you happy now?" said Sheikh Annour.

"May Allah care well for you," Amna replied. "Now that Fatima is no longer there, he may ease his views a little."

A BOLT OF CLOTH

At that time, on the east bank, our camp was still up at Khireissab and in a few weeks we were to descend to our dry season site at Shehateib on the riverbank. One very late afternoon, just before the sun grew large on the western horizon, I was playing with Atalmula Junior in front of their tent when I heard people shout out from different tents that Sheikh Annour was coming. I could see a turbaned man in impeccably white clothing, riding a fast white donkey. As the man approached the camp, men, women and children ran out to meet him. Clearly he was a man of consequence. It was the first time for me to see this uncle of mine. Also my first time to see the white clothes which people called *hidoum-massobanah*, clothes washed with soap. And the first time to see *humar Rifawi*, the white Egyptian donkey.

At Khireissab Sheikh Annour went straight to Atalmula's tent, as the man was his nearest of kin and the only Nawaymi in the camp. He was seated there on a large palm leaf mat. For some time men and women each asked him about their relatives and friends among the Arabs on the west bank. Sheikh Annour gave them the news. I heard Atalmula call my name.

"Hamid, come say hello to *Abouk* Annour, your father Annour."

When I approached, Sheikh Annour cupped my head in his right hand, pulled me towards him and kissed the pinnacle of my head, in the manner followed by old nomad men. The gesture gave the message that there was kinship involved. Then he raised my face and smiled at me, a very kind fatherly smile which carried pride and said, "Splendid! Already a man, eh!" I liked that, and hoped my friend Atalmula had heard the comment. *Abouy* Annour then put his hand in his burlap saddle bag and pulled out a folded length of cloth that was as white as his own clothes, and brand new, as its factory smell told. Ibrahim, my brother, and the young Atalmula were given similar pieces of cloth and we were all given dates and groundnuts.

Ibrahim and I showed Father what *Abouy* Annour had brought us.

"Allah bless Sheikh Annour," he said. "He has always been good to me."

Father said our cloth was a material called *dabalan*, only worn by sheikhs and rich people. *Dabalan* was very white compared to the cheaper, loosely woven, off-white calico, *dammouriya*, that clothed the people in our camp, both men and women, although both materials were made of cotton. Women dyed the fabric with *nila*, indigo, to make the blue *tirga* stole.

My father told me that I was to leave with *Abouy* Annour that very day to visit my mother on the west bank. And Sheikh Annour added that I had a great number of relatives whom I should meet there. A man should know people, he said, especially relatives. It was to be my introduction to a wider world, a world that included the Arab tribes on the west bank of the river, the tribal courts, and the government, the distant British and the local Shukriya leader, worlds that met at Khashm el Girba, a nomad township that was the centre, *al Markaz*, of what was then called an Administrative District.

Early in the afternoon Sheikh Annour put me on the back of his white donkey. Soon we were on our way travelling towards the Blue Bridge. The sound of the donkey's footfalls on the steel floor of the bridge was a symphony. I was happy to be exploring a new world, especially wearing white clothes and riding a white donkey. Behind us scampered a baby donkey. Sometimes it would lag behind us, walking absent-minded like a philosopher, and then when it discovered that it had widened the gap between it and its mother it would give a sudden sprint and be right at its mother's tail. Then it would stop to watch a dog, a goat, another donkey. Then it might kick its hind legs in the air and bend its head to the ground. It had huge all-black eyes. I ruffled its down-like fur with my big toe.

At the *khor* called Jummeiza we stopped at *Abouy* Annour's tent. And I was taken to see my mother again. I had not seen her since the day she gave me a tomato at Shangil Bangil. She was confined to a *khulla*, a canopy of thin cloth on the *serir*, lying on her side nursing a tiny infant. When I entered she embraced me and kissed my face all over, with tears coursing down the tribal scars on her cheeks. She did not leave the canopy and I understood that she would do that only after forty days, like other new mothers. She asked our relative Zeena Duman to take me to the tent of my great grandmother, Diya.

Diya's tent was smaller than the other tents of the extended family. Inside I found a old woman of very fine features, shrunken stature but an imposing air. She did not seem yet to have succumbed to the infirmities of age. Everybody in the family called her *Ummi-Immah*, Mother Ma.

"*Ummi-Immah*! This is Hamid," said Zeena.

The old women took my hand to shake it. "Hamid who?" she asked, inspecting my face in the grey light of the tent, tilting her head a little.

"Hamid wad Amna," answered Zeena.

"Hamid wad Amna? Wad Dirar?" she asked for confirmation.

"Yes," answered Zeena.

Now the old woman took my head and kissed it saying "Welcome, welcome." Then she asked me about Ibrahim, my brother.

We heard *Abouy* Annour call us back. At his tent he introduced me to a young man of about fifteen, who looked very much like a Zibeidi. The Zibeidiya who lived with us at Shehateib were pure Arabs, fair-skinned and silken-haired. The young man's forehead carried a crescent-shaped scar. At first sight I did not care for him. *Abouy* Annour introduced the young man to me as *Khalak* Ali – Uncle Ali. *Abouy* Annour asked *Khali* Ali to take me round the camp to see my aunts.

The first tent we came close to was built of all-white, new palm leaf mats and was slightly displaced from the main stream of tents. I asked *Khali* Ali whose tent it was. I was surprised when he told me that it was the animal byre. I believed him, but kept wondering. It was later that I learned that the white tent was a wedding tent, the bride being Aunt Zeinab. Was *Khali* too shy to say that his sister had got married? The next tent was Aunt Asha's. She was married to Shambati, a widower who had two daughters from his deceased wife. The elder daughter was mad; she was kept fettered to a tree in a thorn fence. She pulled at her chains, scratching her dishevelled hair and tried to smooth the filthy rags she wore for clothing. As I passed by her she rolled her big eyes and grunted at me. She was the first insane person I had seen.

Inside the tent we found *Khalti* Asha and Hajwa, Shambati's older daughter. She had a jovial face and a smile that one wanted to see all the time. Then at *Khalti* Nofal's tent we met her two daughters. The younger was so fair-skinned that she was nicknamed Houri. In the Duman family, clearly, as among all the nomadic tribes, there were fair-skinned people with straight hair as well as very dark people with woolly hair; there were always both, whatever Grandma Diya might think. *Khalti* Nofal's husband, Tayalla was a musician who played the *zumbara*, a long bamboo flute, and was known for his hospitality and physical strength.

The farthest tent was Grandfather Omar Duman's. He lived here with his second wife Mahani, probably the most beautiful young woman in all the camp. She was tall, slim, and dark-skinned with very fine features. Her father was Hadendowa, her mother an Arab. But Mahani was famous not so much for her physical beauty as for being a spitfire, as hot as a live coal. She gave Omar Duman two daughters but later divorced him.

Jummeiza was much larger than our camp at Shehateib and the tents well-built and well-kept. It was much richer than our community too, as witnessed by the greater number of camels and the presence of the fast *Rifawi* donkeys. But I also noticed that there were too many girls and not a single boy of my age. That might have been one reason why I had been met with so much love.

THE CUTTING

Toma was the wife of Sheikh Annour. One day I entered her tent to find her two younger daughters, pomaded and wrapped in *firkas*. The girls looked at me with eyes dashed with kohl. Their hands and feet, I could see, were embellished with henna. They looked like brides but they were too young for that, even by nomad standards. It occurred to me that I had somehow intruded into one of the arcane activities of women. Outside the tent I found Zeena mending the tent mats. She told me her younger sisters were to be circumcised. I had heard of girls being circumcised, but knew little about what happened.

The following morning Bit-Saad came from the neighbouring camp. She was carrying a *majlukha*, a razor that folded into a groove in its handle, the kind of knife that men used to shave their beards. That morning one of the girls was laid down on a rug on the ground in the tent. She was stripped naked and her legs parted wide, each held in place by a strong woman. Bit-Saad wasted no time. She dug a small pit in the ground between the thighs, just a few inches away from the little girl's genitals. Other women held the head and the arms of the girl whose thighs now flinched and twitched. Bit-Saad deployed her razor. She filled the fingers of her left hand with the labia majora and the labia minora and put her knife to them, carrying away a thick strip of flesh, which, as the child screamed, she dropped into the small pit. After removing these ridges of flesh, she located the clitoris, which she rooted out with a single slash. Now Bit-Saad brought the two sides of the wound together, leaving an entrance much narrower than Allah's creation, just three match sticks in diameter. The girl's future husband would have to open her again before they could have sex.

Bit-Saad applied powdered sugar to the wounds and advised Toma to add sugar often during the coming days until the girl healed. She tied the feet of the girl tightly at the ankles and the thighs above the knees and she was carried and laid on the *serir*. With singing and drumming the second girl was brought to the operation table, and the same procedure began again.

I did not see the operation itself. No man or boy did. I learned the details later. But I went in the tent several times later and saw the girls with their legs tied together. They had survived their horrible ordeal without anesthesia. When I saw them they were playing, laughing, joking and eating dates. They felt proud as that initiation brought them into the realm of womanhood, joining the millions of similarly circumcised and infibulated women. I did not understand the medical problems entailed in the practice of female genital cutting until decades later. But I learned that when sugar entered a nomad's tent it was not always meant for tea.

DROUGHT

At noon, the *ferig* looked dead. The scorching heat could kill a dove in flight. Goats took refuge from the infernal heat in the scanty shade between the tents. The trees stood like skeletons. Animals in the camp – goats and donkeys – grew thin. The grass on the *karab* land and the *khors* and the pods and leaves on the trees of the river forest had all been consumed. The sheep had been taken months ago to the east bank of the river, but now word came from the shepherds that they were returning to the camp for lack of grazing there. In just a few days all the sheep were back at the camp. In the dark, riddled with night blindness, they blundered unheedingly into the thorns of the *zariba*.

The shepherds included my older uncle Umhummad wad Duman, *Khali* Umhummad, a fine man who became a good uncle to me. My mother left the camp, returning with her husband, Rajab, to the home of his tribe, the Diweihin, at Andala, up-river near Al Markaz village. Sheikh Annour now had to feed an extra mouth during those hard times. We depended on porridge made from *feterita* sorghum, with the few drops of milk we could get from the flock. At night I woke to the *tok-tok* sound of donkeys applying their teeth to the wood of the *laot* shrubs, trying to strip the bark for food. We scanned the skies for white clouds, *um-bash-shar*, the harbinger of rain. The clouds came but not the rain. Then news came of rain elsewhere. "Strike camp in the morning" was the order. A *kherif* rain shower had been spotted in the Butana, far to the south. The following morning all camps in the area started moving south-west. Visitors to the site of our camp that day would have found only abandoned middens, sooty tripod stones at the fireplace, rags, shards, short thongs, and saddle-stone fixtures at the tent site, and a lonely dog howling.

I travelled with *Khalti* Zeinab, the bride, in her *utfa*, the enclosure on the camel's back, together with two small girls. *Khali* Umhummad was armed with a sword, a shield and a stick. I noticed that, like the Hadendowa of Shehateib, he also carried a hooked dagger. The Arabs on the west bank usually did not do that; but they had a knife on their upper arm. Sheikh Annour always carried a sword and a shield, but you could not tell what other weapon he might have concealed on his body.

We traversed the jagged terrain of the *karab* and presently gained the edge of the dead-level alluvial plain. We went on and on over the dark, bare tableland without seeing any signs of rain. We continued travelling as the heat soared, seeing nothing ahead except the dark soil and the mirages. We were going away from the river. The sheep began falling behind or falling permanently to the ground, famished and thirsty and burning. The goats cried for water, their tongues falling out down the side of their mouths.

In the afternoon clouds appeared in the sky and a few green plants on the ground. Then, in the distance, shimmering, a group of trees. Green plants became more frequent. Ahead of us was a water hole surrounded by the flocks of other tribes, camels and donkeys carrying luggage, children and women. Our own sheep and goats began to run toward the smell of water. There was fighting at the water hole. Everybody wanted to water their animals before the water was roiled into mud and muck. A shepherd from one tribe, trying to hold back another shepherd's flock, hit one of the ewes with a stick. The owner of the ewe saw him and hit him with a stick on the head inflicting a bleeding cut. Soon everyone was fighting everyone, like a spreading bush fire. I saw my grandfather Omar Duman throw the reins of his camel to *Khalti* Zeinab and prepare himself for battle with frenzied jumps and screams.

Swordsmen were fighting in between the camels and donkeys carrying women and children. Our camel panicked and began gurgling and writhing. Aunt Zeinab could not control it and the camel bolted. The straps holding the saddle snapped and we came crashing to the ground among the fighting parties as the camel ran off. The bride rose out of the wreck of her shattered *utfa*, with torn clothes and dusty feet and hair.

Sheikh Annour and Sheikh Mada knew that a skirmish like this could grow into an internecine conflict unless it was quelled immediately. They moved back and forth among the young men to cool them down. Finally, when they had managed to do this, we began moving again, the bride on a donkey's back this time, the henna on her hands and her gold nose brooch now the only evidence of her new status.

A cool wind came, with a hint of rain. Clouds passed overhead, heavy with rain and casting shadows. We called them *abu-dulleil*. Finally, in the late afternoon we found ourselves in the middle of a green carpet of *hantout* that seemed to extend as far as the setting sun. Here in the Butana of Abu Sin, as the Shukriya called it, there were no trees. We had to drive pickets into the ground to tether our camels and donkeys when we set the camp. But the breeze was soft and dew-laden, a world away from the harsh hot wind we had left behind us at Jummeiza, just a day's journey away. This is why nomads move. If the good life does not come to you, you go and seek it.

THE SONGS OF GIRLS

The rainy season over, we moved back to Jummeiza again, to be close to the river. There we would spend both the winter and the dry summer seasons. There were celebrations – weddings and circumcisions of boys – and, on moonlit nights, the songs of young girls on the sands of the *khor*. These unmarried girls were a powerful source of energy in the *ferig*. For hundreds of miles along the western bank of the River Atbara, in every camp and settlement, they gathered on the white sands to sing and dance. In Jummeiza Zeena and Hajwa were the leaders, the most beautiful and vivacious girls in the camp. The songs they sang praised the beauty of girls, reminding young men of their duty to protect them. It was men, of course, who decided who a girl would marry. Women had no say in the matter. A young girl could be given as wife to an old man. And these were the things they sang about on moonlit nights.

> *O young men ready yourself*
> *For the young gazelles that are slim and tall,*
> *That feed on clusters of flowers, not on Acacia sayal,*
> *The gazelles who drop their young when mellow.*
> *Towards the seven peaks lightning raises the clouds.*
> *Nugget of gold, I have a suitor.*
> *Nugget of gold, I have a suitor.*
> *Young men make a phalanx*
> *To defend the young gazelles who are so slim and pure,*
> *That feed on upright tassels not on fallen trash,*
> *The gazelles that drop their young in the time of the* kherif.
> *Towards the seven peaks lightning promises rain and coolness.*
>
> *Nugget of gold, I have a lover.*
> *Nugget of gold, I have a lover.*
> *I looked towards the front tents.*
> *I saw the young clove trees sprouting.*
> *I saw Fatima's perfect beauty.*
> *How beautiful her arms and her ivory armlets.*
> *How beautiful her lips and golden nose brooch.*
>
> *Your hair has been braided very fine*
> *And pomaded with shank bone marrow.*

Here is a man who has the habit of divorcing women.
He is like a dog that searches for stashed food.
We do not want an old man.
May Allah place hot embers on his balding head.
We want a young man, even only for his Adam's apple.

The village of Ghurashi and the Kassala mountain, with its seven peaks, lie in a straight line with Mecca, so for us the direction of prayer was towards the seven peaks. And the lightning which appeared towards Kassala was an augury of rain.

The British rulers of Sudan were excoriated in these songs. As girls worked at pounding the stones of the *mahaleb* cherry to make almond-scented perfume they would denounce the colonialists with their green eyes, yellow teeth and alien language, interlopers who came into their land and milked it of its riches:

A yellow-toothed dog arrived in camp,
Its eyes were green,
Its language strange.
It milked the camel in a woven pail.
And swore that no one else would take a share of the milk.
O mother, mother of Ahmed!
Pound mahaleb *on Ahmed's tob.*
Ahmed is away on a horse-borne raid.

They sang also about the traditional enemies of the Shukriya, the Mahdist Lahawin, a wealthy, camel-owning tribe that lived in the area. Some years previously a Lahawin man had killed an ex-slave of the Shukriya. The killer, called Sharaf el Din, disappeared for fear of punishment, so others had to pay the *diya*, the bloodwealth. The sister of the deceased, a freed slave by the name of Wakila, mourned her brother. A Shukriya poet,

CHILDHOOD

Suleiman wad el Faki, from Ghurashi village, recorded her grief in a poem that spread rapidly among the girls at Jummeiza and along the western bank.

> *Look what Sharaf el Din did:*
> *All that his mother got from begetting him is a fistful of earth.*
> *He forgot that a life is borrowed time.*
> *He did not remember the girls with pomaded hair.*
> *Those Lahawin have unknown ancestry.*
> *His mother was put in jail; his father fettered to a tree;*
> *He forgot he was a man and did not remember the girls.*
> *He did not remember that life can end in death at any time.*
> *The ancestors of the Lahawin are not of Shukriya origin.*
> *His fleeting heart fluttered off like a dove.*
> *He fled with his debts unpaid; other people paid the* diya.
> *Don't expect him to come back.*
> *The Shukriya mock the shame of those who fled.*
> *Your brother, Wakila, died with pride.*
> *He never forgot the beautiful girls of our tribe.*

The girls of the camp sang when they were working too. Early in the morning they would saddle their donkeys, put a pair of water skins on them and move in a group down to the river. The water skins would be filled by hand, orienting the mouth of the skin upstream and scooping the water into it. If a crocodile was to prey on them, the song went, let it take a Lahawin girl not a Shukriya girl with her long hair.

> *O sheep skin, ho-wa-ha*
> *Your owner is thirsty, ho-wa-ha.*
> *He is fasting for Ramadan, ho-wa-ha.*
> *The girls have filled up their water skins, ho-wa-ha.*

They left me behind by the river, ho-wa-ha,
But I am the sister of the strong young man, ho-wa-ha.

The crocodile took its prey, ho-wa-ha.
It took the girl with the thick tresses, ho-wa-ha.
No, No! Allah save that one! Ho-wa-ha.
Take the Lahawin girl instead, ho-wa-ha,
The one with the eyes that challenge men, ho-wa-ha.

Cleaning the sorghum at noon, as they picked impurities from the large wooden bowl, the *gadah*, girls might sing a song that imitated the cooing of doves, *gogai*. These were sad songs about days of youth, before a girl was married away, expressing longing for home, for an absent brother:

My mother's people, gogai, took me away
They pitched my tent, gogai, in the little wadi
They milked for me, gogai, new milk
My mother's son, gogai, the dear one
He slung his sword, gogai, on his left shoulder
He took the whip, gogai, by the right hand
My mother's son, gogai, they say will return
And I shall be happy, gogai, to run out and receive him.

A DANGEROUS GAME AND A CLOSE ENCOUNTER

Ibrahim, my brother, stood with his hands on the wheel in the driver's cabin of the huge black steam locomotive. I pretended to shovel coal in the furnace of the engine. The derelict train was overgrown with all kinds of plants. It lay below the eastern end of the Blue Bridge, completely covered by the river forest. It had probably been used to haul materials for building the bridge back in the 1920s. Or perhaps it had been hit by bombs during the war with the Italians. Playing on the abandoned engine was one of our most absorbing pastimes.

We had another, more dangerous pastime, also bequeathed to us by modern civilization. Early each morning, Ibrahim and I would take the flock from the camp and let it browse in the *karab* around Kibeirizzan, the Timber Bridge. This small bridge was built for the railway over a watercourse about two kilometres away from the Blue Bridge. Kibeirizzan was not really made of timber. It was made of heavy steel but painted in two colours, perhaps to camouflage it during the war. The *karab* where we grazed our flock was called Karab el Ahmar, or the red *karab*, because of the colour of its earth. It was an area of deep gullies, creeks and high knolls and thick trees that had sheltered troops during the Second World War, drawn from Sudan, India and Britain. Their legacy was a collection of unexploded ordnance that no one cared to clear.

No-one told me or Ibrahim. We found old shells, which we called bombs – *ganabil*. They were smooth and grey, half-metre long, spindle-shaped devices, carrying each a small fan at one end. We tied them by the fan to the end of a rope and dragged them around. For some reason they were always found in pairs. We raced those projectiles across sands, rocks and rugged ground until we became bored. Then we began to wonder what could be inside. We fetched large stones and hit one, but nothing happened.

Ibrahim said we were not using the right kind of stone and so we went to look for flint, as used by the nomads to strike sparks for fire. Ibrahim found a big rock and raised it high and brought it crashing down on the bomb. There was an explosion and a profusion of smoke and we ran for our lives. Other boys were not so lucky. Later we heard of two of them being killed by one of these abandoned weapons. Ibrahim and I stopped playing with them and the men in the camp went and buried any shells they could find in deep pits.

Our life that summer went on uninterrupted by anything else out of the ordinary. Then, suddenly something utterly new took place. It was a hot summer's afternoon and Ibrahim and I were inside the byre with the sheep when we heard someone outside. Ibrahim asked me to go out and see what the matter was. As I looked I saw, standing on the escarpment of the railway, just before the entrance of the bridge a *nasraniya*, a Nazarene, an English lady! She was wearing a flowery dress, and was standing near one of those fast railcars, a small self-propelled cubicle-like locomotive that we called *autombil-sikka-hadid*. Were there other people in the car? Who knew? I was concentrating completely on the woman, She seemed to be beckoning me to come over. I shouted to Ibrahim that the *nasraniya* up there was signaling that I should go to her. Ibrahim said, "Well, what are you waiting for? Go on."

But the *Nasara* were *nijus*, unclean. I knew this from religious teaching. They would be the wood-gatherers in *Jahannam*, in Gehenna. They had been disobedient to Allah and He would surely punish them in the hereafter. Should I speak to this *kafir*? This infidel? It would be like speaking to a Martian, not that I knew what a Martian was, either. My mixed feelings metamorphosed into fear, but I climbed up the high embankment of the railroad and timidly approached the woman. When I raised my eyes I saw a sweet, motherly smile. She extended her arm to shake my hand. And despite the fears of a wild five-year old child of Muslim upbringing, I found my tiny hand held gently in hers as if it were a young sparrow.

In broken Arabic she asked me to bring her some milk. She gave me an enamel jug and I ran back to Ibrahim who milked a few goats and sheep to fill the jug. After I had given her the milk, the lady asked me to wait until she came back. I noticed that her legs and arms were bare and that one of her legs had a large red blotch, perhaps as a result of the heat. Her hair was not braided; it was short and shiny. A single hair was as thick as the hairs of a donkey's tail, the ones we used to trap birds with. She was tall and slim, yet not bony.

Presently she came back with a can in her hand. She handed it over to me and I noticed the can was freshly opened and was full to the brim with meat of the strangest colour I had ever yet seen. It was pink! I took the can to Ibrahim. He said it could be *khinzeer*, pig meat. I thought of our father, a man of religion. But Ibrahim had already tasted the meat. I reminded him that pork was *haram* – forbidden – and that we were the sons of a *feki*.

"I didn't say it was pork for sure," said Ibrahim. "I only said it may be pork, just may be, you understand? How would I know?"

"It certainly tastes good." he added. "Have a bite, Hamid."

We ate it all and Ibrahim turned the empty can into a coffee bean roaster, a *tawwa*. Our father knew nothing about it to the day he died, nearly half a century later.

A DOG DIES

At the beginning of the rainy season we moved up from the *karab* of Shangil Bangil to the tableland of Wadi Khireissab. To the west of our camp was a large Hadendowa camp. Between the two camps ran the upper reaches of Shehateib creek. The Hadendowa camp belonged to the cattle-owning Kimeilab tribe.

One day, in the early afternoon, we noticed an unusual stir in the Kimeilab camp. Soon it became clear that something serious was the matter, as raised voices wafted to us across the low valley. A little later, we saw droves of men move towards our camp. The majority of the men were young men armed with swords and shields. The men in our camp took up their swords and shields, too, just in case. As the saying went, "he who comes to you with rolled up sleeves, meet him naked."

The Hadendowa group stopped on an open ground behind our tents. They sat down and waited, which meant they expected us to come in order to discuss a matter of some gravity. Our men moved towards the visitors while the women, apprehensive, watched from their tents. I went with the men to see what the problem was. The Hadendowa group consisted of some fifteen or twenty young warriors accompanied by four or five older men. The young men looked restless. They were in a continuous state of urging themselves to action, while the old men were trying to calm them down.

The issue at hand turned out to be a problem created by a dog, Deira, Ahmed Jubar's huge woolly dog. The dog had marauded calves belonging to the Kimeilab. The old men were trying to solve the problem peacefully by dialogue while the young ones thought that the Arabs had been intimidating them for quite a while and that the matter now needed a radical solution. This meant resort to the sword. The older people in both camps were aware of the fact that in nomadic life even an incident so trifling as the one at hand could engender major conflict. The elders saluted each other like brothers then they moved together towards the groups of young warriors from each camp saying appeasing words while the two groups were kept well apart. The old men began their parley in the space between the two groups of young warriors. Every now and then two of them would go to one or the other group and discuss some idea with them. In their large *tobs*, looking like Roman senators, the elders went back and forth until they came to a solution they thought would be accepted by the two parties.

To announce the solution the oldest man of all, a Hadendowa, was asked to be the spokesman. Just as he rose to talk, one of the older Arab men went and stood close to Ahmed Jubar. The decision stipulated that our camp should pay a pecuniary fine acceptable to the owners of the calves. However, the young Hadendowa warriors could not care less for that solution. They wanted to appease their swords; they wanted blood to be shed. They stood up making battle cries. The old man told them to sit down and listen to him for he had a solution that would result in the bloodshed they wanted. There was silence. The old man paused for a while as if waiting for some feeling or message to register in the minds of the young warriors. Then he said, "That dog, Deira, should be brought to us here and now to try our swords on it." Ahmed Jubar jumped up, his hand on his sword's hilt, showing vigorous objection but the man who was standing near him calmed him down. The young warriors accepted the solution and the dog was brought to court. Deira was as sturdy as one of the Dobermans I came to know later, as woolly as a Hungarian Kuvasz. But he belonged to a distinctly Hadendowa breed. Ahmed Jubar left the meeting, his eyes red.

We made a wide circle and the dog in the centre was held by two long ropes, one attached to the neck and another to a hind leg. It struggled and snarled at the spectators but all that to no avail; it was doomed. Two young warriors brandished their broadswords, and, with a battle cry, each jumped high, high in the air, with their swords and the shields. The circle rippled wider to make more room for the death dancers as emotions mounted higher and higher. Near to ten young warriors were now jumping, shouting and raising dust. The others in the circle of spectators shook their swords and clattered them against their hippo-hide shields as they chanted inflaming words to help the dancing warriors divest themselves of the last scintilla of mercy.

The confused dog was at the centre of the circle, its muscles twitching, its whole body shaking with fear and anticipation of death. Wherever it tried to escape a rope pulled it back in the opposite direction. Suddenly a young Hadendowa lept very high and lighted close to the dog, then feinting to hit the neck, took off the free hind leg. Blood gushed out on the ground and the poor animal fell on the stub left of the leg.

As a child who raised and loved dogs, I was horrified. A shudder went through my body as I winced under the effect of the vicarious feeling of pain. I could bear the sight of a ram being slaughtered, but the killing of a dog in that manner seemed unbearably cruel. The warriors were laughing at its suffering. Now a front leg was chopped off and it fell on its belly. The amputation of the two remaining legs then followed. Finally the head was lopped off.

In truth the affair had nothing to do with the dog. It was an exhibition of force, a reminder from the Hadendowa to us, the Arabs, that the land on which we lived, the land on the east bank of the river, was Hadendowa land, not Arab land. The jamboree over, the satisfied party of Hadendowa warriors disbanded. We dragged the bloody ropes home. Deira, decapitated, disembowelled and dismembered, was left to the vultures.

CHILDHOOD

LOST IN THE FOREST

The day that followed I came down with *wirda um berid*, chill-fever. Every one in the camp could easily diagnose malaria. Its symptoms were unique: chills, nausea, vomiting and loss of appetite, sometimes backache. The fever skipped a day and appeared again the next. Nobody ever connected mosquitoes with the illness. Only one medicine was prescribed then: endurance. I got malaria practically each rainy season; it appeared in no other season. No one ever died of it as far as I know.

I lay low on the *serir* while Ketira kept covering me with the coarse *shamla* blanket whenever I threw it away from me. The prickly goat-hair *shamla* with its thorny bristles felt like a million hedgehogs on my bare skin. As I retched and vomited, Ketira would prop up my forehead with her hand to prevent the vomit coming out through my nose. She would release a chain of "Oh dears!" and "Oh Muhammads!" as part of the treatment. Once in a while she would give me either a bowl of thin sorghum pap or a gourd of water-diluted sour milk to drink from.

For days, the high fever kept on recurring. Then Ibrahim took me to *teb-el-Jennah* or Paradise Pool. When a *khor* stopped running, water pools formed in the meanders under high steep banks formed by landslides. One of these big pools, which we called *tebs*, was overhung by a canopy of trees and its water was always much cooler than the other *tebs*. Ibrahim discovered that bathing in that *teb* usually rid one of fever and so he called it Paradise Tub. It was I who made good use of the *teb* not Ibrahim, though, because it was almost always I who contracted malaria or other transient fevers.

THE AMULET

ASUBRI

My uncles and cousins, the Dirars, in the village of Asubri and vicinity, further downstream from Ghurashi, had always been concerned with my well-being in what they considered the wild land of the Hadendowa on the east bank. In spite of the fact that they had been on bad terms with my father, they never totally severed relationship with him. They were happy at one time when they heard that Sheikh Annour had taken me to my mother on the west bank. Now they sent Khalid, my oldest cousin, to fetch me from Shehateib.

Khalid arrived at our camp one early afternoon. Like Sheikh Annour, he came riding a fast, white *Rifawi* donkey. Among the Dirars, Khalid held a status close to that of Sheikh Annour among the Dumans. His clothes were always white and his *tob* long and large. By local standards he was pale of complexion and fairly good-looking, but much younger than Sheikh Annour, perhaps in his late twenties then. He laughed and smiled often, displaying well-set white teeth. At times, however, he could get very serious and his face showed it, when discussing matters of gravity. He was extremely intelligent, shrewd and quick at sorting out entangled situations. Unlike Sheikh Annour, Khalid had grasped the vital importance of education and had taught himself how to read and write when he was a *muhafiz* with Sheikh Awad el Karim Abu Sin, without attending any formal school.

Khalid knew all the men in our camp although not as closely as Sheikh Annour did. He called my father *Abouy* Ahmed. He stayed with us at Shehateib for a few days, apparently enjoying the life of the nomads and the abundance of milk. He spent the moonlit nights on the sands of the *khor* talking to the men of the camp and listening to the music of the *rababa*, or the *basinkob*, as the Hadendowa called it, a stringed instrument played with a bow. Then he asked my father to let him take me to visit my relatives at Asubri. Father agreed reluctantly.

Asubri was a relatively large village whose houses were *tukuls* of old, dark grass like all villages in the area. The village had two shops, each a large adobe cubicle with a thatch lean-to which served as awning against the sun. It lay on the demarcation line between the *karab* and the clay plain. The small creeks were lined with the ugly *usher*, the Sodom apple, with its inflated fruit like a shaven devil's head. The creeks joined to form a *khor* that flanked the village on its southern and eastern sides. A large *hafir*, an artificial reservoir dug by the people of the village, lay to the north, and held rainwater which supplied the village for the three or four dry months that followed the rains.

The layout of the village was similar to that of Ghurashi, but whereas the latter was a religious centre, Asubri had been the political and administrative seat of the tribal government of the Shukriya before and under the early British rule. When the British took over the Sudan from the Mahdists at the turn of the nineteenth century they ruled over the nomadic tribes through their existing leaders, who thus ruled, as *nazirs*, with the clout of the British behind them. In the case of the Shukriya before the Second World this was Sheikh Awad el Karim Abu Sin. He spent half the year at Rufa'a, a town on the Blue Nile, and the other half at Asubri in the north of the Butana. In later years, Sheikh Awad el Karim moved the seat of his rule from Asubri to Khashm el Girba, far upstream. But most of his retinue of lesser sheikhs of the Abu Sin clan remained at Asubri.

Sheikh Awad el Karim was adamantly against the modern education that was introduced by the British. He had a strong conviction that a tribe of educated men could not be ruled over properly and resisted any attempt at establishing schools for the nomads. After Awad el Karim died, in 1944, his nephew, Sheikh Muhammad Hamad Abu Sin, became the leader of the Shukriya. The young sheikh had a completely different attitude from his late uncle with regard to modern education. The day he acceded to leadership he started the process of establishing the first school in the Atbara region at Asubri. It was a school called *madrasa-sughra*, sub-grade school, and by the time I came to the village it had been in existence for three years.

Khalid and I arrived at sunset and spent the night in his house at the navel of the village. The following morning he took me to a nomad camp down near the creek where I met the rest of the family in their single tent. Khalid's father, *Abouy* Muhammad, was a big man, dark and squat, with broad shoulders. But what drew my attention the most was the thick entanglement of curly hair covering his broad chest. In fact Uncle Muhammad's chest hair was so phenomenal that a joke ran in the family that when one of his children lost his pet baby hare it was found hiding in the forest on *Abouy* Muhammad's chest.

Next, Khalid took me to another nomad camp where I met *Abouy* Hassan wad Dirar. He was a fair-skinned man of fine features and certainly the most good-looking of all the Dirars. Like Sheikh Annour, he had been a playboy of repute in his youth; like Sheikh Annour, too, he was a friend of poets and his name was already heard in poems circulating in the land of the Shukriya. And like all the Dirars he was a carpenter. He specialized in making camel saddles; and he raised racing camels. Both were lucrative, but a good portion of what Uncle Hassan earned went in acts of generosity and to please the many women in his life. Locally he was described as a *fenjeri*, a man well-dressed and generous.

III

Schooldays

GOING TO SCHOOL

News reached Khalid that my father was expected to arrive at Asubri to take me back to Shehateib. My uncles and cousins felt alarmed and began to seek a way to prevent this. But they knew very well that their argument had to be very convincing to make my father yield to their demand. Khalid quickly came up with a solution. He went to the sub-grade school of the village and explained the situation to the two teachers there. He told them that my father was a man of religion and would only leave me with my cousins if he knew I was enrolled in school. They knew I was below school age, but they agreed on the proviso that he brought me to school just on the day my father came and that I would leave after he left the village.

Father arrived at Uncle Muhammad's house. Khalid had already taken me to the village and into the school where I was placed at the end of the class behind the regular pupils. I was issued a slate and crayon for writing. The classroom itself was a wood-and-grass *dahar-tor*, an ox-back, named for its humped shape, similar to our animal byre at the Blue Bridge. Father came the day after and when he was told that I was at school, he left without even seeing me. The ruse had worked. Or it seemed to have. Khalid thanked the teachers for their help.

I was not expected to go to school the following day, but early in the morning Khalid saw me preparing to leave. He asked me where I thought I was going. I told him, matter-of-factly, that I was on my way to school. He did not try to stop me. At the school the headmaster was taken by a surprise when he saw me walk past him straight into the classroom, without a word. I sat in my seat of the day before. I knew it was where I should be. Most of the pupils in the school were there because their parents or the sheikhs of the tribe wanted them there, not because they chose. In my case things were the opposite. Months passed and nothing disturbed my education except for the rare moments when my classmates laughed at my bad Arabic. I loved school as I had never loved anything before. But my happiness was not destined to last.

KIDNAPPED FROM CLASS

On a certain day, following the sinuous course of the creek that skirted the village, muffled to the ears with his large, dust-and-fat-soaked calico *tob*, came a man on camelback. He proceeded quietly towards the school, dismounted and approached warily, hidden by the lush growth of broad-leaved Sodom Apple shrubs. From that vantage point he could command a clear view of the courtyard of the school. He waited.

Half an hour later, I and the other pupils were released from the classrooms for the nine o'clock breakfast break. The other pupils played in the shade of the *sayal* trees in the school courtyard. I wandered towards the creek in a reverie. Then I felt a heavy hand on my shoulder. Before I knew it I was dragged down the creek to where the hidden camel was waiting and hoisted onto its back. In an instant we were trotting away into the wilderness. Over my shoulder I could see my school mates far off in their white garments, looking like grains of sorghum.

Zaki wad el Faki Beshir, who had just kidnapped me, was telling me that Allah would not accept that a man like my father should work so hard as to harm his health when he had a son who could help. My father and Zaki had a sorghum farm on the clay plain near Sharafa village, not far from the Blue Bridge, at a place called Rigayig. When they came from Shehateib on the eastern bank, they had brought with them a flock of goats for milk. My father, said Zaki, would be very happy if I proved man enough to take care of the goats. School was a luxury, I was given to understand, and my first duty was to help my father, like other nomad boy.

It was Zaki who had persuaded my father that he should collect me from school. Since when, he said, did nomads take their young to these *Nasara* schools? So I wound up working as a goatherd for them. I took the flock for grazing up on the clay plain every morning and in the afternoon I took the goats down to the river for water, then I let them roam the river forest. There was nothing goats liked better than browsing here and there on different trees. In the late afternoon I took them up to the farm. At the farm we slept in a small improvised thatch of sorghum stalks, on rush mats, rugs and pallets on the ground. For cover, I had a small stretch of calico that we called *fitga*. I had nightmares about *marafin*, the hyena.

One day I spotted a he-goat of ours that had been lost a year before. I chased it for hours through the buckthorn underbrush and finally brought it back. My father was happy.

"The speckled *ambalok!*" he shouted.

"I tell you, Ahmed," said Zaki. "You should always keep that boy with you. He is *mabruk* – blessed."

The following day I took the he-goat to Shehateib across the river. I used my *fitga* as a leash and dragged the goat behind me to the Blue Bridge and across the river to Shehateib. There in the camp I found my mother and my brother Ibrahim. What I did not find was my dear dog Maigulu, of the tawny fur. Ibrahim said he had been stolen by Zibeidiya who lived at a nearby camp.

LOSING MAIGULU

I picked up Maigulu's leash rope, folded it in the nomad way by wrapping it along my left forearm around the elbow and a fork formed by the thumb and the forefinger. After releasing the circles of rope from my arm, I secured them with the end of the rope. I left the camp and walked towards the Zibeidiya camp, climbing up the knolls and down the creeks until I found myself walking along the top of a steep slope of *goz* soil. I knew that my destination was just below it. I had a full view of the camp. There they were, their wool tents perched like a grounded swarm of bats. I felt powerful, standing there looking down on them.

It was noon. I had no shadow. I stood on the crest of the *goz*, like a sugar ant posing on its hind legs. I started the descent to the camp intending to demand my dog back. But I slipped on stones and crashed down the slope. Now I could see the inside of the tents. There were no beds; the Zibeidiya slept on rugs on the ground. (How did they keep snakes and rain water away?) Men – and women in cowrie-studded veils – came out of their tents and converged on this small boy holding a rope, who had just appeared in their midst.

One of them asked me what I wanted.

"I want my dog," I said.

"And where is your dog?"

"It's here in your camp. You stole my dog," I said.

The old man looked amused.

"You mean of all animals we stole a dog?"

"Maigulu is no animal, she is my dog and you stole her,"

"What makes you so sure we have your dog?" the man asked.

"Ibrahim and Hassan said you do. They wouldn't lie."

"No, of course they wouldn't," said the man. "Ibrahim and Hassan – who are they?

A young man holding a camel by the reins answered the old man's question. It seemed he knew us.

"Ibrahim is his brother, the tall thin boy the *Ujman* call the Noon Devil," he said

"And can you identify your dog?" said the old man.

I was certain I could. The man asked the boys to summon their dogs. Among them I saw my dog Maigulu my dog with her slick tawny fur.

"That is Tarha" exclaimed a boy in the crowd. So they had given my dog a new name.

I was given the dog on a leash. But Maigilu would not respond to my commands. I pulled as hard as I could. Suddenly the dog growled and came charging at me, as though to bite me. I hit her hard with my stick on the muzzle. She retreated in pain. I tried again, and fell over. The spectators laughed. The dog snarled and lunged. She clearly did not recognize me or want to come with me. I left, cursing them all. I did not tell Ibrahim, or anyone else in our camp, but they were all bound to know the story sooner or later

A FLASH FLOOD

Huge bald-headed vultures and buzzards were fighting over the carcass of a Hedendowa cow on the sandy bed of the Shehateib River. Ibrahim drove them off with his throwing stick. The birds made a circle around us, unwilling to relinquish their find. We began to hack at the hide of the flank of the animal, ignoring the stench of the scattered entrails. We would make shoes from the hide, after the custom of the Hadendowa. And Ibrahim cut along the sides of the backbone to release a pair of tendons which he intended to use as the string of a bow, a weapon he was fond of.

We took the pieces of hide to the river and beat them with rocks on the shore, then buried them deep in the mud until the following day. Then we beat them again, using a wooden mallet. We put them under our feet to take measurements, cut them and laced them round our feet to make shoes, *ni-ilat*. These *ni-ilat*, were soft as moccasins when damp, but when they dried they gave us sore feet and were noisy when you walked. The nomads believed that at that stage the cow had come alive, reincarnated in the pieces of rawhide, and that it was bellowing. They called the hide footwear *bagara-hayya*, live cow. You could not use such shoes for hunting. Women never wore *baggara-hayyas* though they also had their own noisy wood clogs called *kerkeb*, noisy ones. Women hated *bagara-hayyas* for a special reason which I will come to later.

The Shehateib River was a hundred yards wide. In places it was ten or fifteen foot deep. In the dry season there was no water in it at all. The blazing summer months slipped away and the first two rain showers came. Water flowed in the river for a time then subsided again. In the clean sands it left behind we dug shallow wells. The wells belonged to a Zibeidi by the name of Hamid Iyoun; they were located just behind our tents, thirty or forty yards away. I was down one of the wells filling up a water skin, scooping water into it with a small half-gourd when I heard Katira shouting.

"Hamid! Hamid! Get out quick! The *khor* is coming!"

I looked up and saw a tall bank of foam rushing towards me, roaring. I leapt to safety with my half-filled water skin. Within minutes the Shehateib was in spate, from bank to bank. Huge uprooted trees came down with the flood. In places, it overflowed its banks. The people of the camp came out and lined up to watch the flood. Where we were there was no rain at all, but the headwaters of the Shehateib were far away.

The wadi had developed good pastures. There was enough water to sustain life until the full *kherif* came. Soon preparations were underway for the annual migration. Older women went into the forest to cut and char and mould the wood for the *utfas* of young brides. Other women rolled up the tent mats and smoked them so they would resist decay during the wet season. Carpenters like my father received a spate of demands for the wooden augers used by farmers to make shallow holes in the ground for sowing sorghum. Young men prepared tinder for fires by rubbing old rags on ash and then on the outside of a sheep's udder. A bag of tinder would also contain flint and steel, and, usually, tobacco. Bit Burbur had a speciality at this time of year. Before the rains came, she would prepare *gutran*, a kind of tar. She heated the seeds of the wild melon in order to extract the tar. *Gutran* tar extract was used to treat skin disease in sheep and goats.

When a storm came women began pounding the pegs of the tents to drive them deeper into the ground. They threw heavy ropes over the tent to tie it down. The animals would be quickly milked and closed in the *zariba*. Wood and kindling were moved where rainwater would not reach them and dry soil was kept in a safe place to provide a fireplace following the storm. Ibrahim and I would be compelled to move our live-cow sandals away from the camp and hide them: the women insisted that these *bagara-hayya*s attracted lightning. This was the reason women did not like shoes of this kind. I was worried that a thunderbolt would discover their hiding place and destroy them. I had heard also that when a bolt of lightning hit, a slug of iron would appear and sink into the ground. If a man poured milk on it it would stop sinking. This iron would make the best kind of sword, *seif-assagaa*, a thunderbolt sword, so sharp that no scabbard could hold it. But I never found such a thing.

A rain storm at night could be terrifyingly violent. "*Ya Latif! Ya Latif! Ya Latif!*" people would cry, as they rushed to secure livestock and posesssions. "O Gentle God! Gentle God!" Storms bred frogs. After the storm had passed the silence would be filled by the croaking of thousands of them in pools. Frogs were venerated by the nomads; they augured an abundance of rain and food.

A STOLEN CHILD?

A bull was to be slaughtered for the wedding of Garja, a man from a famous Diweihin family, the in-laws of my mother. The Diweihin camp was at Khor el Jurab, Leather Bag Creek, far up-river, on the east bank, just across the water from the village of Khashm el Girba. The tents were at the upper edge of the river forest in a flat area strewn with shady large *sayal* trees. My grandfather

Omar Duman took me at the request of my mother, who heard that there was a food shortage where we were at Shehateib.

As the animal was about to be slaughtered it broke its ropes and ran amok, turning the whole Diweihin camp into bedlam. Men tried to catch it using ropes with running nooses but failed. The bull, with its mouth foaming charged the wedding guests, and charged again. Finally four young men appeared brandishing swords like matadors. As the bull charged at them they cut him down, aiming at the hock tendons of the hind legs. The animal, hamstrung, lay foaming on the ground. And was finally dispatched by a blow to its jugular

An argument then arose over whose sword was best among those in the camp. The test was which of them could cut clean in one thrust the two shank bones of the slaughtered bull. There were two normal-length broadswords and a half-length horseman's sword. It was this sword which won the contest. It belonged to my step-father who had bought it from my grandfather Omar Duman. Grandpa was a spearsman and had little use for a sword, especially one that needed a horse to function properly. The next time I was to see that sword was forty years later when it was presented to me on the occasion of my wedding.

All the guests at the wedding of Garja were Arabs except for one man who was a Hadendowa. He sat alone on a large rock under a balanites tree playing his *basinkob*. I went with a group of boys to listen. The man became vexed by our presence and waved his stick at us, muttering in the Hadendowa language "*Haramj-ar*! "Sons of bitches!" It did not occur to him that any of the Arab children would understand what he was saying; he was surprised to see me glowering at him when all the other children scurried away.

THE AMULET

I later learned that he began an investigation of the identity of the boy who could understand his language. It was known that tribes stole the children of other tribes. The man suspected that I was a Hadendowa child stolen by the Diweihin. Finally he spoke to Rajab, my step-father, who explained the story of my Hadendowa upbringing.

A few weeks later the Diweihin decided to move the camp to their rainy season site, Andala, across the river on the west bank, before rain in Ethiopia brought flood water into the river. So we all moved to Andala, taking with us the few cattle that we had with us. In the summer months the Diweihin sent the bulk of their cattle away south along the river to the Ethiopian border, where pasture abounded in the Humran region, comprising Seiteet, Humara and Fashaga. Just a few cows in milk would be left back at the camp. The group of cattle that left for the border area were called the *hanon*; those left at home were the *homah*.

THE YEAR OF THE SYNDICATE

In the famine year of 1948, however, the rains were late and the cows gave no milk because of lack of pasture. Sorghum stores were depleted and famine spread fast. Children began to suffer as their condition deteriorated.

The British colonial government was not taken by surprise and had already secured the necessary provisions of sorghum. All tribal sheikhs were alerted to inform their people that there were sorghum supplies at Khashm el Girba for them, but priority was to be given to families with young children. So heads of families took some of their kids with them to Khashm el Girba. My step-father took me with him to the village. The picture that stuck in my mind was a great mound of white sorghum grain in an open space near the dispensary. The mound was guarded by khaki-clad *muhafizin*, carrying their carbine rifles. A circle of Arab men, old women and children surrounded the sorghum and the carabineers. Everything was organized and controlled so that we got our fair share of sorghum and rode our donkey back. The nomads called that year *Sanat el Sindica*, the Year of the Syndicate, after the committee established to deal with the food distribution.

Good rains began to fall and the cattle that had been sent to the south were brought back. The day they appeared on the east bank, we went to the bank of the river to see them cross over. The river was in spate. The huge body of Diweihein cattle on the east bank paused on the brink, then entered the water. The herdsmen wrapped their clothes into a bundle carried on their heads and seized the tail of a steer. The crowd roared their approval. Tree trunks collided with the mass of cattle and men; there were snakes and scorpions sheltering in the trees and crocodiles in the water. All but the weakest cattle made it across, though.

Rajab, my step-father, had a son, Jabir, whose mother had drowned in the river at Ain el Jamal, the Camel's Eye Pond, near Andala. Remarkably, as she was drowning, she managed to throw the child out on the shore to be picked up by his grandmother. Rajab was extremely affected by the loss. He suffered the difficulties of raising a motherless child. Perhaps he felt compassion towards me for this reason. He always treated me as if I were his own son and Jabir treated me as if I were his younger brother. And I made another friend, Adlan, the son of Sheikh Yousif Umara Abu Sin. He approached me and offered his friendship after he learned from his father that it was my grandfather Ali Dirar who established a fruit garden for his grandfather at Asubri. Sheikh

Yousif was a powerful man. Most of the west bank of the river from the borders with Ethiopia to the confluence with the Nile fell under his jurisdiction.

One evening Adlan told me he was going to be taken to school at Khashm el Girba. This struck a spark in my heart, a renewed yearning for education. I told my mother and Rajab, her husband. Rajab spoke to Sheikh Yousif Abu Sin. He was pleased. The *nazir* of the Shukriya, Muhammad Hamad Abu Sin, had decided that the school in Asubri should be upgraded to a full elementary school and transferred to the village of Khashm el Girba, where there was a railway station, a telegraph line and a main road. But a rumour had spread that the school encouraged homosexuality, which had led many families to shrink from sending their sons there. The *nazir* had asked his sheikhs to each send a quota of boys from his tribe. Faced by the reluctance of the Diweihin to contribute to the quota, Sheikh Yousif volunteered to set an example by sending his own son to school. When he was told that I would like to go too, it was quickly agreed that I would accompany Adlan.

THE ROAD TO KNOWLEDGE

Early in the morning of our departure I walked up to Sheikh Yousif's tent to find Adlan being made ready for school. He had been bought a full attire of white *dabalan* clothes, *surwal*, *jibbah* and turban, together with leather sandals. I had only my usual Shehateib *fitga*, a dirty coarse cotton piece of cloth, hardly larger than an oversize kerchief. I was barefoot and bareheaded. But the son of a famous tribal leader had to look good, of course. Adlan was proud of his new clothes and strutted around in them with his turban coiled on the top of his head like a nut on a bolt.

Sheikh Yousif entrusted us to one of his *muhafizin*, named Yaru, to take us to school. Later I discovered that Yaru was a West African, a Fulani by descent, though Sudanese by birth. His Arabic was so good that most people who knew him mistook him for a Shukriya Arab. Only when he got married and chose a Fulani wife did they learn of his Nigerian roots. Today Yaru was wearing the *muhafizin berdaloba*, a khaki tunic with his legs swathed in khaki wool puttees. He had a khaki turban, a rifle and a bandolier over his left shoulder. He checked repeatedly on the eight-year-old sheikh. Adlan was not keen on going to school and might try and run off. For me, though, school was the focus of all my hopes. I was determined not to let myself be kidnapped again.

The school had one classroom. The only employee was the headmaster. He was teaching when we arrived, wearing a dazzlingly white garment that villagers and town folks called a *jellabiya*. His skin was white like an Egyptian or a Turk. When he shook hands with us I noticed the soft touch of his palm. With his voluminous *jellabiya*, he looked like what nomads called a *Jaa-li-ab-khurtaya*, a Jaalin wearing a bag, though he was from the Magharba tribe, originally from Morocco.

"What's your name?" the headmaster asked me.

"Hamid wad Ahmed wad Dirar," I answered.

"Do you know anyone here in the class?" he stepped aside and I surveyed the faces.

"Yes, sir, Khidir and Daw, the sons of Shawish Yousif," I answered. The headmaster said "OK, go in and take a seat."

I entered the crowded classroom and wedged myself between the two boys tightly. I wanted to make sure nobody would ever again pluck me out.

KHASHM EL GIRBA

Khashm el Girba was a very small village. Its few buildings ran to the very edge of the deep river gorge which gave the village its name. On the far west, on the edge of the clay plain, were the railway station buildings. The maintenance workers lived in ten white stone and brick *guttiyas*, five at one end of the station and five at the other end. A large red brick building, lying between the two complexes, served as the station's administration. Close to this was a huge steel water tank raised high on steel supports. Midway between the railway station and the river was the village proper, the houses of which were all dark *tukuls* roofed with old *nal* grass. The inhabitants were freed slaves and their descendants.

In the marketplace there were adobe shops arranged in a square with their doors opening into the central space. The arrangement was not Sudanese, but the work of the British District Commissioner. There were government buildings scattered over a large area. The *nazir*'s rest house comprised a few buildings of grass and adobe inside a grass fence. Close to this was the school building. Then came the Zabtiya, the department of legal affairs, headquarters of the *muhafizin*. The head was Shawish Yousif. He was married to Halima Bit el Tom, my mother's aunt. There was a telephone fixed to the mud wall of the Zabtiya that was operated by cranking and shouting. Here, complaints could be filed and cases prepared for the *nazir*'s court. Affiliated to the Zabtiya was a clerk whose duties included taking a record of the rainfall and the water level in the river.

South of the Zabtiya was the prison, a large thick-walled adobe hall with a door of steel bars and small ventilators near the roof. The bars of the tiny windows were made from barrels of rifles captured from Mahdists by the British. The prison held *mahajra* – camel thieves – and murderers waiting to be sent to Port Sudan to be hanged. The guards stayed in the Karakon, a three-walled room. The missing wall faced the prison door, an arrangement that was meant to promote vigilance on the part of the guards. Khashm el Girba prison was called Abu-Debeeb, Snake Haunt Prison, for it was the home of a great cobra that no one was able to kill.

The last group of buildings towards the river constituted the District Commissioner's house, the *istiraha*, on raised ground overlooking the river. The *istiraha* had three large, spacious rooms with well-polished white walls. It was made of adobe with grass lean-to verandas supported by brick pillars. The windowsills and the floor were all of cement and the internal bathroom had a porcelain tub. The *istiraha* commanded a view of the lowlands surrounding it as far as the Ethiopian border. The river below formed a deep pool, green most of the year because of the reflection of the lush growth of tamarind trees that lined the banks. The deep pool was infested with hundreds and hundreds of dark-skinned crocodiles. The nomads called the pool Um Aswad, Black Crocodile Pool.

Khashm el Girba had been the creation of Mr A. Paul, the British District Commissioner in the region (later to become a notable chronicler of the Beja people). Before his arrival there was no village. Even nomads avoided the place. One peril was the teeming crocodiles of Um Aswad pool, the other the marauding packs of hyenas in Kireib Assi. The village was a byproduct of the advent of telecommunications in the British time. During the early years of British rule a telegraph line was installed between the towns of Gedaref and Kassala. The line passed through Khashm el Girba, but nomad shepherds and children played such havoc with the line that the government was forced to station a guard there. The guard built a *tukul* but had no neighbours. During the rainy season when the camps of the nomads moved away from the river to the clay plain, he was left alone in his lonely hut. He was nicknamed Addireikan, little man in danger, and his *tukul* was called Tikeil Addireikan, the little hut of the little man in danger. Eventually the whole area came to be called Tikeil Addireikan.

Shortly after Mr Paul built his headquarters, he decreed the emancipation of the slaves owned by the nomadic tribes. In the years from 1919 to 1921 he worked relentlessly to see that all the slaves in the district were freed from their nomadic masters. The action brought about a disruption in the social fabric of nomadic life. Until then, men in bondage had tended the camel herds, grown sorghum and fought their masters' wars, while slave women and girls did all the household work – fetching water, gathering firewood, milling and cooking sorghum, and looking after the children. In addition they were obliged to satisfy the carnal desires of their masters. The free Arab women lived for beauty and child bearing.

Following the emancipation of the slaves, Arab nomad women found themselves face to face with the realities of daily life. And who was the person behind all that misery? It was Mr Paul. Arab girls, tasting for the first time the rigours of milling hard sorghum grain on a saddlestone, sang this song:

> *Oh daya over daya,*
> *Grinding grain breaks my hands.*
> *May Mr Paul taste pain*
> *For he has made this free girl grind grain*
> *Oh dana over dana*

SCHOOLDAYS

May Mr Paul taste humiliation
For he made the mistress of the house grind grain.

The abolition of slavery did not pass without casualties. Many slaves were flogged by their masters for trying to leave. Others were killed by the sword. Many were forced to flee during the night. Former slaves arrived at Khashm el Girba in droves seeking government protection. They were the first civilians to settle in the area. The former slave women brewed sorghum beer, *merissa*. Some were sex workers, courtesans catering to wealthy nomads. The men, not having cattle or camels, cleared the bush and grew sorghum.

LIMOUN

The school at Khashm el Girba was a boarding school. The nomad boys were lodged in a boarding house. Each of us had a wooden bed – an *angareib* – and a heavy black Sudan Government blanket. At nine o'clock in the evening the spirit lamp was put out and we all went to sleep by order of the headmaster. Three meals of stiff sorghum porridge and dry okra sauce were offered per day. The preparation of the meals was the responsibility of three old women from the village. We sat in groups of five under the scattered *sayal* trees in the open space surrounding the kitchen. One boy from the group would get the bowl of porridge and place it between us to eat. When we needed more sauce one of us would go to the cook to get some. We gave her the name *Habboba Mulah*, Grandma Sauce.

There were some pupils known by their mothers' names instead of their fathers' names, children of courtesans who could not be sure who had fathered their child. Sheikh Annour met with the mothers and elicited the names of the most likely father of each boy. Then, with the consent of those men, he gave the children the names of their putative fathers.

One day I woke up early in the morning and was surprised to see that half the residents of the dormitory were not there. There was no sign that they were out in the courtyard.

Sherif, who always did his morning prayer very early, was awake and noticed the questioning look on my face.

"You're wondering where the missing students are?"

"Yes, where are they?"

"They went home. They escaped," he answered.

"Escaped? Why?"

"Well, you know nomads don't like school. Every night we lose about half the residents, but almost every day we get an equal number back as the sheikhs of the tribes return them. The influx roughly balances the truancy," Sherif talked as though he was part of the school administration.

Just a few days later I found my immediate neighbours in the ward, Hamad, Zubeir and Babiker, of the Jawamiss tribe, missing.

"My neighbours have escaped," I said to Sherif.

"But this is different," he said. "They are conjugal escapees."

"You mean they are married?" I said.

"Yes," said Sherif.

"But these are only seven-year-old boys," I said.

"No, they are eight-year-olds," said Sherif matter-of-factly.

"But don't worry," he added. "They usually come back of their own accord."

On another day I found that not a single boy was missing.

"Sherif, it appears that things settling down," I said.

"No, I don't think so", Sherif said.

"Then how come everyone is here today?"

"Today is Wednesday. It's fruit day," Sherif said. "Every Wednesday the school receives a crate of fruit from Kassala. The fruit seems to keep boys in school. We haven't received fruit for the last two months but it is almost sure that we will this Wednesday."

Sure enough, in the early afternoon just after we had lunch a man in a *jibbah* came carrying a large basket on his shoulder, sewn up with thick thread of jute. Sherif ordered the man to open up the basket. The man rolled up his left sleeve, pulled out his knife, cut the basket open and pulled the contents out. I was disappointed to see the fruits were neither yellow nor orange. They were small, round and very dark green. But the other children were used to them.

"*Limoon!*" They shouted in exhilaration. Limes! Green limes! Sherif immediately set about distributing the fruit, two limes for each of us. It was a British idea to make sure we were all supplied with vitamin C.

In another attempt to keep nomad children in school Sheikh Annour suggested to the headmaster that he allow each pupil to have his own goat on the school premises. He told Rahim that those nomad boys could not possibly live without milk and that they escaped partly because they wanted milk. He told the headmaster that when a nomad did not get milk for some time he or she would develop *eima*, a craving for milk. A few days later, confirming this, my brother Ibrahim arrived at Khashm el Girba with a goat in milk. He also brought me a pair of shoes. From Kassala, too.

Ibrahim tethered the goat to the trunk of the prison tree and decided to sneak into the classroom by the rear door. He sat not far from the open door where he had a good view both of the teacher and the goat. He now paid attention to the surprised teacher who just saw a man with a shock of hair wearing a *tob* and carrying a heavy stick enter his classroom without permission. However, Rahim continued to teach, barely faltering. Suddenly the goat outside gave a shrill bleat, which Ibrahim considered as disturbing the progress of education. He immediately replied from where he was inside the classroom with an even sharper deterring shout.

"Tek!" he said to the goat.

Everybody in the classroom now turned towards the end of the room to see the source of herdsman's cry, and laughed. I was mortified, but kept my countenance. Ibrahim was laughing; he never had feelings of embarrassment. The teacher went back to his Arabic lesson.

"The older hyena chewed the rotten bone *ghuruntush! ghuruntush!* The younger hyena chewed the rotten bone *ghirintish! ghirintish!*"

Both Ibrahim and I felt at home with that kind of lesson.

The Bata shoes which Ibrahim brought me lived two whole days. The black rubber soles of the white canvas shoes were as brittle as bad cakes. They broke in two halves after two days of chasing monkeys. I did my schooling barefoot for the next five years.

The wonders of that first year at school were endless. After the nine o'clock bell tolled Sherif would put out the spirit lamp in the dormitory. Initially there was silence but then Gilbos would break the silence. It was always Gilbos, a precocious sixteen-year-old.

"Let us revile him whose penis is not one handspan long!" he announced.

One handspan long! Mine I couldn't even find! I went groping for it in the dark. I had no doubt that the other pupils were doing what I did, taking measurements. Gilbos, I supposed, was busy fondling his. Everything about him seemed to be tall or long. He was a tall, thin young adult. His limbs were long, his fingers long and his neck was long. In fact he had a number of features in common with camels, especially in his neck and gait.

"When I inserted it into that wench, Dugaga..." Gilbos might begin. No one spoke. Then he would doze off, snoring loudly.

Sherif, urbane and decorous, never asked Gilbos to stop his blasphemous talk. Sherif was a pious boy who came from a deeply religious family who lived around Sharafa village near the Blue Bridge. He was about the same age as Gilbos but behaved as if he were an adult. He moved quietly, spoke gently and in a low voice. He must have suffered greatly from Gilbos' rogueishness.

WRESTLING

When I returned to school after the first long vacation, I found that a new school complete with four classrooms, staff residence, pupils' hostels, water stands, bucket latrines and a kitchen had been built of adobe halfway towards the railway station. The new buildings occupied a spacious area.

The headmaster was now joined by two young teachers wearing unmentionables. They were the first trousers ever seen in Khashm el Girba. One of the new teachers was a thin, tall gaunt young man with vertical tribal facial scars. The other was a stocky squat man of lighter complexion and unmarked round cheeks who looked more sophisticated than his colleague. It was clear that the former teacher was from a rural area and the latter from the city.

This new academic year was characterized by a special emphasis on medical care. Various diseases afflicted the boys at the boarding school. Those who had worms were frequently vermifuged and the malaria patients were given a bitter, saffron-yellow drink called *keena*, quinine. A disease that was endemic was *kala-azar*, visceral leishmaniasis, which we called *tohal*, or spleen. Its outward manifestations included a hideously distended belly carried on an emaciated bodily frame. A strange ailment that often appeared in winter was the one we called *um-simeigha*, the gummy. It was a kind of a sticky ulcer around the mouth, especially on the lower side of the lower lip. This skin disease is caused by an insect and characterized by the oozing of a sticky serum-colored substance that gave it its name.

We were all infested with lice. These insects were most abundant on the inner side of the waistband of the *surwal*. We were asked to loosen a bit our drawstring and then DDT powder was strewn on the waistband. When the insecticide was not available, an empty petrol drum was filled with water and brought to the boil. We would then throw our *surwals* into the boiling water to kill the blood-sucking pests.

I shared with other boys all of these vermin and diseases. And I had my own specific case of ill health that none of the boys shared with me. That ailment was a profuse nasal haemorrhage, a nosebleed. I got it quite often but at one time it seemed to have reached its peak. I sat down on the ground, dug out a small pit in the sand and succumbed to draining my blood out. The process took a while and the pupils who gathered around me sent for the headmaster who brought Sheikh Annour and Shawish Yousif with him.

I heard Sheikh Annour say: "He will be all right; his mother had similar bouts of bleeding when she was his age."

SCHOOLDAYS

That year I had a problem called Salim, a boy in my class. He came from Asubri and knew my folks there, the Dirars. For a long time, my relatives and his family were not on the best of terms. Salim had the same stature as myself and was equally thin but he was healthier, coming from an important lineage. He was much richer than me and looked at me as an indigent of some Jaali family of unknown, probably negroid, roots. His ambivalent feelings were manifested in wanting to wrestle with me. Wrestling was the major game of the nomads; every nomad child had experience in the art of this sport. There were many other nomad children of our age and weight, but Salim would not ask them to wrestle with him. He always approached me with a big smile and laughter whenever he wanted us to wrestle. But I felt that behind his ostensibly guileless smiles and his jovial face, there was hidden spite and ill-will. When we wrestled, he usually lost, but insistent like a puppy, he would relentlessly ask for another round. Sometimes, however, he would play a dirty game. He would sneak like a cat behind me and then, holding me by the legs, he would throw me off balance. In all cases, however, whether he gained or lost, he would smile it all away, seemingly like a good sport.

One day, I went to class but discovered that I had forgotten an important notebook back at the dormitory. While I was looking for the book, Salim materialized out of the blue and as I turned to face him, he grabbed me by the legs and threw me on the dirt floor. We were alone because all the boys were at school. I was in a hurry to catch up with my classes, but Salim, who never really cared much for schooling, kept wrapping himself around me like an octopus while I tried to get loose.

I looked into Salim's face at that moment and I saw a different boy. His expression was deadly, cadaverous. I saw him look around, as though for a weapon. I became truly alarmed and used all my force to extricate myself. I decided to keep away from him at all costs. Salim ended his education at elementary school level and just a year or two later, when he was still in his teens, he took his first life, a man twice his size, stabbing him following a wrangle over a card game. Because of his influential family, Salim was acquitted and subsequently enlisted in the police force where he was given a gun. He was posted in a remote outpost with another policeman with whom he picked a quarrel. With the duty rifle in his hands, Salim took the life of his colleague, then turned the muzzle of the gun on his own head and pulled the trigger.

THE RIVER FOREST

Back home I came to understand the blessings of the Shehateib river forest where we lived half the year. Food, medicine and peace of mind came from the forest. We respected its fauna and flora and held them in high esteem. After the *dom* palms, the tall athel trees that the Hadendowa called *amab* were the most imposing of the plant species, with their stout trunks and boughs, These trees had no thorns and their leaves were modified into a series of tiny salty green granules like beads. Camels liked to eat them. Carpenters like my father loved them for their timber.

The tallest trees of the Shehateib forest were the *dom* palms, scattered here and there towering above the rest of the forest. *Dom* palms lived the longest and provided us with food and medicine as well as materials to build our dwelling places. Their fist-sized fruits were our coconuts; when green, we split them, drank the sweet water of the core and ate the white flesh containing it.

SCHOOLDAYS

When ripe, the fruit provided abundant edible outer flesh which could be turned into syrup to treat children's coughs. The once-white and soft core, which contained the sweet water, dried up into a dark hollow container which was used by women to store kohl. The long, bladelike leaves of an old tree and the numerous baby sprouts underneath it made our tent mats and ropes. Nobody ever felled a *dom* palm; they only died of old age.

Small trees and thorn bushes, creepers and runners made parts of the forest impenetrable, a haven for bird life. The sounds of cooing doves, cawing crows, the cheeping sparrows, the chirping insects all mingled there. Nobody killed the hoopoe: it was King Solomon's messenger to the Queen of Sheba. Nor the *umajjanna*, the linnet, because it came from Paradise. Nor the *simbria*, the black stork, nor the *ab-koo-koo*, the red-billed hornbill, because both birds brought rain. Wildlife in the forest included the wart-hog, a small gazelle we called *morah*, monkeys, wild cats, jackals, hares, ground squirrels, snakes and boas. Even, one day, a leopard that came loping across the dry bed of a branch of the river.

IBRAHIM'S ARMOURY

In many respects my brother Ibrahim was the exact opposite of myself. While I was somewhat clumsy and lacked self-confidence, Ibrahim was a boy of great craftsmanship, deft and industrious, perhaps a little over-confident. I was looked upon as patient and taciturn while Ibrahim was considered energetic, talkative, audacious and pugnacious.

At thirteen he was already selling crockery he made. He would travel to distant places in the area to fetch special type of earth which he used to make household pots such as the *ibrig*, the pot for absolution before prayer, and other earthenware articles, which he then burnished, fired and sold to the Hadendowa. And he excelled in making metal tools: knives, spears, cutlasses, gaffs, pokers, skewers and the like. The materials for these products he brought from the Blue Bridge area. He used them to catch large fish from ponds cut off from the river in the summer time. Ibrahim was the only nomad in the region to catch fish, a practice nomads generally detested. He occasionally followed the fishermen who came from far outside the region and camped on the banks of the river.

And most unusually, Ibrahim made bows and arrows, something we never knew in Shehateib. Where he got the idea could not be said. Throughout the Sudan that kind of weapon was only used by people of West African origin, such as the Takarir – the Hausa – and the Mbororo, or Fulani. Where we lived one only rarely saw a Tekruri. They came selling beads and baubles to women; they did not carry bows and arrows.

One day, Ibrahim made a terrifying bow with its cord made of cow tendons. The arrow, made of solid *hijlij* wood – *Balanites aegyptiaca* – was tipped with a cone of corrugated iron which Ibrahim called zinc. It had been especially brought for the purpose from the vicinity of the Blue Bridge. When the weapon was ready, Ibrahim handed the weapon over to me and explained how I was going to use it, knowing that although I lacked the dexterity and deftness that he had, I was nevertheless a good disciple.

"Now aim at me! OK?" said Ibrahim. "Pull the bowstring and the arrow the hardest you can. No! No, Hamid that's not enough. Pull harder, man! That's it. Now let go!" he shouted enthusiastically.

I let go. The ballistic missile whooshed through the air, grazed my dog and entered Ibrahim's ankle. Ibrahim fell back under the pain but quickly pulled the metal-shod harpoon out, leaving a gaping wound with blood gushing out. With great composure he cut a long swath of cloth from his *tob* and wrapped his ankle. I helped him stand up and prop himself on his stick. Back at the camp the wound was dressed with sheep's wool. Lying on his back on the *serir* at the tent he said

"That is a mighty good weapon, isn't it, Hamid?"

It took Ibrahim some days to recover from his wound. But the Noon Devil, as he was known in the camp, still had many ideas in his quiver.

Ibrahim had a special dislike for the Zibeidiya boys. He called them bad names, quarrelled with them and laughed at them. They were bigots, he said, arrogant people who considered others inferior. The fact that they called all of us, both Arabs and Hadendowa, by the derogatory term *ujman*, meaning non-Arab, infuriated Ibrahim who considered himself better than them in every respect.

The Zibeidiya were pure Arabs who had came from Saudi Arabia across the Red Sea only two or three centuries before. Our ancestors had been in Africa thousands of years before them. We were black and our hair woolly or kinky. And our women were not veiled. For the Zibeidiya these were all signs of inferiority. Just as we looked at the darker and more negroid peoples to the south as inferior and enslaveable, the Zibeidiya looked at us as halfway to the same state. Everybody had to be somebody's slave in order to prove their opponent's worth and self-importance.

One day Ibrahim was fighting a Zibeidi boy called Hassan. As he raised his *bilbil*, the Hadendowa boomerang, to hit his adversary, the latter got hold of it with both his hands and the pointed end of the curved stick hit Ibrahim's forehead and drew blood. Seeing the blood, the Zibeidi boy let go of the stick and took to his heels. The whole Zibeidiya group watching the fight took off, the cloaked and veiled girls scuttling away like ostriches, the clang and rattle of their silver trinkets fading away with the dust. Father took Ibrahim immediately to the Zibeidiya camp, which was on a little creek not far from Shehateib. The issue was settled by giving my father a sum of money. The Zibeidiya in the area feared my father and strove to avoid the wrath of the man they called a *fechi*.

THE STORY OF ZAHIN AND NAJI

Zahin was the jewel of the camp. She was a natural beauty, with round hips, a narrow waist, firm breasts, long neck and bright eyes. Because she was the daughter of a slave she could never marry an Arab, but she was free to consort with anyone she liked, while other unmarried girls in our camp would have been put to the sword by their own families if any of them were found in a compromising position with a man.

Naji was the most handsome young man in the camp. He was brave and strongly built. His eyes were red and his moustache long and thick. His hair was silky, like a true Arab; his smile radiant. The ends of his *tob* dangled over his heels, the drawstrings had been woven by his doting sisters with tassels of silk.

Zahin and Naji were in love. Their liaison was accepted; they suffered no opprobrium. Zahin was not called ill names. She was referred to as Naji's *sahiba*, his friend, an honourable epithet in the speech of the nomads, for the Shukriya are famous throughout the Sudan for their love of poetry, and half of it is about *sahiba*s, while the other half is about the camels which carry the poet to his *sahiba*'s home. Such poems are not written about free Arab women, at least not directly. That would instigate hatred and war.

Zahin and her lover had various meeting places – *wadis*, creeks and forests. But she could not leave the camp on her own. I became her chosen companion when she ventured out of the camp – I, a taciturn boy who would not reveal her secrets,

It was the time of the early rains, the *rushash*, when rainwater had washed the sands of the *khors* clean. The *ghaba*, the river forest, had turned green and was thickly carpeted with undergrowth. Canopies of *arak* trees preserved the fragrance of the clusters of tiny fruits and flowers populated with bees and other insects. Small birds and butterflies fluttered between the trees. This mild, spring-like season had a special name, *sheg el oud*, the season when seemingly dry branches split along their lengths to let out delicate new buds. It was the season, people said, when women most wanted men.

One day Zahin was restless; she had to see her lover. She grabbed a *girba*, an empty waterskin and dragged me out of the camp with her. She said she wanted to fetch some water from the river, though she usually got water from water-holes in the sands of the creek close-by. She asked me to take the *girba* and proceed straight to the river. Then she turned right and went down the bank of a large creek. Turning round I saw Naji with her, holding her by the wrist and pulling her towards the green carpet of grass under a tree. She was resisting and smiling at the same time.

"Hamid, save me!" she cried. But I realised that she was joking.

Later we visited her mother, Maimona. Zahin fell asleep there while her mother talked. I knew Maimona had been a *sahiba* of my uncle Karim. She had been taken as a slave when she was already grown – her Arabic bore the traces of her original language – she had been captured in a raid on her home village somewhere to the south and had never seen any of her family again. She told me she was taken to Ethiopia and sold to a Sudanese who brought her back to our camp.

"It was your grandmother Hukm-el-Gadir who taught me Arabic," Maimona said.

When slavery was abolished in Sudan, Maimona told me, she chose to live a sedentary life in the village. But her two daughters and son preferred the nomadic life. Thus it was that she lived alone in her hut in the village.

I returned to school soon after, and it was months before I learned of the sad end to Zahin and Naji's affair. When I arrived back at the camp at the start of the school holidays and asked after them no one wanted to say anything. Eventually my brother Ibrahim told me that Zahin was dead. This was a great shock to me. It was old people who died. It had never occurred to me that young beautiful people could die also. I did not even ask about the cause of her death. All I knew was that it meant that I could never see her again. It crippled my thinking.

In the days that followed I learned the details. Zahin had fallen pregnant. Because she was a *sahiba* that was not a scandal, while if she had been a free woman her father or her brother or uncle would have killed her by the sword. It was a breech delivery. The old women of the camp strove to help Zahin in her struggle to give birth – even jumping on her chest – but to no avail. Naji's mother and Zahin's former owner quarrelled, each accusing the other of committing a crime. Meanwhile the throes of thwarted childbirth became groans and ebbed away. And mother and child were carried to a world from which no news ever came. After that, no one spoke of Zahin any more.

SCHOOLDAYS

A NOMAD WEDDING

That year there was a big wedding, planned by Grandma Diya with the express purpose of showing the importance of the Duman family. Umhummad, the first-born male in the family, was the bridegroom. He was to marry the eldest daughter of Atalmula. The Atalmulas lived alongside us in Shehateib. The Dumans invited all and sundry to the wedding. My aunts, the sisters of the groom, were the busiest of people. In particular, they prepared *dilka*, the smoke and perfume-imbued abrasive material of sorghum grain, employed like fine sandpaper to massage the groom's and bride's bodies, removing dirt and sloughed scales of skin. Uncle Umhummad, a shepherd who was always out in the sun and away from water, was relieved of his duties with the sheep and kept inside the tent away from the sun for forty days to gain a lighter colour. *Khadimas* – women of slave background – took on the job of massaging him with *dilka* night and day. The evenings in the camp were spent in singing and dancing to the rhythm of the *delluka* drum and the songs of valour performed by two *ghaniya*s, celebrated female singers – also *khadima*s – by name Um el Yem and Bit Issa. The day was spent preparing for the wedding procession to Shehateib: Aunt Asha and Aunt Zeinab sat under a large *arak* tree in front of Diya's tent pounding the ends of long bamboo poles which they soaked in animal fat. Each day for three or four days they brought more bamboo poles and did the same thing with them, spread out like a painter's brushes, impregnated with fat.

The day of the wedding finally arrived. Women and adolescent girls put on their best attire: nose-studs of gold, heavy silver anklets and bracelets, armlets of coloured beads, all kinds of necklaces and chokers, with lines of threaded cowrie diadems in their hair. These made their wearers tinkle and clang at the least movement. With their bodies anointed with perfumed sesame oil, bare-breasted, their hair braided and pomaded, they counted on catching the eyes of young men as they dashed about.

The nuptial procession began moving in the early morning. The *delluka* drum sounded – Um el Yem beating it with the flat of her palms while Bit Issa hit the smaller drum, the *shetem*, with a small stick that made it whine like a puppy. Men fell in with the beat with the eagle dance, brandishing hippo-hide shields and glinting swords. As the cortege finally set off, a great number of men, women and girls moved with it. Men straddled their favourite camels, their swords and shields hanging on the saddle pommels, their whips dangling from their right-hand wrists by a loop of soft leather.

Khali Umhummad, the bridegroom, was given the most beautiful camel of all, one of the *as-hab* breed of racing camels – white, thin, narrow-waisted, narrow-hipped, broad-chested and smooth-coated. Its ears were small, its eyes alert and its muzzle pointed. It had been tied and fed for months on *feterita* – sorghum grain – with soft dates and butteroil. The bridegroom's saddle was carved of wood that had been anointed to give it a mahogany colour and make it water-resistant, secured on the back of the camel with a multitude of cinches and girth straps, some broad, some thin, some of leather, others of woven wool. Tufts of soft leather and tassles of coloured hair swayed beneath the flanks of the camel as it moved. The saddle was made comfortable by a folded cotton mattress called the *hiliss*, then a red-and-black-striped woollen plaid of tartan called *hiram* and, finally, a *tweili*, a Persian caracul sheepskin with long dense silky black hair still covering its upper surface. The *tweili* hung down on both sides of the camel. A large piece of soft leather, the *firaya*, covered the camel's withers, where the rider's legs were crossed in front of the saddle.

The bridle of the camel consisted of two thick goat hair ropes, each running from one side of the head back to the saddle, with a collar round the neck bearing leather-bound amulets. A steel nose brooch passed through the wing of the animal's nose, attached to a long thin leather strand that ran parallel to the bridle back to the saddle. This auxiliary bridle was for the effective control of the camel. Finally the rider's sword and shield were hung on the pommels of the saddle.

Atop this work of art sat my uncle Umhummad, resplendent in new raiment. His hands and feet were dark with henna; his feet were fitted with moccasin-style shoes, *merkoub*. His long white *surwal* was secured by a cord with vermilion tassels. There were *baniga*s, small triangular, dark-coloured cloth pieces sewn at the inner face of the legs at knee level. Over his *jibbah* he sported a black *sideiriya*, with many pockets. And over these, the *tob ushari*, a ten-forearm-length stole of *sakubeiss*, the thinnest white muslin.

The groom did not wear the customary headgear of skullcap and turban. His shaven head was daubed with a mixture of dry perfume of ground sandalwood and *mahaleb* cherry-stones. A red headband was wrapped around the head just above the level of the ears but not covering the top of the head. A *hilal*, a large gold crescent, was fixed to the front. His right hand carried the *harira*, a tuft of deep red silk with symbols of good luck including a green bead in the form of a beetle, a fish bone and a string of silk-threaded beads. On his neck was *sibhat-al-yassur*, a long necklace of large black beads. There was an air of royalty about the groom, with his sword as his sceptre and the headwear his crown. But in reality the articles adorning him were primarily to ward off the evil eye. Since *Khali* Umhummad was a very good-looking young man, it was all the more reason that he have the complete set of traditional articles of protection.

And then it was my turn to be raised high and put on the camel behind the groom. This was Diya's idea. She was acutely aware that, apart from Ibrahim, all thirteen children in the family except me were female. The Duman clan badly needed more males. I was put behind the groom as a good omen in the hope that *Khali* Umhummad would beget male offspring. (I bungled the job, though: my maternal uncle later begot only females, like the rest of the family).

The procession moved on. Shepherds grazing their sheep in the *karab* abandoned their herds for a while and joined in dancing and making passes at the girls before they turned back to their flocks. Small boys and girls came running and followed the procession, their fingers in their mouths. Young men on camelback raced their camels ahead of the procession and back. They flourished their swords over the heads of the women crying "*Abishri! Abishri bel-kheir!* Be happy! Don't worry! We will protect you all, women of the tribe!" And the women would release a shriek of acknowledgement. The camel race – *shayom* – was repeated many times throughout the journey whenever there was an open land. I clung tenaciously to the rear pommel of the saddle as *Khali* Umhummad's camel galloped back and forth. The rubbing of the camel's hair against my bare thighs made them bleed, but I scarcely noticed and did not complain.

We reached Shehateib at nightfall. The moon rose late. Here the bamboo poles my aunts had spent the week soaking in fat came into their own, lighting our way across the river. At the river's edge the sword dancers drew sparks from the stones as they leapt up and down. The river ran like a dark broadsword below us, reflecting the stars and the flickering lights of our procession as we waded across it. The place seemed to be filled with fireflies. On the back of a camel my feet were too short to touch the water as they would have done had I been riding a donkey. There at the *ferig*, the celebrations went on till dawn. I fell asleep back in the place I knew best, Shehateib, the closest thing a nomad boy could have to a home.

THE BLUE BRIDGE CAFES

When I went back to school I did not find anything new. In fact, life at school – and even in the village – seemed to lack variety. It was not like life with the nomads, where the action was. School had one interesting thing as far as I was concerned and that was knowledge. So I returned home with a sense of excitement at the start of the vacation, sometimes not knowing even where our camp had moved to, making my way on foot to the Blue Bridge. This time, as I arrived at the west bank end of the bridge, I found a surprise waiting for me. A shanty town had developed in the middle of the forest, where no tent or any house was ever built before – right on the edge of the riverbank. The idea had come to someone that the lorries which crossed the bridge carrying passengers and goods should have catering facilities at that strategic spot. Some twenty or thirty grass-hut shops, cafés and restaurants appeared out of the blue. Tea, coffee, tobacco as well as cloth, sugar, salt and spices were offered for sale. Lorry drivers found the opportunity to get some rest during the long journey on dirt roads between Khartoum and Port Sudan, somewhere they and their passengers could eat and drink and take a nap and go down to the river to swim and bathe. The name Gahawi el Kubri – Bridge Cafés – caught on. The cafés were manned mostly by the sedentary inhabitants of Sharafa village.

Nomads and village dwellers and travellers mixed at the Blue Bridge Cafés. Those from the area who wanted to travel to Kassala, Gedaref or Asubri would wait there for transportation. Peripatetic Jaali merchants and vendors of small household articles came there, and nomads who had lost livestock came looking for the thieves, while the thieves found a convenient point of sale. (*Salat*, a Hadendowa dish of hot-stone-barbecued lamb, was a feature of the menu and demanded ample supplies of sheep for slaughter.) Police from the town began to show up, pursuing suspects. Soon a police station was established on the east bank at the Blue Bridge. There were frequent altercations there between people of different backgrounds, especially nomads, yet life at the Cafés gave us all an introduction to civility and urban tolerance.

By government decree lorries did not travel during the rainy season, between July 15 and October 15, when roads were generally impassable. The Cafés were closed up during this period and their work force directed towards growing sorghum up in the clay plain. During the *kherif* months tall grass and creepers took over the area and wild animals and game lived there. The rest of the year people in our camp made increasing use of the Cafés. Women found a market for their butteroil, and men sold sheep and goats when they needed to, exchanging news there with nomads from other camps. Some of the young men sold stolen animals; some robbed the freight train of sacks of sugar or sorghum, which they sold at the Cafés.

SCHOOLDAYS

ATALMULA AND HIS SONS

The fact that our camp lay among hostile tribes and was relatively close to the border with Eritrea and its jagged hills made stock theft a constant danger. One day we heard that Atalmula's flock had been taken. The news fell like thunderbolt on the camp. The loss of a whole flock could mean the end of a family. Immediately men fanned out into the bush looking for the flock. But at sunset the livestock had not returned. Atalmula's daughters that night for the first time did not build the evening fire before their tent. The lambs and kid goats in their corral gave out heart-rending bleats, calling for their lost mothers. The men of the camp returned empty-handed. They gave orders to the boys in the camp to feed the motherless lambs and take enough milk to Atalmula's tent. Meanwhile they saddled their camels, took their arms and lit out in the gloom. Atalmula's daughters were crying loudly.

The men travelled all night in all directions, gathering information from other tribes. In the morning they solicited the help of known trackers in the area and continued their search. It became clear that the flock had been driven towards the border with Eritrea at a spot close to Kassala. The robbers had divided the flock into three groups, and each was driven along the bank of the Gash River into the hilly wilderness of Eritrea. By the time the pursuers got to the border they were gone forever.

Atalmula had been the richest man in our camp. He had the largest flock. He also had the most beautiful daughters. Of the five girls only the oldest was married. It was she who had been the bride of *Khali* Umhummad. Because of their beauty and their father's riches, men had been reluctant to ask their hands in matrimony even though, by nomad standards, they were all of marriageable age. In the days that followed the catastrophe, people donated goats and sheep to the bereaved family but not enough to restore their fortunes. Atalmula at first took the calamity with great equanimity but it wasn't long before he passed away. The four girls were hurriedly married to the first men who came asking. The older of the three was married first but she died shortly after. When the pall-bearers brought the *angareib* bier back from the cemetery, her husband, the widower, threw his body down on the ground and held firmly to its leg. That gesture was well known in nomadic culture to mean that the man demanded to be compensated by being given the deceased wife's sister as wife – or else he should be buried himself too. Accordingly he was given the youngest of the girls. One other girl was given as a second wife. The fourth married a Hadendowa. She refused to live with the Arabs. Atalmula's two boys joined the Bridge Cafés and tried to sell coffee and tea, but they were unlucky in their endeavour.

    Their business came to an end in a fracas that took place at the Cafés. Omoro, a Sudanese Hausa of Nigerian extraction, worked as assistant to a lorry driver. Their lorry was carrying goods from Port Sudan to Khartoum when they stopped at the Bridge Cafés. At one of the cafés, Omoro asked for a cup of tea but the café attendant ignored him. Omoro repeated his order but once more the man went on serving the others while ignoring him completely. It did not take great wit to understand the racist character of the gesture. Omoro became furious and dashed to his lorry where he pulled out the crank, a crooked heavy steel rod used then to fire the engine, and with it he ran into the crowd cutting down men and property. Atalmula's sons lost all their cups and pots and with those the meager capital they had mustered for their new enterprise. The event was chronicled by the poet Suleiman wad el Faki who praised the valour of Omoro and the cowardice of the onlookers. The poem spread like fire among the various tribes. The poet Suleiman even mentioned the names of the *sahiba*s of those men who ran away, suggesting that they should reject their cowardly lovers. And they did. Such was the power of poetry among our people. The Atalmula brothers moved to Eritrea to live with their Nawayma tribesmen there in Abu Gamul, but both died young, one of them from snakebite.

A FIGHT TO THE DEATH

In the summer months that year, when Atalmula's flock was robbed, famine loomed. Children began to be visibly affected, losing weight quickly. The grain supplies of all the families in the camp dwindled rapidly and they finally ran short. I drank goat's milk in the evening, but that was all. My belly grew in size, my neck thinned, my head looked larger and my hips shrank away.

But Ketira prepared a thick disc of sorghum bread for me with the little grain we had, which I took over to my father. He kept a goat-skin bag, a *hilbateeb*, full of butteroil, flavoured with *dom* fruit. Father added ghee to the sorghum bread and I was kept on that food until I had consumed the whole contents of the leather bag. My health improved further when *Khali* Umhummad started to give me sheep's milk.

On my way to the Blue Bridge to meet the flock, I noticed two young Hadendowa men, lithe as cats, engaged in a duel. I took it for a mock fight, and continued on my way, but it turned out that it was a real duel, and it ended in the death of one of the opponents. The deceased was called Minni. He was said to have killed a man in a long-standing vendetta between two Hadendowa tribes. The victim had had no son, or brother or any other male member of the family to avenge his death.

But he had a sister Teila, then a young girl, who had witnessed the killing of her brother by Minni. As the years passed she became a great beauty, but her bitterness against Minni grew too. She did not talk about it, but she never smiled or laughed. One after the other the young warriors of the tribe aspired to marry Teila, but she refused all of them. She sought a man who could measure up to the strength and bravery of he brother – and avenge him. The man she had her eyes on, Ohaj, was too shy to ask her hand in marriage, so she took the initiative. They got married, but Teila held back from Ohaj. She told him she loved him but she was not able to give herself fully to him because the man who killed her only brother before her eyes was still at liberty. A man who could not avenge the death of her brother, Teila told her new husband, was not worthy of her. Thus the young man, whose marriage had been barely consummated, was lured into taking on the feud. He arrived at Shehateib on his camel, armed with a broadsword, a shield and a throw-dagger.

Ohaj waylaid Minni at noon when he was driving his cattle for watering. While he was brewing coffee Minni saw a man on camelback heading his way. The stranger took his sword and shield and advanced towards Minni telling him he intended to take revenge on behalf of the man he killed years back. Minni now recognized the man as Teila's husband. Minni put up a brave performance for a man armed with only a stout stick against an adversary armed with a sword and a shield. In the end, however, the sword won the day. When men from our camp arrived at the scene the killer had already left and Minni, whom they all knew, was dying. My father, being a man of religion, took Minni's head and put it on his thigh. Minni's blood and bone marrow flowed down my father's leg. As he died he said was sorry that he had left no son to avenge his death. Father told him the government would do this for him and he would report the crime himself. My father was as good as his word. Ohaj was apprehended, tried and convicted, and hanged at Port Sudan. What happened to Teila history does not relate.

THE VAST GREEN LAND

The summer days at Jummeiza turned mean. It was atrociously hot. The landscape became bare and grey in the *karab* and the creeks. The soil of the tableland was an expanse of cracking sun-baked brown crust. The land revealed its desert nature. Nothing green, except for the tops of a few balanites trees dotting the bleak terrain. Camels and goats had nipped off all the smaller twigs of the trees and divested the lower branches of all leaves. Distances between neighbouring trees seemed to have increased. The assembled bones you could see walking among the tents were the wraith of what had once been a cow. Camels used up their humps and ants kept to their nests. Women's skins turned dry and grey and their hair became dishevelled. Young children began the game of counting the ribs of their younger siblings. The early white patches of clouds, *umbashar*, appeared in the skies, but they did not keep their promise. By now the south ought to have sent dark, water-laden clouds. Clearly, the rains were very late. Once more the spectre of a famine hung overhead.

    Omar Duman looked ceaselessly towards the east. One evening I sneaked behind him and scrutinized the far horizon where he had fixed his gaze. Sure enough, far and away at the meeting point of the sky and the curvature of the earth, a faint pulsation of a lightning could be discerned. Then I understood my grandfather's preoccupation with the horizon. He had been monitoring the distance to work out where the rainy season had already set in.

"Rain is like a fawn," he liked to say, "it always haunts the same area."

A few days later, he summoned *Khali* Umhummad and instructed him to saddle his camel for a scouting mission. *Khali* Umhummad asked a young man from the camp, Adam wad Misslih, to accompany him. Early in the morning the two scouts trotted their camels out of the camp heading for the Blue Bridge where they would cross the river. They did not return for a week. I saw them as they approached and recognized the good news imprinted on the camels' bodies. Mud covered their fur and each carried a load of green wilted fodder for goats.

The two scouts reported to the elders, Sheikh Annour, Omar Duman, Tay Alla, Misslih – father of Adam – and Shambati.

"How far does the green land extend?" asked Misslih.

"Almost endless," replied his son. "We travelled across it for two days towards the border without reaching an end. That is why it took us so long to come back here."

"How many camps are already there?" asked Tayalla.

"Only a few Zibeidiya camelherds are there at the moment," said *Khali* Umhummad. "But unless we move the camp quickly I am afraid many nomads will be moving there soon. We met two scouting teams there and many camps along the way took the good news from us,"

"And water?" asked *Jeddi* Omar. "The river is far."

Uncle Umhummad assured the elders that there was plentiful

water, and the elders gave the order to strike camp at daybreak.

I slept very little that night, but lay looking at the stars, at the four rather crookedly arranged stars in the form of the four legs of a bed that make up the constellation we call the Angareib. The bed is said to carry the corpse of a dead man and the three stars that follow the pall bearers are the dead man's daughters, Banat Naash. The one in the middle is the divorced daughter and the tiny star close to it is her own daughter. (If you can see this one then your eyesight is excellent.) The girl farthest back is the lame girl Ireij. The star nearest the coffin is the unmarried daughter. The Angareib is the constellation known in northern lands as the Great Bear or the Big Dipper. If you draw a straight line joining the two front legs of this Angareib and extrapolate it northwards it will pass through the Jedi, the gazelle fawn, the Pole Star.

But as a infant star-gazer I was more fascinated with Majar el Kebish, the Track of the Dragged Ram, elsewhere known as the Milky Way. When Allah incited the Prophet Ibrahim to slaughter his son Ismail as a sacrifice to Him, Ibrahim told his son about the matter. The young prophet consented and told his father to obey Allah's orders. Allah willing, the young man said, he would endure death. Thus Ismail lay down and Ibrahim brought his knife to slaughter his son. At this point, Ibrahim, the Friend of Allah, heard a sound in the sky above him. When he raised his face to investigate, he saw an angel dragging a ram bringing it to him to redeem his son. The track of the dragging of the ram is marked by the myriad stars of Majar el Kebish.

THE AMULET

THE BLUE BRIDGE AT NOON

Early in the morning when I woke up I found nearly all tents down. Everyone was busy. I joined in, unlashing tent poles, wrapping and folding mats, loading camels and asses, milking goats. Everybody was doing something. We were in a race with time.

Both Grandpa Omar and Grandpa Annour, with their *tobs* wrapped round their waists, were busy loading the sorghum sacks on a big camel. Older women were busy decorating their *utfa*s, the camel hoods in which they were to travel. These cabins were built by women from slender branshes of *sidir* wood and lashed permanently to a camel saddle using rawhide strips. In preparation for the journey, the *utfa* would be ornamented with various fabric, leather and woollen ropes hiding the wooden frame. The camel chosen to carry an *utfa* had to be large, broad-backed, broad-bellied and good-tempered.

The Lahawin poet Umhummad Zein described the making of his sweetheart's *utfa*. The carpenter who made it was not in a hurry, he said. He had had his breakfast and tucked his chewing tobacco in his mouth. The saddle was made of sandalwood, the poem continued. And the camel that carried it was one familiar with *utfa*s: when it sat it gave wide berth to its knees so that the cabinet would not topple off.

Koor hoorik mo lignig
Fis sandal oudu shagig
Najjaru mahu mdig
Mijjadim u fak arrig
Jabolo el biarif leh
Fil barka bifij rakebeh

Diya was given a camel carrying a small ramshackle *utfa*, known as a *shibriya*, meaning handspan-size, reserved specifically for old women to protect them from the hot sun. She was then above eighty years of age. Diya had spent most of her life roaming the vast expanses of the Butana steppeland and the eastern territories, as we were doing now, running after the good life of new pastures and fresh water. Even in her shabby camel cabin, Diya kept her noble mien and regal bearing. The belief that she was above all others never left her. She insisted that she was the purest Arab in the land, as, of course, were Omar and Annour, her two sons. She called them *al-safyeen-dhahab-el-zuman* – the pure gold of the nose brooch. Once Diya had been the owner of a hundred black slaves given to her by her brother el Tom. At the age of 80, this grand-daughter of the legendary Tajuj of the Humran still showed signs of the beauty and hauteur that had earned her the name Diya.

Nothing marred our journey until we came to the Blue Bridge at noon. There we found great numbers of herds and camels and donkeys carrying nomad gear. They had been held up by a freight train occupying the narrow steel bridge. The hustle began immediately the train left the bridge. Each group of people began pushing their animals forward. When our turn came we had to send the flocks in first and then follow them with the camels and donkeys. The confusion caused by the cries of the sheep and goats and the shouts of the shepherds who tried to urge them on was confounded by the loud mechanical booming of the bridge. This panicked the sheep, which bolted or tried to jump off the bridge into the roaring flood water. The bridge was littered with sheep-droppings, making it slippery. The young and the weak among the sheep and goats slipped, fell and were trod on as the mass of animals stampeded back and forth. Some sheep broke their legs when their thin limbs went through the drainage holes of the bridge floor and they had to be removed from the way. The shepherds, however, kept pressing, beating the huddling sheep while giving little attention to mishaps and accidents. They were competing with each other in the rush to pasture and afraid that another train might come and flatten them.

It took us from noon to late afternoon to take the flocks across the bridge. Then the bleating of the sheep was replaced by the gurgling of the camels. Each animal was pulled by one man in front and urged by another from behind; they were resistant and nervous, with twitching muscles. They would often make as if to jump off the bridge, or bite the camel drivers, or fold themselves up and sit down, blocking the way.

Eventually the flocks and the ladies and the camels and the children and the donkeys all managed to cross safely. Remaining were me and my donkey. Try as I might I could not make it move. Unlike camels and sheep, donkeys do not cry out under these circumstances. My donkey, true to its kind, just stood there with no particular expression on its long face. All attempts to get it onto the bridge were met with failure. I was thin and weak; my donkey was stronger than me. I pulled as hard as I could on the lead rope, but the animal would not follow. I got hold of its ears with both my hands. It probably thought I was going to talk to it. But I bit its ears until my mouth ached. It was unmoved. Then I looked across the bridge and saw, to my joy, Zeena and Hajwa, my maternal relatives, racing towards me. Zeena began hurling imprecations at me, the most gentle of which was her favourite: "Hamid, may Allah dispatch a thunderbolt to your head!" Had Allah always responded positively to Zeena's wishes I would have been struck down a thousand times in my early life. Hajwa, though, led the donkey calmly across the bridge while Zeena shouted at it from behind. It obeyed them placidly. That donkey clearly preferred women to men.

When we reached the tableland, with its scattered thorn trees, we found that we had already straggled far behind the main body of the moving flocks and herds. Soon darkness fell and we reached a more difficult terrain, where we were forced to follow hardly discernable porcupine and jackal trails. We decided to stop and stay where we were for the night. We unsaddled the donkeys and tied them to the trees. I did not sleep much. I wished I had had a dog with me to protect us from hyenas. Then in the early hours we saw firebrands being tossed up high in the sky not far from where we were, the beacon of the nomads, sent up for those lost in the dark nights. We quickly saddled our donkeys, and were off, fighting the thorns, to join them, Zeena reminding me all the way that it was I who brought all the trouble.

There was a sudden transition from the dry, parched summer landscape to the green *kherif* land that now opened up before us. This is why nomads say that rain can wet one horn of a cow and leave the other dry. There were flowers and butterflies and cool breezes. After the rigours of the dry season it seemed like paradise. Our animals cleared their rumens of worms and the indigestible rubbish from the barren Jummeiza summer site and began to put on weight. Ewes in milk doubled their yield. Soon we could regale ourselves on milk and butter. Women became beautiful. Even Zeena's temper improved.

One afternoon while I was driving the sheep to Garada creek to water them I had to cross some very wet ground. Large herds of sheep had been moving eastward and I found an abandoned lamb covered in mud. I quickly picked it up and carried it with me to the *khor* to wash it. With the tip of my tongue I cleaned the inside of its eyes, spitting the mud off. Then I sucked the mud that clogged its nostrils and removed the mud from its mouth. I took it to a large, dry slab of a rock where the sun's rays fell; it shook its body shedding a spray of water all around. It was a beautiful male brown lamb with a blaze at the very centre of its forehead.

In the evening, at the camp, I asked *Khali* Umhummad whether it was right to keep the lamb as my own. He told me that according to accepted nomad tradition, unless the lamb was genuinely claimed by someone to be his or hers, it was mine, especially since it was still unbranded. He suggested that I exchange the male lamb with a female one which he would give me from his own ewes. *Khali* Umhummad believed that sheep flourished with those who loved them and he knew I liked them very much. When I agreed he asked me to go into the herd and select the female lamb of my choice. I did so, and called her Garada after the place where the he-lamb had been found.

One afternoon, with the sun a spear's-length above the western horizon, I went down to Garada creek to look for a young goat that the girls said they had seen there when they went to fetch water. It was late in the rainy season now. Standing in the middle of the wide sandy bed of the seasonal river, I became suddenly and acutely aware of the beauty of nature around me. The two steep banks of the large creek were thick with *guddeim* trees. The trees were heavy with shining fruit – gold, red or still green. The kid I was looking for was a black dot on the white sands of the riverbed. The picture imprinted itself on my mind, even as the rainy season was ending.

As the rainy season ended the grass became dry and yellow. And the danger of fire increased. Omar Duman insisted that we move from the site in spite of the protests of many in the camp.

Years later a group of Jawamiss nomads, who established a camp in the middle of a vast area of dry elephant grass, was wiped out when a fire started at a spot away from the camp in the middle of the night. By the time the inhabitants woke up it was too late. Camels, goats, sheep, dogs, donkeys and people exploded as the flames swallowed them all, leaving only barren blackness in its wake. The Jawamiss from that camp were no more. They were obliterated, people believed, because of the poor judgement of their elders.

IN THE TENT OF LOVE

During the winter that followed, we lived in a sprawling camp at Jummeiza comprising a number of tribes including Bawadra and Hudoor as well as us Shukriya. Early in the evening one day as I was carrying milk from the corral to Sheikh Annour's house, I saw a middle-aged woman, wearing what looked a rather expensive *tob*, approach the tent. I poured the milk into the large enamel bucket in the tent and retraced my steps back to the corral. When I returned with another batch of milk, Toma, Sheikh Annour's wife told me that Nayla, our neighbour wanted me to keep her daughter, Ineiba, company that night. It was one of the tasks of young boys who had not reached adulthood to guard young brides like Ineiba. She was about sixteen. I was favoured for such tasks, as Zahin had once favoured me, a silent boy who would not gossip. Rich nomad men might marry young girls more for pleasure than for begetting children. Such girls would not be mature enough to get pregnant and so there would be two or three years of love without the inconveniences of children. Today we would call it paedophilia, but not back then. As

Muslims, men could have up to four wives, though it was rare for a man to have more than two.

Following her engagement, Ineiba was confined to her mother's tent and subjected to a rigorous programme of fattening and beautification. She was prohibited from leaving the premises of the tent in order not to subject herself to sunlight. Her mother and elder sister worked on her day and night to prepare her for the husband-to-be, who paid generously. She was given fattening foods and made to refrain from any kind of work that demanded physical exertion. She simply had to lie down most of the time, like a queen bee, and accept the services of those who waited on her. Her young body was massaged with the depilatory *dilka*, her hair meticulously braided, her lower lip tattooed blue-green, her nose pierced and fitted with a cleft nose brooch of gold and her ears also pierced and fitted with large golden earrings. The gold of her complexion was accentuated by rubbing the skin with saffron powder.

When Ineiba was delivered to her husband on the night of the consummation of their marriage, we boys were hiding behind their tent to monitor her vocal response, as we were meant to do. She screamed as she was taken for the first time. During the next few days the bride would be given to the groom only once every two days during the night. The daytime she spent at her mother's tent. Then the bride was shown how to lead her own life with her husband in a gradual manner. She would first be asked to make coffee for the man. It was during that coffee break that the couple began to talk to each other and get better acquainted.

Ineiba's husband was a married man of middle age and had sons and daughters far from Jummeiza. He was a big man with a powerful build, a rich *mihajri*, camel thief. The day I came to keep

Ineiba company, her husband was out on one of his mysterious errands. They expected him back, or else the bride would have been staying at her mother's tent. When I approached Nayla's tent that evening I was greeted by scents of civet, musk and myrrh. I had not seen Ineiba for months. Now I could hardly recognize the skinny kid I had known before, just six years older than me. She had just got off the smoke pit and was bent down trying to rub her left instep, her breast exposed. She was now a full-fleshed, voluptuous woman. As I entered she raised her face to meet me with large kohl-fringed eyes and parted lips.

I retired to the bridal tent and Ineiba came and took her place on the bed, at a distance. We talked a little before each drifted into sleep. I spent two nights in that manner. Whenever Ineiba came to the tent, she came wearing a *firka*, a red and black perfume-soaked silk garment in the form of a one-piece wrap-around, used only for bridal purposes. Late in the night of the third day, when Ineiba and I were asleep, I was woken up by some stir outside. In the darkness I saw a sitting camel. Then a big man came in the tent carrying the saddle of the camel, complete with its covers. He placed it at one side of the tent, finding his way in the darkness. He fed some grain to the camel, then climbed on the bed next to Ineiba. I pretended to be asleep.

"Who is the boy?" asked the man. "Hamid", said Imeida.

Then I heard the sound of him dragging her body across the *serir*. There was no more talk. Imeida cried out. There was a series of rapid inhalations and exhalations, a rattling of beads and bracelets, the sound of whimpering and pleading. Not a sound from the man. The whole episode was taking place only one handspan away from me. I saw she was on top of him. I was mesmerized. The man now pushed his bride away back in my direction. She slept; I didn't. Before daybreak I was off.

THE INTERVIEW

It was the fourth and last year for our class at Khashm el Girba Elementary School. We were preparing to go to Kassala to sit for the intermediate school examination with pupils from many other schools in the province. As a dry run we were examined at the end of that year at Khashm el Girba. I was top of the class. And Ibrahim my brother, who had just joined the school, was the top of his first year class at the same time. The announcement was made out in the school yard when all the pupils were standing in their customary morning lines. Sherif, who had been top of the class every year previously, had already enrolled in the intermediate school at Kassala, and Beshir Dirar, my cousin from Asubri, was absent too. That was how I came to be the top of the class. Had Beshir been there he would have beaten me – he was six years older. The fact that I was the top of the class did not please everyone. My history teacher in particular was one of those city-dwellers who hated nomads. He considered us primitive. I learned later, when I lived in cities myself, that this was a national problem, though poems and plays were written by educationalists to combat the attitude.

We took the train to Kassala, the first time for many of us. I found the examination quite easy, but I made one mistake. I did not write my name on the general knowledge paper. The competition was fierce; from some 700 candidates the government intermediate school would admit only the top forty. There was another non-government school, not so good, that would admit another group of forty, but they had to pay a tuition fee, which was out of the question for me. I was so depressed on the day the results were announced that I stayed back alone on the high cement terrace around the dining hall at the back of the crowd. The accepted students were called for interview in order of excellence. The first was named Zein Yasin – I still remember the name – from Ali Gidir in Eritrea. Each time a name was called, the pupil would step up accompanied by his father or some relative to discuss the terms on which the pupil was to be admitted.

Suddenly I heard my name. I was number eighteen. Everyone looked around for me. It took me a while before I made myself visible and stood before the committee: barefoot with my head uncovered. I had never undergone an interview and did not know what it was. I saw there was a man sitting behind a large desk, probably the chairman of the committee, and four others, two on either side of me as I stood facing the desk. There was a pause before the man behind the desk asked me where was my *wali amrek*, my guardian

My grasp of Arabic language failed me. What was a *wali amrek*? What was a guardian?

"Guardian, sir?" I said perplexed.

"Yes, guardian."

"What is wrong with you, boy?" said the deputy headmaster.

"Nothing is wrong with me, sir," I said. The deputy headmaster was angry and made as if to strike me.

Another member of the committee intervened, a small man in khaki shorts and a short-sleeve white shirt who was holding one of those large British tropical pith helmets. Later, I learned that he was a Hadendowa by the name of Okair and was the inspector of education of the province. He asked me very quietly whether my father was with me. When I answered in the negative, he asked whether any adult relative came with me to Kassala. Again I answered in the negative. The members of the committee deliberated the matter. I wondered what my father could be doing at that very moment. He was probably chasing wart-hogs at Shehateib. I knew that he and Sheikh Annour did not really take my education seriously.

The committee asked me to fetch one of the teachers who accompanied us to Kassala to act as my guardian. And the committee spelled out its decision: "Six pounds a year and no boarding!" It was unfair, considering my circumstances, but at least I had a place in the school. It was my cousin Beshir Dirar, who came up with a solution to my absence of familial support. He took me to town and at one of the cafés he introduced me to a man whom he said was a cousin. They agreed that I would stay at that cousin's house in the village of Khatmiya, at the base of Jebel Kassala, six kilometres away from the school. I was given the address of the house.

THE YEAR OF RATS

So began a period of transition between nomadic life and village life. I left for Khashm el Girba to seek out my family at Jummeiza. I was more part of Sheikh Annour's family now than my father's. At Jummeiza, I found the Dumans were about to move. There was an endless struggle between Sheikh Annour, who wanted to pull the family towards settled and more civilized life, and his elder brother Omar Duman who wanted to take the family further into ungoverned places like Shehateib and Shangil Bangil. Omar Duman's objection to the village stemmed from the presence of liberated slaves, who brewed, sold and consumed *merissa*, the local sorghum beer. He was further antagonised by the introduction in Khashm el Girba – by the Crop Protection Inspector, Beshir el Shafie – of the apparatus called "radio". Omar Duman

SCHOOLDAYS

said there was no difference between a radio and an *indaya*, a local bar.

The compromise was Kireib Assi. It was close to the village of Khashm el Girba, so Sheikh Annour, as village sheikh, could go and meet important people and attend meetings. And for me the proximity to the village gave me the chance to see my great-aunt, *Habbobti* Halima and her husband Shawish Yousif, and their sons Khidir and Daw. But Kireib Assi was still wild. No one else set their camp there because of the ferocity of its hyenas. The day we arrived the hyenas began to howl around us even before sunset. Sheikh Annour gave orders that we fix seven or eight scarecrows scattered around the camp. We did that and strengthened the enclosure that protected the flocks. We had three vicious dogs that helped.

No one was happier with the new site than *Khali* Ali, the natural hunter. Since Kireib Assi was virgin land that the nomads avoided, it had become the haven of many wild animals. Late in the afternoon the day after we arrived *Khali* Ali called me to get the gin trap and come with him. We walked to a wild spot in the *karab* where you would think no human had ever been. We chose a thin trail beneath the high banks of a *khor* and began to fix our gin trap on the sands, hiding it with earth and a wisp of grass.

Suddenly I looked up to see around us a hundred gazelles swishing their tails and fixing us with their eyes.

"Hamid, we are under attack," said *Khali* Ali, taking his stick and standing up.

"By gazelles?" I said, taking my stick too.

"They could trample us, if we are not careful," said Uncle Ali.

I had never occurred to me that gazelles could be dangerous. Who had ever heard of men being chased by gazelles? Gazelles were gentle. They were what you likened beautiful girls to.

The herd was becoming nervous. *Khali* Ali had a large knife girded to his waist. I had a smaller knife around my upper arm. The gazelles were snorting and dashing around like crazy. We moved away from the trap, hoping that one of them would inadvertently step on it. We stuck together each holding a stick. Encouraged by our retreat, the gazelles began to dash one after another towards us, past us, feigning attack. One, a female, came so close to me that I swung my stick at her.

"Don't throw your stick away at them," said *Khali* Ali. "Keep it in your hand and never mind the females. Watch out for the bucks over there, with the mighty horns and darker colour."

Gazelles were dashing everywhere, snorting and bounding. It was as if they had never seen human beings before. *Khali* Ali said they behaved as though we were jackals or hyenas, trying to frighten us away. He was still hoping that the gin trap would catch one of them. But it did not. The snorting and swishing of tails continued and we rattled the blades of our knives and beat the sticks together to chase the animals far enough to clear our route home.

It was during those days that *Khali* Ali decided to teach me how to swim. He took me to a deep pond cut off from the river just below Goz Gadala at a great bend in the river. The pond was infested with crocodiles. My idiosyncratic maternal uncle simply threw me into the deep water and drew my attention to the crocodiles as they launched themselves towards me from the spit of sand on which they were basking. So I swam, fast, though I came out gasping and sputtering water from my stomach.

We may have saved ourselves from the gazelles, but we could not save ourselves from the rats that attacked the camp at night. The tents crawled with them. They would fall from the top of the tent and bite uncovered toes. Children screamed all night. The rats climbed all over the *serir*, the tent mats, the grain sacks, the cooking pots, the eating bowls, everywhere. The touch of a rat sent chills through my body. I was so squeamish that whenever one fell on me I gagged. As nomads, we were supposed to be tough, but my courage failed me when it came to rats. Sheikh Annour's young daughter kept crying all night, "It is gnawing at my feet!".

We soon discovered that the rats had invaded the entire region, not only Kireib Assi. The nomads dubbed that year *Sanat el Far*, Year of the Rats.

One afternoon, when I was taking the flock to the river, I saw a man sitting in the shade of a tree just on the edge of Darb-el-Khatur. It did not take me long to recognize my father, even at a distance. He was on his way from Shehateib to Khashm el Girba when he recognized the branding on the sheep and goats crossing the road. He knew that I would be tending the flock and was waiting for me.

I approached and saluted; he kissed me on the head in the custom of the nomads. But we talked to one another like strangers because we had rarely seen each other the past few years. Father told me that he heard that I had been admitted to Kassala school and that he was proud of me. He offered to rig me out when school started and said that I should contact him at the end of the vacation. I took this as a promise.

INITIATION

Sheikh Annour and Shawish Yousif decided that the boys in the family had to be initiated, arabised, that is to say circumcised. There were four of us: Shawish Yousif's three boys and myself. Khidir, the oldest, was fourteen and I was twelve years old. Daw my peer, like Ibrahim my brother, had been arabised by Diya one week after his birth.

Shawish Yousif suggested that the event be held at his house at Khashm el Girba since two of us were his sons and that he would bear the bulk of the cost. I was happy when Sheikh Annour asked me to take a goat from the camp to Shawish Yousif's house as our contribution to the festivities. There was no greater shame for a boy than to remain *aghlaf*, a heathen, an uncircumcised gentile. The word for the circumcision ritual, *tahoor*, means purification. Once circumcised I would be a man, and more of a Muslim. I could milk a goat and people would drink that milk. Boys who were *aghlaf* – uncircumcised – were not allowed to do any milking.

Shawish Yousif, like Sheikh Annour, knew about the difficulties I had faced during my childhood, following my mother's divorce. He told me that when he himself was a baby his mother and father had divorced. She had disappeared completely from his life. Once, he said, for lack of any other nutrition, he had been fed the milk of a gazelle. Then his father died and he was raised by his uncle Adam. Most of his early life he spent as a nomad in the Butana, in Shehateib and with his Humran kinsfolk at Wad el Hileiw. Later Shawish Yousif joined the Sudan Defence Force. When he left the army, he went back to his life as a shepherd at Shehateib. But when Sheikh Awad el Karim Abu Sin moved his court from Asubri to Khashm el Girba, he sent for Shawish Yousif to join and train his new *muhafizin* gendarmerie. Shawish Yousif kept the post for half a century until his death in 1979. He was one of the tallest and strongest men in the region but he did not boast. He talked very little, but was popular among the freed slaves who made up most of the inhabitants of Khashm el Girba.

He was married to my great aunt, who I called *Habbobti* Halima. She was the sibling of Ghaniya, my mother's mother.

Habbobti Halima was superstitious and believed in the powers of *fekis*, demons, ghosts, spirits, *jinns*, devils and hovering souls. She told us that Fellata, the West African immigrants to Sudan, could turn into hyenas and eat people. They would roll in ash, she said, and the first thing that appeared was a tail. *Habbobti* Halima swore to Allah that, years back at Um Khanjar, near Gedaref, men found hyenas with human hands, one still kneading sorghum dough.

The idea of me being circumcised with her own boys was accepted by *Habbobti* Halima with certain misgivings. But the whole village was happy to hear that Shawish Yousif was going to have his sons circumcised. They had been waiting for the occasion for a long time. Following the announcement of the *tahoor*, the evenings of Khashm el Girba became riotous. There were large pots of *merissa* beer available and bottles of distilled *araki*. Each evening, after I had dinner and penned the flock, I would leave the camp, sporting my arm-knife and stick and urging my dogs to follow me, and walk to Khashm el Girba to attend the evening party.

Zayda bit Faraj, a *ghaniya* singer, led the festivities. Her full voice, her battle songs and her enthusiasm in performance had made her famous. She drove both men and women to excel in their dances. As she beat a drum and sang her small head moved back and forth with such force you would think it would shoot away. My grandmother Diya would have despised her Africanity, but Zayda knew better Arabic than most Arabs; she spun ballads out of the language like spider-silk.

"Beat the drum, *khadim*!" One rough nomad would tell Zayda, standing over her. The word *khadim* meant a slave, but the word had been more or less divested of its original meaning. Zayda would begin beating the drum. A pair of nomad men might stage a mock fight, the *sagriya* or eagle dance, each with his *tob* wrapped round his waist, leaping and locking horns.

Then Zayda might sing a song to make girls dance. It might be one about a bridegroom who set the pace for other young men to follow by paying a bridewealth of a hundred yellow camels and a hundred red cows and a hundred speckled sheep. How beautiful his brandished sword shone, sang Zayda, how powerful the beat of his drum:

> *Miya naga safra*
> *Miya bagara hamra*
> *Miya naaja barga*
> *Samahat seifu salla*
> *U dagdag nihassu alla*

Then shepherds and herdsmen might stand in a line with their backs towards the women and with bare torsos, bracing themselves for *dharb-el-sot*, the whip lash. They would whip each other's backs till they bled. The herdsmen, living for months on *gariss*, fermented camel milk, far away from any human habitation, became demented at the sight of women. They behaved like buffaloes in rut. They would do crazy things to prove to the girls how virile they were. To them a lashing with a whip was not of much more concern than a silk handkerchief.

The young women of Khashm el Girba were the offspring of freed slaves. Their freedom included the sexual liberty denied by the patriarchal structure of the Arab family to the Arab women who had once owned them. They had the privilege of choosing the man they liked. After a group of young men had gone through their whipping bouts, they would remain in line waiting for the reward from the girls of a *shabbal*: a girl would toss her hair over her chosen suitor and dance for him. A group of six or seven young women stepped into the dance stage, wrapped in thin stoles, and began to dance, swaying and bending back until their heads almost rested on their hips. They were led by Mahalik, as bright as the moon, with her long neck and silky hair and cinnamon-coloured skin. To the chagrin of all nomad men Mahalik chose a young Hausa man as her lover. Perhaps because he was the driver of the only lorry in town.

MY PRIVATE PARTS

The day of the circumcision operation arrived. We were prepared almost as bridegrooms might be, with dry perfumes, a red handkerchief, and a tuft of red silk hanging from our wrists. Sheikh Annour had sent for my mother to come from Andala. It was a modern circumcision. *Habbobti* Halima insisted taking us to the doctor to be operated on, not to the traditional *tahhar* or circumciser. Although *Habbobti* Halima was highly superstitious, she shunned everything nomadic, considering it very primitive and never mentioning her life as a nomad at Shehateib and Jummeiza, where I had first met her and her sons in their tent.

The dispensary was half a kilometre away towards the river. As Zayda beat the drums, the dancing, the flogging, the shrill *zagharid* and the mock sword fight all continued until we came to the rocket-shaped British-built, white, mud-brick buildings of the dispensary. All four of us were taken into the dispensary. The medical assistant had his tools ready. There was a medical smell and kerosene pressure stove hissing loudly. A chipped, white enamel-coated jug stood like a spotted dog on the window sill. An oblong container of water was boiling on the stove, with scalpel and cheese cloth visible. The medical assistant inspected our *shamboras*. When he came to me, he discovered that the foreskin was stuck to the glans. He shook his head in disapproval and shouted "Negligence!" The crowd fell silent, as though birds were perching on their heads.

"An abandoned child!" said the medical assistant.

He looked around and asked: "Who is the father of the thin boy? Where is his mother?"

My mother spoke up.

"You should have done your homework, woman. I cannot circumcise this child."

So I was publicly identified as the boy whose prepuce was stuck to his glans.

Mother looked ashamed and her aunt *Habbobti* Halima showed a flicker of alarm. Sheikh Annour saved the day by announcing to the crowd that I was to be taken back to Shawish Yousif's house to be circumcised. He sent Daw to summon Haj Hassan, the village barber, to the house. I was put on Sheikh Annour's white donkey and, followed by all nomad members of the crowd, made my way back to the house. With my defective private parts no longer private, I felt rather miserable.

At Shawish Yousif's house, they sat me on an inverted *gadah* and women and men stood around me. Haj Hassan, a Hausa man, sat on the ground in front of me and opened his tarnished leather bag of surgical kit. He examined my *shambora* and asked for ash. He dabbed his thumb in it and simply pushed the foreskin back. From his bag he took a cut-throat razor and a leather strop. He held one end of the strop with his toes and the other in his left hand. I watched as he unfolded the razor with his right hand and sharpened it.

Haj Hassan started searching in the dirt with his fingers. I was sure he was looking for stones. Hausa circumcision was said to involve the insertion of tiny stone fragments, so the penis of an adult Hausa would look like a crocodile. This was meant to elicit unlimited erotic enjoyment in a woman. But all Haj Hassan was looking for was a piece of straw. He muttered an incantation, spat on the straw and passed it round my foreskin. That was all the anasthaesic I was to get. But I felt almost no pain as he cut off two rings of the foreskin and rolled what remained back to heal. I was mortified, though, when my mother picked them up and put them as rings around her left-hand fingers, a nomad tradition intended to remind everyone that she had begotten male offspring.

Once the operation was completed and the wound wrapped with bandage secured from the dispensary I was handed Grandpa Omar's barbed spear and asked to throw it. I shook it well and as the crowd cleared the yard before me, I took a few steps forward and threw the spear to stick into the ground a few metres away. I performed this javelin ritual three times as women ululated in happiness. This was a symbolic gesture that ushered a new warrior into the army of fighters of the Shukriya tribe. *Habbobti* Halima took the incident of the stuck prepuce as a portent of calamity and insisted that I did not join her sons in their hut. This, she said, would cause them harm. My mother was indignant, but Shawish Yousif – who did not want to anger his wife – eased the situation by giving me his sword to carry.

THE SHADOW OF SLAVERY

Sheikh Annour's relentless attempts to pull our camp towards the village now brought us to live for the first time in our lives in dark, straw-roofed *tukuls* instead of tents. He convinced everyone that it was best for us that particular rainy season to live at the edge of the village in order to be close to a farm where he planned to grow sorghum. We took over a small group of *tukuls* that originally belonged to Shawish Yousif in Kumur just across the main *khor* at the southern edge of Khashm el Girba.

Only two families lived at Kumur when we came. Both were families of freed slaves of the Jawamiss Lahawin. Abu Saeed (father of Saeed) and Um Saeed (mother of Saeed) lived with their daughter Zeinab and son Saeed in one hut. The other family was Bilal wad Ukud's family. Nobody knew the actual names of Saeed's parents but they were sociable and friendly. The day we arrived at Kumur they came to see us and brought food for us. They used to be neighbours of *Habbobti* Halima and knew we were her kin. Saeed's parents spoke broken Arabic with a heavy accent like Grandma Maimona. But their son, Saeed, a *rababa* player of fame, was similar in skin colour, features and clothing from *Khali* Umhummad. Zeinab, their daughter, was fair-complexioned and famous for her beauty. But we did not have much time to get to know her before she was taken by the crocodiles while bathing in the river, becoming, as people said, yet another bride of the Nile.

Abu Saeed told us how he and his wife had escaped from their master and run to the government post at Khashm el Girba to get their freedom cards. But the shadow of slavery pursued them. His back was criss-crossed with scars from whippings. Sometimes I would see nomad men – Jawamiss – with swords and whips enter Abu Saeed's hut and kick him out, while they took their pleasure with his wife. Both his children were fathered that way.

But nobody could touch the wife of Bilal wad Ukud. Bilal was the opposite of Abu Saeed, despite the fact that they were both freed slaves. Bilal had no scars. He had been a killer, a killer of other slaves at his masters' behest. If he was given orders to kill, for instance, a certain slave camelherd, Bilal would wait for the camels to come to the river. There he would chop off the herder's head, install a substitute slave as a camel herder and take the head back to his master.

One day his master had told him to kill a child. The mother, they said, was too preoccupied with the child and not minding her duties well. Bilal obeyed. He took the infant of the slave woman and simply flung it into the river alive to be eaten by crocodiles. The mother, crazed with grief, took her master's child to the river. Standing on a high rock on the edge of the water, she shouted to some bystanders to tell her master that she had taken her revenge. Then, clutching the child to her bosom, she jumped into the water. Today the rock is called Hajar al Khadim, Slave Woman's Rock. Bilal wad Ukud was never punished for his misdeeds.

LOOKING FOR MY FATHER

The rainy season over, we abandoned our *tukuls* and went back to nomadic life. But it was time for me to leave for Kassala and begin my new phase of schooling. I wrapped my few articles in a bundle, and throwing it over my shoulder left for the Blue Bridge in search of my father, to ask him to fulfil his promise to kit me out for school.

At the outskirts of the camp at Shehateib I found Hassan Jubar singing and tending to his donkey. Ketira was delousing the blind Zahara, Bit Burbur was disentangling a skein of yarn. I started to make the necessary enquiries concerning the welfare of each person in the camp. The women asked me about my people at Khashm el Girba. They asked me about Sheikh Annour, about Grandfather Omar and about my mother. The young girls asked about Aunt Zeena and her sisters. Most of the men of the camp were out at work, they said, looking after their flocks, visiting other camps, or cutting wood in the Shehateib forest.

The women at the camp told me they had heard that I was successful in some business in Kassala town, but they were not sure what it was. They asked me about my experience riding the train and whether I had seen *himar-el-hadid*, the iron donkey – a bicycle – when I was in Kassala. They were awed by many things I told them: that I was going to learn how to speak and write English, the language of the infidel British, that Jebel Kassala was not blue but actually brown and that it was a chain of hills not a single mountain with seven peaks, and that I had visited Sidi al Hassan of the Khatmiya sect at the foot of the Jebel and kissed his silk-wrapped hand and swallowed some of the sand on which he walked. I told them that I was on my way now to Kassala where I would be living close to Sidi Al-Hassan, near the Khatmiya shrine at the base of the great rock. None of them had ever seen Kassala.

I told them that I came to see my father, who had promised to help me with my schooling expenditure. I noticed an unfavourable expression pass across Bit Annour's face. She said she was not sure if my father was going to keep his word. Sheikh Annour should have helped me out himself, she said. Bit Annour knew my father well, as he had been married to her daughter Melka Tajouj. Melka Tajouj had died many years before.

But I did not doubt that my father would keep his word. He would surely be happy to know that I had been admitted to school in Kassala. The women told me that he was near to Kassala, still at the rainy season camp, with the Hadendowa who had not moved yet down to their summer site on the river. I realised I should have asked about his whereabouts earlier. It was now late afternoon. Bit Annour advised me to stay for the night because it would be dangerous for a twelve-year-old to venture in the wilderness ahead close to nightfall. But I told myself I could make the journey to my father's camp before sunset, though I worried about the hyenas that descended by night from the eastern hills to eat goats and sheep – and the odd twelve-year-old human.

I set off, traversing the Shehateib *karab* knolls and made my way through the thick *kitir* forest. Finally I came to the Hajiz railway station and went looking for water. I found a water tanker on a side track and quenched my thirst from a dripping water outlet. By the time I slung my bundle once more over my shoulder and picked up my stick, the last light of the sun was gone. Fear gave me the impetus to move faster as I set out on the road, heading northeast. The sun took cover behind the earth. Barefoot and bareheaded, I moved faster and faster. It crossed my mind that I might have travelled all day in vain, that I would not find money in the hands of my father. I knew that none of my family wanted me to go to school. They wanted me to know how to read and write, but not beyond elementary level. They had not openly tried to discourage me and I had not expected them to help defray the cost of my education. It did not occur to me to blame anyone for my poverty. But I was running after my father because he had promised to help.

I continued, alternately running and walking, keeping direction by the *Jedi*, the pole star, with an ear cocked for the barking of dogs, keeping an eye out for my father's *tuggaba* fire. I heard only the sound of my own footfalls. The trees grew tall. Then I saw firelight. Was it real, or was it a will-o'-the-wisp, *Abu Fanous*, perhaps, the lantern devil? Dogs barked and charged towards me. Then I was sure I could see my father's bonfire. The men guarding the camp jumped up. I waved my stick at the dogs and entered the camp, with bleeding feet and cracking lips.

By the fire I found my father surrounded, as usual, by a gang of young warriors. One of them offered me his hippo shield to sit on. An old man sent a young man to bring me food, sorghum porridge with cow's milk and a dish of *rebit* – greaves – the fibrous remains after rendering fat from an animal. I told my father of my intention to go to Kassala for school the following morning and reminded him of his promise. He went on stoking the fire. I could see what he was thinking: he was alone now, no sons, no daughters, no wives, no relatives except for the Book. I decided to wait till morning to pursue the matter and curled up to sleep, like a hedgehog.

A short time later I was aroused again by a great commotion in the tents of the camp. Men were shouting *"igalaba!"*. It was the Hadendowa word for hyena. I heard my father shout: "W-or! W-or! Oroon! Oroon!" – the boy, the boy, my boy! And the silhouette of the hyena came speeding towards me. I snatched a burning piece of wood from the dying fire and waved it in the face of the animal. It veered and headed for the far valleys in the east. The dogs followed it, but they could not close the distance.

SPEAKING A NEW LANGUAGE

At first cockcrow I was up to find the others in the camp already awake warming themselves by the fire, which had been replenished with fresh fuelwood. At a distance, father was doing his *subuh* prayer. I could see the *ibrig*, the water vessel, standing by his side. I took the *ibrig* and washed my face. How could I reach Kassala if my father reneged on his promise? I went to pass water and as I was walking back to the *shafat*, I caught sight of the high peaks of Jebel Kassala in the distance. The great bright rock seemed as close to me as a blackboard to a teacher. It felt as though I had already gone the better part of the distance. I could walk there on foot! It was no longer such a critical matter that my father should keep his word.

I went to say my prayers. Then sat by the fire. There were many men there now, some making coffee, some saying prayers, others clutching their knees against their chests. I could even run to Kassala, I told myself. The childhood diseases that I suffered and the medical treatments by fire and the knife had made my body sturdy. The continuous physical exercise to which a nomad boy was subjected made me even stronger, even if I was thin. And I knew that schooling was my destiny.

An old man, of my father's age, asked me: "*Hallan isawad tikana?*" Do you know the blackening? What he was asking me was whether I knew how to write. To prove it I wrote my name on the dirt. The old man smiled.

Father gave me twenty-five piastres. It was a quarter of a pound, a paper denomination that was then called *tarrada*. He also told me, when I reached Kassala, to go to a certain merchant there and to tell him that my father asked him to give me a pair of shoes and clothes. After a breakfast of stiff porridge with buttermilk I set off again for Kassala, some thirty kilometres away. While I was walking I reminded myself of the kinds of cars and trucks I knew. There was the Bedford, the Canada and the Dodge. And there were small cars or sedans, called Ford or Studebaker. When Sidi Bakri, one of the leaders of the Khatmiya, had come by Khashm el Girba some time before, I heard people say: "Sidi Bakri is riding a Sidi Baker".

And after an hour, I heard the rumble of a car behind me, a Dodge loaded with sorghum from Gedaref and passengers perched on top of the sacks.

"Where are you coming from?" said the driver.

"From over there," I pointed my finger in the direction of the camp.

The man looked and saw nothing but the bush.

"What village is there?" He asked, probably thinking of future travellers on his truck. "And where are you going?"

"I am going to school in Kassala," I told him.

The man hesitated for a while and then asked, "What school?"

"Kassala Government Intermediate School, sir," I said proudly.

"You speak *ingiliz*?" he laughed.

"No sir, I don't speak English. I am going there for the first time."

The driver told me to climb up with the other passengers. His assistant, riding on the sorghum sacks with us, flicked his fingers at me asking for money.

"How much do you want?" I asked.

"How much could you offer?" He asked.

I held out my *tarrada*, a quarter of a Sudanese pound and said, "This is all the money I have." He took it without compunction.

Kassala, the oasis city, appeared in the distance, with a green line of orchards running along the foot of the great rock that stood formidable against the blue skies. A white streak of a cloud ran across the rock below the peaks. The lorry stopped under a huge *neem* tree, one of the many lining the tarmac road linking the railway station on the west bank of the Gash river. The driver said he was sorry but he had to drop us all there because although he was going to the city centre it was illegal to cross the bridge with passengers seated on the cargo.

So I had to travel on foot another ten kilometres to reach my destination: the Khatmiya village at the foot of the rock on the other side of the city. It was early afternoon when I set out. I was hungry and now completely impecunious. I walked across the bridge, making it a point to avoid the city completely. I followed the eastern bank of the Gash River, skirting the town and crossing the tall *sunut* acacia forest on the riverbank, where my ancestor had felled trees for waterwheels, and the dense *dom* palm groves between the city and the village.

It took me hours to reach the Khatmiya village. I could not find the house I was looking for. They all looked alike. Finally I stood at a large fenced compound with a door made of flattened petrol cans nailed on a wooden frame. The fence itself was built of closely stacked thorn-bearing *dom* palm fronds. In the centre of the enclosed space there were three huge *neem* trees with thick trunks, which meant that they were very old and well watered. Their foliage touched, forming a canopy.

Running for a short distance was a line of henna shrubs. Close to my left was a roof-less latrine. It had a *boussa*, a pipe of tinplate like a chimney which sent foul fumes up into the air. There was a spacious courtyard that was immaculately clean, except for a small depression close to the centre. Here, where earth used to build the wall of the courtyard had been excavated, straw, leaves, small twigs and sand and gravel were dumped as a landfill. The distribution of the huts at the edges of the compound was meant to keep the boundaries intact against any encroachment by the neighbours.

I knocked on the door timidly. No answer. What if the people I had come to see had moved to some other town? A grizzled figure came out of a hovel built of wattle. I guessed he was an ex-slave.

"You have to knock harder," he said, without salutation. "The women are indoors and they won't hear you."

I knocked so hard on the door my knuckles hurt. Then I waited, looking through the gaps in the fence. A huge woman, who looked Egyptian or Turkish appeared, followed by another who turned out to be her daughter. It took them an age to reach the gate.

The old woman opened the door and greeted me in a soft voice.

"*Marhab*," she said.

"*Ahlan*," I returned the greeting. "I am Hamid wad Ahmed wad Dirar,"

Her eyes were cat-like, bluish-green. Her hair, which peeped from the *tob* over the forehead, was definitely frizzy. These were my relatives, then.

"Oh, you are the boy who is coming to school?" the mother asked with a smile.

"Yes, that is me, madam," I said quickly.

"Sayed told us about you," She said. Sayed was my cousin whom Beshir Dirar had introduced me to a few months back in a café in Kassala.

"Come in," she said. She noticed the old ex-slave outside his hovel and greeted him: "Abul Hadiya, *izzayak*."

The two fat ladies and myself walked back through the compound – two tortoises and a jumping frog. I had yet to learn that obesity was considered something beautiful in the city. It was referred to as *sahha*, meaning "good health".

"So you are the son of Ahmed, son of Ali, son of Dirar," she said with an edge of bitterness.

"Yes," I said, a bit alarmed.

"I am your aunt Macaroni. But I have not seen your father and your uncles since their family left Khatmiya village. My husband was their cousin. He passed away leaving me with my three small children, but no one came back from Asubri to see how we were faring. They did not even come for the land that Sidi Ahmed al Mirghani deeded to their father here in Khatmiya. And now it is lost to some Tekruris."

I said nothing. Macaroni, I thought, what a strange name. It had never crossed my mind that my father had lived here. He certainly hadn't mentioned it. I began to fear I might not be welcome. But it turned out the two fat women were in need of an agile boy who could move around and accomplish things. They offered me food and an *angareib* to sleep on. And early the following morning I took off to Kassala to report to school and to get the shoes and clothes from the merchant that father had mentioned.

The house of the women lay on the very edge of the village, close to a long high earth embankment, the Jasur, raised against the seasonal flooding of the Gash River. The flat land between the village and Kassala was a thick forest of *dom* palms. The road to Kassala tunneled through the forest for three miles or so. On both sides were upright palms, fallen palms, palm stumps, *dom* saplings, and fallen *dom* fruits. Its nocturnal inhabitants were the dreaded brown hyenas, *karai goad*. Their haven was high in the Jebel, the mountain above the town; they descended at sunset to roam the palm forest. My school was at the far end of the city; I had to walk every day six kilometres and back without breakfast, and without shoes or headwear. But I was happy now.

After the first day, I went downtown and looked up the merchant my father had told me to see.

"I am Hamid wad Ahmed wad Dirar," I said after greeting the man.

"So?" was his reaction.

"My father said you could give me shoes and clothes and when he comes here he would pay you," I said.

"If I clothe everyone who comes here asking for clothes, I wouldn't be in business," he said.

"But I am a student," I said. "And I depend on this to go to school. My father said you were his friend and would solve my problem."

"I see your father once every year. Business cannot wait for Ahmed wad Dirar to emerge from his hiding places once a year. Besides, your father knows how to write, now why didn't he write a quick note for me?"

"Are you saying you cannot help me?" I asked.

"I'm sorry," were his last words.

I continued my schooling wearing clothes from my old elementary school. Each day I went to school and came back along the Dom Road. The other boys laughed at my nomad language. They used words I had never heard before. One of them said that he would like to be a *sahafi*, a journalist. I wondered what a journalist was. I had never seen a newspaper in my life. Another asked me if I had a *shageeg*, a sibling.

"Only a brother," I said.

With English, though, we all started from the same point. Within a few months we were saying, "An ant is in the tin," and "Peter Piper put the pencil on the paper." Our English teachers were Sudanese, of course.

Back in Khatmiya, Aunt Macaroni introduced me to the neighbourhood grocer, the greengrocer and the butcher. She showed me the well from which we drew our water in the grounds of the neighbouring Toteel football club. And she introduced me to the headmaster of the boys' elementary school there. I played football with his sons in the afternoon.

I made trips into town for her, even selling chickens in the market. The two women grew still fatter and more sluggish, a sign of beauty and affluence. They received meagre monthly sums of money from Macaroni's sons, who worked as carpenters in Aroma, a town down the Gash River. Sometimes Aunt Macaroni would give me two piastres for my breakfast at school, but I saved the money to be spent on other things. With two piastres I hired a bicycle for fifteen minutes and taught myself to ride the iron donkey. I also ate my first orange. It came from Beirut, in Lebanon, wrapped in tissue paper.

I filled the compound with dogs and cats. Macaroni had never had such animals in her home. One night she asked me to carry a basketful of blind puppies to the river for the hyenas to eat. I did it with tears in my eyes.

PROBLEMS AT SCHOOL

One Wednesday at school a janitor put his hand on my shoulder and said: "Hamid Dirar?"

"Yes," I said.

"The school principal wants to see you," said the messenger.

"The deputy headmaster?" I asked. The headmaster was away this time too.

"Who else?"

"What is it he wants to see me about?" I asked, apprehensive.

"How would I know? Why don't you ask him?"

I had a feeling that the deputy headmaster did not like me

or my rustic demeanor. And I was going not only barefoot and bareheaded, but in old clothes, and emaciated as a wraith.

I knocked on the open door and waited.

"Come in," the deputy headmaster shouted.

I stood at attention before the desk, making sure to be at an arm's length from him in case he tried to hit me. The deputy headmaster was looking at some papers. He gave me a cursory glance and returned to his work. Finally he peered at me over his glasses.

"You are Hamid Dirar?"

"Yes, sir."

"Hamid Ahmed Dirar?"

"Yes, sir."

Now he slowly removed his glasses and placed them on the right side of the desk. My eyes followed every move he made. I noticed that the spectacles hung from his neck on a long snake-like black thread. The deputy headmaster clasped his fingers on the desk. When he raised his face again it had already undergone a convulsive transformation, with a deep-furrowed frown. I prayed my knees would not fail me.

"You think you are going to get away with this, don't you, boy?"

"This, sir?" I said in my rustic accent, at a loss for what he meant.

"Yes this!" he screamed at me

"Sir, I swear to Allah….."

"May Allah break your neck," he said.

"Sir, honestly I have no idea what you are talking about," I said.

"Oh yes you do! You know it like you know the hunger of your stomach."

I knew the hunger of my stomach well, but I did not then know that this was just a proverbial expression.

SCHOOLDAYS

"Have you paid your school fees, boy?" he said

Fees? Fees? Tuition fees? What fees? The matter had completely slipped my mind. For a moment I could neither move nor talk. Then I remembered that when I was admitted to school I was told that I had to pay six pounds per annum. In the bliss of the moment then, I had forgotten about the tuition fee. I never mentioned it to my father or to Sheikh Annour. What difference would it have made in any case? They were not going to pay such a large amount of money every year! Their whole annual income put together would not amount to that sum. My tacit agreement with them was that they were not going to stand in my way to school so long as I did not ask for help.

The deputy headmaster took the opportunity to rub salt in the wound.

"Do you hear me?"

"The matter, sir, completely escaped my memory," I said.

"If it did, now you know it. Today is Wednesday. If you do not get that money by Thursday, you won't set a foot in my school on Saturday."

I left his office. My education had always been a precarious enterprise. Now his words seemed like the death knell of my hopes of acquiring knowledge. Would I have to return to the nomadic life in Shangil Bangil and Khireissab now? I told myself that that was how life was: things waxed and waned. Maybe I could find a solution. Then I fell into pessimism again. My luck had run out. In the words of an Arabic poet, my fortune was like fine flour – strewn on thorns that barefoot men were asked to collect on a windy day.

At the end of the school day, clutching at straws, I went to see the merchant my father sent me to before. I reminded him of my first visit to him. I knew what he would say, but I had nowhere else to turn. And, as the proverb goes, *he who has lost something would search the mouth of a cow.*

"I haven't seen your father throughout this past year," said the merchant. "I am running a business here not a charity organization. I just can't dole out money to strangers. I am sorry. Why don't you go back to your father and help him with his animals. This is no way to go to school,"

The deputy headmaster's words kept coming back to me as I walked along the *dom* road. "If you do not get that money by Thursday," he had said, "you don't set a foot in my school on Saturday." Had he noticed that I was barefoot and bareheaded, the only one among the boys, and that my face was thin with hunger?

At home, the two women became aware of the fact that something was the matter. I told them what had happened. They were sympathetic. I lay on my *angareib* with open eyes all night, nursing the misery that had befallen me. I was thirteen and my education was at an end. No more Peter Piper and ants in tins. It was back to swords and the nomadic life. In the morning I left for my last day at school. I attended my classes as if nothing was the matter. I had taken the decision to leave school and that left me calm. As I left the classroom one of my classmates, Sherif, who came from the same area as myself, said: "What is wrong, Hamid?"

I told him about the deputy headmaster's ultimatum.

"What? The deputy headmaster? You should still come to school on Saturday," he said.

"I beg your pardon?" I asked, perplexed.

"I think you have no problem," he said.

"What do you mean I have no problem, Sherif?" I asked.

"You have no problem. Your fees have already been paid, like mine.

"But by whom?" I asked still not believing.

"By the North Gedaref Rural Council," said Sharif. "By the Shukriya Tribe Council. The headmaster has a letter signed by the nazir, Muhammad Hamad Abu Sin, and Kudi Adduma, the Executive Officer."

"I did not know that," I said.

"Well, now you know," he said.

"Sherif, are you sure that the letter concerns me?" I asked.

"I have seen it with my own eyes," said Sherif.

I did not ask why any council should pay my fees for me. On Saturday morning I went to the administration and asked to speak with the deputy headmaster. He took some papers out of the drawer and ran his finger down a short list of names on one page. His finger stopped against one of the names.

"Hamid Ahmed Dirar, right?" He asked without raising his head.

"Yes, sir."

"You are lucky, boy. Go join your class," he said.

I felt very indignant. His mistake almost cost me my future. But who was he accountable to? Who was going to reprimand the deputy headmaster?

Later, when my mother heard the story she said it was the guardian spirit of Feki Beshir who solved my problem for me. She often imputed the good things that happened to me to this long deceased holy man and the amulet that he had shown her in a dream.

A CHANGE OF FORTUNE

My health was not good. I was not eating enough. I was lucky if I could secure a meal and a half a day. In most cases, I returned to the house in the afternoon without having had breakfast. There I would find just *kisra* – unleavened sorghum bread – with water and salt. Sometimes, when I had to return in the afternoon to school for physical exercises, I walked the distance from school to Khatmiya four times the same day. When I returned to Khashm el Girba at the end of the year, people were horrified to see me, sallow and thin. They thought I should leave school before it brought my doom, but that was something I could not do.

At the start of the third year I had a change of fortune. I saw the headmaster, Ali Hamid, accompanied by the mathematics teacher, Mamoun. The mathematics teacher called me and I went up to them, thinking that they wanted to send me fetch something or someone for them. I was surprised when Ustaz Mamoun asked: "Do you want to join the boarding house?"

"Yes, sir, I do," I said unbelievingly.

"OK then. On Saturday you bring your things and you will be provided with the necessary accommodation in the hostels," said the headmaster.

How it came about I do not know. My mother knew, of course. It was because I was the amulet of that holy man, Feki Beshir.

"You could have expired, my son," she said later. "But your guardian spirit was watching you. I have no doubt about that, believe you what you may."

I broke what I thought to be good news to the two women where I lived, but to my surprise they did not share my happiness. What was wrong? These same women were talking sympathetically to me about the difficulties I was in till yesterday. What was wrong now? They were adamant I should not go to the boarding house. Pressed, they told me that boarding houses encouraged immorality and to homosexuality and that was why they did not want me to go there. As a nomad boy I did not find it becoming to talk such talk. I had heard this in the days when the nomads around Khashm el Girba said the same thing about the new school there. I had lived for four years before in a boarding house and did not notice anything untoward about life there.

The next day, as the two women and I were sitting in the shade of the *neem* trees, we noticed the top of the head of a young man peering over the fence near the doorway. It was Ibrahim, my brother! I introduced him to the ladies of the house, but it was clear they did not welcome him. He had left school some time ago and they were alarmed at the sight of what looked like a Hadendowa man with thick hair and tattered clothes, fearing the neighbours would discover that they were related to this ragamuffin.

If Ibrahim sensed this, he did not show it. He said that he would rather stay in the city where the action was, not in the village where I lived. He said he had practically no money but he would meet me on Saturday when I was on my way to school. It was the first time he had seen Kassala, but it seemed as if he knew the town. Ibrahim was the opposite of me. He was completely happy in the city.

Early Saturday morning I started packing my things into my suitcase. Macaroni snatched away the two metres of calico which she had bought me to use as a cover when I slept. And she seized my half-size football. I did not have much to pack other than a *jellabiya* and a *surwal*. I packed those and my books in my beautiful little leather-and-cardboard suitcase and went to the large *rakuba* to bid the ladies goodbye.

Macaroni said: "Hamid, you can't take that suitcase because my daughter wants it."

So I left the house as poor as I was the day I entered it two years before. But in my relentless pursuit of knowledge nothing else mattered.

Ibrahim, meanwhile, on his way to Kassala, had found a circle of young men on the outskirts of the town gambling. He watched them for some time, learned the rules and decided to risk the little money he had. Within an hour or so he had all the men's money in his pocket. When he stood up to leave, they threatened him but he held out his stick and drew his arm-knife and walked away backwards and disappeared into the town. When we met later he gave me a good sum of money, the proceeds of his gambling escapade. He asked me how to find the two young men, our cousins, who worked in Aroma. I told him that they worked as carpenters with a contractor there called Ibrahim Fadl el Mula.

Ibrahim had finished third year grade school and that was about all the formal education he ever got. When he heard of my difficulties at Kassala – and before he knew that I was going to join the boarding house – he decided to quit school and travel to Kassala to find a job so he could help me in my education. Ibrahim was resourceful. In the vacation he went back to Shehateib and Khireissab. He found he needed money to get back to Kassala. One day he was passing my father's cultivation area when he noticed a herd of cows entering the farm. It had been already harvested except for a few heads of sorghum here and there, but Ibrahim maintained that the cattle destroyed the farm. He drove the herd to the police station at the Blue Bridge and claimed compensation in cash. When the cattle owners came they paid the money and Ibrahim took the lorry to Kassala, and left nomadic life forever. Thus the old man, our father, was left alone.

A WRESTLING MATCH

At the boarding house, I entered into my new life easily. Three meals a day and regular study programmes improved my academic performance. I excelled in basketball and wrestling. Tagi, my colleague and friend from Khashm el Girba, dared me to fight against the most feared wrestler, a boy nicknamed Mutwahish, the Wild One. The Wild One was a town boy, well-built, almost twice my weight. His body was smooth, no knots or sinews. I was deceptively thin and wiry. I looked like the underdog and most of the boys supported me.

The boys gathered in a wide circle and the Wild One and I stood at the centre. From the days of Shangil Bangil and Jummeiza I knew wrestling was more of a skill than a question of sheer weight and physical strength. At first the Wild One kept his distance. Then suddenly he attacked. A wild scream arose from the audience. Tagi kept close to me. I pushed the Wild One away. Because I was thin, he thought he would hold me by the waist and swing me down. But I surprised him by wrapping both my arms round his own waist. The moment I touched my adversary's body I became confident that I was going to win. His flesh was soft; stripped of all fat, he would have been the same weight as I.

The Wild One tried to free himself, but I placed my foot behind his legs – the move known to the nomads as *hakla*, and tripped him. The Wild One came down like a sack of sorghum, stirring the dust. I won that round, but the second round was inconclusive and finally we were separated by the umpires.

The Wild One turned out to be a good sport and became my friend. The son of a rich merchant, when he discovered that I was poor he helped me in many ways. One of the presents he gave me was a torch, which I took to my people at Shehateib – the first modern technology in a nomadic camp in the area. (Torchlight was a wonder, but only, of course, while the dry cells lasted.) I could not afford to go to the cinema, but sometimes one of the boys would take me out of kindness. I liked Tarzan movies and westerns because they reminded me of the environment I knew: mountains, rivers, creeks, forests, livestock and wild animals.

And one day Ibrahim returned. He was wearing slacks of English tweed, an impeccably clean shirt, a lustrous pair of leather shoes and a wrist watch, with his hair cut like a film star, combed smooth to one side. His tanned nomad complexion was now pale. In his hand he held a pack of Navy Cut cigarettes. He said he had come to take me to the cinema. In just a few months, it turned out, he had learned the trade of modern carpentry, got himself a salaried job as a carpenter and transformed himself into a city slicker. I had to explain to him that I could not just leave to go to the town, that I had an evening class, so he gave me some money and left, strutting like a peacock.

A CIRCUMCISION PARTY

Two boys invited me to Kassala for their circumcision. We stayed in their rather unkempt house. What happened there put me off city life even more.

SCHOOLDAYS

One day I was sent to the marketplace to fetch groceries. When I returned I found only the daughter and the mother in the house. They told me that the others had gone away to spend the day with their grandmother. I went to prepare myself to leave but I heard the mother call me. She told me her daughter wanted me in the other room.

When I entered I found the daughter stark naked. I retreated, but she called me back.

"Stay!" she said. "And close the door, Hamid. I just want you to help me rub my back." She was laughing.

I was fourteen years old. The room was dim. The young woman was crouching in an aluminium tub used for washing clothes, and in front of her was a bucket of water with a small cup floating on the surface. In her right hand was a new bar of red carbolic soap. On a nearby *angareib* were her clothes. Her well-set white teeth and her wide gazelle-like black eyes were beaming at me.

She had already poured water over her light-brown body; her long hair was sticking to her shoulders and her back. Rivulets of water were coursing down her body, glittering like stars.

"Sit behind me and please rub my back from the neck down," she said

I began rubbing her neck. She bent forward and with both hands held her hair up high. I strove not to look at her buttocks. She was smiling and giggling. Suddenly the bar of soap slipped away from my hand and disappeared in the water beneath her. The thought of retrieving it from there caused me to jump up and leave the room. Her laughter rang in my ears.

With that family there was worse to come. The next day there was a stranger in the house. A huge man, the size of a gorilla, dark-skinned and obese. Fat women were one thing, but the sight of a man like that with huge buttocks and a potbelly was repulsive. The teachings of Sheikh Annour came back to me: "What's the use of a man with large buttocks?" he used to say. "Allah blessed a hirsute man and a heavy-bottomed woman." These teachings, he claimed – though I doubted it – were *hadeeth* from Prophet Muhammad, peace be upon him.

The man in front of me was nude except for a tiny pair of shorts. He was dark and covered in hair, like a derelict building overgrown by plants. He surely could not qualify for Allah's blessing. He sensed my presence and raised his head to look at me. His eyes were large and his eyeballs mottled as if a bird had laid its eggs in their sockets. He looked as if he had been fighting a battle – and lost. He rolled a fat cigarette, twisting the ends in opposite directions.

"Who the hell are you?" he said.

"Hamid, sir". By then I had stopped saying my full name the nomad way.

"Hamid? Hamid who?"

"Hamid Dirar, sir."

"And what is your business in this house, Hamid Dirar?"

"I'm a friend of the boys, sir."

"What boys?"

"Asim and Kamal, sir; I came for their circumcision."

"And are you going to stand there forever? Go!" he said.

I knew something was wrong in that house. The old woman explained that the man was her son, Jumaa. He had been away a long time, she said, seeing the world, gaining experience. But in the days that followed I discovered that Jumaa had not been wandering the world at all. He had just been released from jail in Wad Medani, on the Blue Nile. And the fat cigarette was *bongo*, cannabis. Jumaa was a drug addict. No one talked about the crime he had committed. The mother, meanwhile, distilled and sold *aragi*. I contemplated leaving the house but decided it was unbecoming of me to do so before the circumcision party had taken place.

The day of the circumcision feast arrived. Women gathered in the rooms and courtyard at the venue, cooking food and serving it. Young men carried the dishes on large aluminium trays and presented the food to groups of invited men. Then the place was swept clean by old women, and chairs, hired from a local café, were arranged in the large courtyard where the dance was due to begin under bright electric light. A band arrived, all male, city-style, with lutes, violins and small drums, more elaborate than the entertainment at my own circumcision. Women and young girls sat on large mats facing the band.

The girls of Kassala, then and now, are famous for their beauty. I wondered if it was thanks to the abundance of fruit and vegetables in the region. I watched them intently but, knowing now what one of them looked like naked made me shyer than before. When they danced, I noticed a difference between what I saw here in the town and what I knew back at Khashm el Girba. It was free women who danced here, not ex-slave courtesans as at home. And yet the Kassala dancers, with all their beauty and affluence, were no match for their counterparts in Khashm el Girba. They were less spontaneous, and less sexual. None of them knew how to bend their head back until it rested on their hips, as the courtesans of Khashm el Girba did.

Suddenly the figure of Jumaa broke into the dancing arena. Huge and hirsute and still clad only in white shorts. Everyone stood stock-still. My premonition was about to be proven true. In his hand was a butcher's knife. His head turned left and right. He was looking for someone. And soon he found her: it was his own mother. He lunged towards her, running into the crowd of women. She ran from the house and through the narrow alleyways. I took off for the forest by the Gash river, the only place I felt safe.

How could a man raise a hand against his parent? "The Lord has decreed you worship none but Him," says the Qur'an, "and that you be kind to parents." And again, "Whether one or both of them attain old age in thy life, say not to them a word of contempt, nor repel them, but address them in terms of honour." On one occasion the Prophet Muhammad – peace be upon him – was asked by one of his disciples who deserved the best of his company?" The Prophet replied "Your mother."

"Then who?" asked the man.

"Your mother," answered the Prophet.

"Then who?"

"Your mother."

"Then who?"

"Then your father," answered the Prophet.

As Jumaa hurled himself into the crowd, his knife flashing, everyone ran for their lives. Not a single man stood up against the madman. He was left free to deal with his mother as he wished, right before the other men's eyes. He inflicted some wounds on her but cut himself due to his clumsiness with the butcher's knife and his mother managed to escape to a neighbour's house. Jumaa returned to the family house and fell asleep. The case was never reported to the police.

I left that place as soon as I could. How I hated city people and city life. Better the hyenas of the forest, I decided, than the hyenas of the town. The only thing I wanted from them was their schools.

SCHOOLDAYS

MY BIRTH CERTIFICATE

We were just completing the fourth and final year of Kassala Government Intermediate School and were soon to sit for the secondary school entry examination. An important requirement for this examination was a birth certificate, or an official assessment of date of birth. Of course I did not have a birth certificate, so I had to go to the hospital to see a doctor for an informed guess of my birth date.

The doctor was an Egyptian Copt, a portly type in his forties. He had a completely bald head, pink, the same colour as his face.

"What's your name?" he asked, holding a pen in his right hand while his left hand rested on a paper laid before him.

"Hamid Ahmed Dirar," I said.

"Any relation to the Dirars of Port Sudan and Suakin?" he asked.

"No, not that I know of," I answered.

"Well, Hamid, when do you think you were born?" the doctor asked.

"In the Year of the Bombs," I said confidently.

"I beg your pardon?"

"The Year of the Bombs, sir," I answered.

"Year of the what? Bombs?" He asked, putting down the pen. "You say it as if I am supposed to know this year of the... Bombs."

"Well, sir, that's what my family always said. I was born in the Year of the Bombs, they told me."

"So where do you come from?" he asked.

"Shehateib, sir."

"Where is that?" the doctor asked.

"Close to Shangil Bangil and Karai Kadan; near the Blue Bridge."

"Now tell me about the Year of the Bombs," said the doctor.

"My people say in that year airplanes flew over the area dropping bombs around the bridge which made people run away along the riverbeds," I said.

"Very well," said the doctor. "So you were born on the first of January of the year of our Lord 1940". I protested because that was the same date he had assigned a moment ago to my friend Abdel Hameed Jabr whom everyone knew was much older than I. But I was ignored. The first of January 1940 became my birth date.

SMUGGLERS

The secondary school entrance examination over, I returned for a time to my nomadic life with the Dumans. Our camp was now located at Kireib Assi. I went about the business of tending the big flock of sheep and goats in the ups and downs of the *karab*. One late afternoon when I brought the herd home, I noticed in the nearby creek two camels I had not seen before. At first I thought we must have guests that day, but as I approached the tents I saw no signs of a guest either in the house or under the trees around it.

I unslung my *ferwa* – a sheepskin sling – from my shoulder and put it down at the tent. I had tied the four legs of it to use as straps over my shoulder. The sling contained a new-born lamb and the empty aluminium vessel in which I used to carry the thick sorghum dumpling I took for food as I followed the flock. I summoned Jenna, Sheikh Annour's daughter, to take care of the lamb and descended to the creek to cut some branches to mend broken parts of the *zariba* enclosure.

SCHOOLDAYS

I was adding the last thorns to the weak points of the enclosure when I saw Sheikh Annour heading towards me from the other end of the camp.

"Hamid, I would like to have a word with you," he said.

"Yes, sir," I said

We moved away from the *zariba* and its dung-strewn surroundings to a small elevated space, which had once been a *karab* but was worn down now by water erosion.

"My son," said Sheikh Annour, addressing me formally, "there are things in a man's life that one has to give a special attention to. Every now and then a man should stop to think and plan his life. That makes him differ from all kinds of other creatures of Allah."

"For instance," he continued, "how old are you now? Fifteen, sixteen?"

"Sixteen, sir," I said proudly.

"By nomad standards, as you well know, you are a fully grown man and have responsibilites to shoulder for the community and for your own self," said Sheikh Annour. He continued:

"Hamid, you know I consider you my son, the brother of my daughters, and you know that I would like you to lead a happy and prosperous life. I know you well and you are a resourceful young man. As a nomad, you could do better than most young men in the usual daily activities of nomadic life. You are successful as a nomad just as you are successful in your schooling."

I was wondering what Sheikh Annour had in mind.

"By our standards, you should have already entertained the idea of getting married. This is something inevitable; it is in the nature of men."

Ah. Was that the issue?

"But married life is one of the responsibilities and obligations that demand a reliable source of income. Naturally you would think of raising a flock of sheep, but that requires capital and time. If you decide to raise a flock from the few ewes that you have now, that would be a very long and tedious job. So the best way is to get some capital in the shortest time possible."

Indeed, I agreed, to make money and invest it in sheep would be the smartest way of raising a flock within a short time.

"There is, son, one way of achieving this," said Sheikh Annour. "And that's why I am here talking to you, to tell you how. You are luckier than all of us in that you have erased your illiteracy. But, the way I see it, going to school on and on is not going to provide you with a living."

I could only concur. In this matter, though, both Sheikh Annour and myself were mistaken. He had not grasped the full potential of education as a route to wealth – to becoming a doctor, an engineer, an agriculturist, a veterinarian, or a lawyer. And, at this point, neither had I. The possibility had not crossed my mind in my endeavour to educate myself. Never had I thought of education as a possible source of income, as a livelihood. What motivated me was simply the pursuit of understanding. Meanwhile, for Sheikh Annour, my education was a matter of bringing prestige to the family and the tribe, and the useful fact that I could write or read letters for him and follow him from tribe to tribe to collect taxes, marking the names of those who paid on the list in a large ledger that he carried with him.

"Tomorrow, son, we are going on a mission," Sheikh Annour returned to his theme. "One that is fit for brave men of nomadic upbringing who are not afraid of dangerous tasks. We are going on a *barashot* – parachute – mission. On a smuggling expedition."

Ah! The camels! That was why they were there. I had never figured out why the nomads referred to such ventures as "parachutes", but my mind was racing.

"We will be going into Al Habasha – Ethiopia – then into Eritrea," he said. "Our relatives the Nawayma are there in the area of Abu Gamul, near the border, and they will help us. You will meet your aunt Zeinab there. We'll bring back goods and sell them at a high price. And then you will be able to make enough money to begin an independent life."

I saw myself in skirmishes then with the Sudanese Police, especially the celebrated Shawish Khidir of Kassala. Or maybe in a fight with Haile Selassie's gendarmes, or with the Baza warriors with their huge shields and spears. I had heard of the dangers involved in smuggling and the difficulties that smugglers met with. But I had also heard that Haile Selassie's Ethiopia was a place full of cheap goods and beautiful girls.

"As you know," Sheikh Annour continued, "your uncle Muhammad is hospitalized and your uncle Ali is working with the Lahawin as a camelherd. I've just come from Misslih and he agreed that his son Abdallah would take care of the flock in your absence. I have also borrowed two camels from friends in Shagarab village. They're there down by the creek."

Sheikh Annour asked me to collect the camels from the creek and bring their bridles and saddles from the tent. I raced down to fetch the camels and found them nipping at the topmost twigs of the bushes – the dove branches, as we called them – swishing their tails as camels do, to repel insects. I put a noose with a running knot at one end of the bridle and put it over the first camel's head. I tightened the slip knot around its neck and undid the hobble from its front legs. Then the second camel. They were unusually easy to control. Normally camels protested and took some persuading. But these were smuggler's camels, quiet, obedient, fast and strong.

By dawn the following day, Sheikh Annour and I were on our way to Shehateib. Here he had recruited two more men: Taha, an experienced old smuggler who knew the roads, and Jubar, a strong young man, a man of proven courage. We tried but failed to find a third member for our party, a man called Amran, an expert in tribal genealogies and the languages of the area.

I was given a sword and a shield, which I hung on the front pommel of my saddle. We packed coffee beans, tea and sugar and left Shehateib at dusk, travelling at an easy gallop eastwards. We traversed the railway line at a point just south of Hajiz station, following a road that cut through the steep up-and-down of the *karab* where it merged with the flat clay plain. At Mirmidayeb creek there was a sprawling Kimeilab Hadendowa camp. These were cattle-owning Hadendowa. They gave us porridge with milk. Then Jubar made us all tea, which was much savoured by our hosts. They told me that my father was a few miles to the north-west at another Kimeilab camp. But I felt completely detached from him now – and from my mother too.

The night was moonlit and a cool summer breeze blew across the land as we urged our silent camels on. Eventually we moved beyond the eroded terrain of the *karab* and entered the clay plain and the thick, thorny *kitir* forest. Here we bivouacked in a glade among the trees. The saddles were down and the camels had their folded front legs toggled together. I cleared away some of the grass and fallen leaves and twigs from the ground near my saddle and went to sleep on the bare ground. At dawn we were preparing to set off when Taha called me over to the fireplace. He gave me an enamel mug of tea. Then he took a piece of solid porridge from his saddlebag, proffering it with a gnarled and deformed finger.

"Here, *effendi*, take this cake," he said.

Effendi. It was a Turko-Egyptian word denoting a delicate school-educated government official. Taha addressing me in this fashion put me in confusion. I had been leading a full nomadic life. I had not thought of school for two months. The word *effendi* made me suddenly acutely aware of the tension between my two lives. What would my schoolmates, my classmates, be doing at that moment? Reading a book? How many of them were riding camels in the wilderness, toting swords, on a smuggling expedition? And which of those two lives was I destined to lead? The life of the pen or the sword? The car or the camel? The life of the *effendi* in clean, ironed pantaloons and a white shirt? Or the life of the nomad in a dirt-soaked *tob*?

For now, anyway, it was the way of the nomad. I had to go through with my apprenticeship in smuggling. I was vague about the implications, legal and otherwise. What was a border, anyway? I had no papers. I did not know what a passport was.

HOW TAHA LOST HIS FOREFINGER

Taha's deformed forefinger had a story behind it. Before Mr Paul, the British district commissioner, gave the slaves in the area their freedom, the nomad families at Shehateib, like all others, had their slaves. Among the slaves of Ukasha was a beautiful young teenage girl. Each night she was visited by a young slave boy from across the river. Ukasha knew and did not mind. Such slave boys were sometimes borrowed or hired from their masters to sire children from slave women. Strong offspring were helpful for menial work and as fighters in tribal wars.

The two fell in love. The boy had heard of the freedom given to slaves by the British rulers. So he planned an elopement with the girl to Khartoum. They sneaked out of the camp, waded across the ford and, following the west bank forest, travelled on foot north westwards the whole night till their feet were swollen. But their escape plan was doomed. A journey to Khartoum would take many, many days on foot. And back at Shehateib, camel riders left the camp and picked up the tracks of the fleeing slaves. The riders were Ukasha, Zeidan and Taha. Before long they caught up with the runaways. The boy put up a fight using just a club against swords and shields. But he and the girl were captured and tied up. In the night he was able to free himself. He and the girl slipped away again. And this time he took Ukasha's sword. Once again they were pursued and caught. But this time the slave boy wounded Taha, cutting his forefinger to half its length. This was the finger that he had extended towards me over the fire with the cake of porridge, calling me "effendi".

Nobody heard of the slave boy again. And nobody asked about him.

SHEIKH ANNOUR THE PEACEMAKER

The second person in the company, my childhood friend Jubar, was from one of the most prominent Humran families. The Humran were celebrated as hunters, of elephant, rhino and buffalo. Later I learned that the explorer Samuel Baker had written about them. And they were famous because of Tajuj and Mahalag, the star-crossed lovers whose story is famous throughout Sudan, depicted in poetry and songs – and on film.

Jubar's family gained fame among their tribe because of their grandfather Abu Makna. In Abu Makna's day the leader of the tribe was Sheikh al Hakin. Autocratic and unchallenged, Sheikh al Hakin had a young nanny goat, as a pet, that he loved. He fixed a collar to its neck with a bundle of salt and pepper. It was a challenge to all not to kill and eat it. No one would have the courage to do that, he said. The goat wreaked havoc in the camp for months. One day Abu Makna was drinking *merissa* at the hut of a slave woman who sold beer, when the goat wandered into the hut looking for food. Ah, thought Abu Makna, Allah himself had sent him meat on a silver platter.

"Whose goat is this?" he asked the lady of the hut.

"This is al Hakin's pet goat," she replied.

"And what's that hanging from its neck? An amulet?" he asked.

"No, Abu Makna. That's salt and pepper," said the beer brewer.

"What for?" he asked.

"Abu Makna, you will be damned if you touch that goat," she said. "The sheikh said no one would have the courage to kill his goat. And he hung the salt and pepper as a warning."

"Is that what he said?" asked Abu Makna

"Yes, that's what he said."

Then Abu Makna took out his knife and killed the goat and said "Kindle the fire, woman."

The news of Abu Makna's transgression travelled fast. A messenger arrived.

"The sheikh wants to see you, Abu Makna," said the messenger.

"Not till I have finished the delicious meat of his goat," said Abu Makna.

When Abu Makna finally appeared before the sheikh, he was carrying a spear, his *tob* trailing behind him. Sheikh al Hakin was sitting on an *angareib* under the shade of a tree. As Abu Makna came closer he threw the spear. It landed in the ground between

Sheikh al Hakin's legs.

Abu Makna was ready to fight the Sheikh, but the Sheikh just smiled. "I was looking for a man like you," he said. "Someone brave enough to defy me. Welcome."

And that, they said, was how Jubar's grandfather became one of the Sheikh's trusted men.

Then there was my uncle, Sheikh Annour. I began to understand how he had become a leader. He was brought up close to the Abu Sin family, the undisputed leaders of the Shukriya. In his youth he worked with Sheikh Awad el Karim Abu Sin as a *muhafiz*, one of the sheikh's police. Sheikh Annour's *tob* was always very white, clean and perfumed. His daughters said he shaved and applied scent twice a day. His favorite perfume throughout his life was Fleur d'Amour, from Paris.

He had a relationship with the most sought-after slave courtesan in the region, Taya um Hujoul, Taya of the Bangles. He was a friend of the famous Nawayma poet, Abdallah wad al Awad. Songs were written about him. But he was also dedicated to administration, to the proper conduct of tribal governance. He was a master of words. My stepfather Rajab once said, "By God, if Sheikh Annour were to praise death for you, you would wonder why in the world you should keep on living!" Yet Sheikh Annour did not know how to write.

Sheikh Abu Sin called Sheikh Annour *Khalig Ruhu* – the man who created himself. He made him sheikh of the Arab tribes on the east bank of the River Atbara, then sheikh of Khashm el Girba itself, the seat of the tribal government. Sheikh Annour presided over many meetings to make peace between one tribe and another – and between men and their wives. He was devoted to that kind of life, solving problems by dialogue, poor throughout his life, never making money beyond that which guaranteed a decent subsistence for his daughters.

And now, here I was setting out with him on a smuggling expedition.

We moved on eastwards, travelling through the *kitir* forest, till noontime when it became too hot for us to proceed. We unsaddled at a dry water hole, which had large shady trees. I felt the place looked like it abounded with game and so I took a tour to explore. I was astonished at the number of jackals, hares and guinea fowl that I aroused from under the trees. I wished I had my dogs with me.

When we decided to move again, Sheikh Annour asked me to hand him his *gemiss*. As I took the garment, an object fell to the ground. It was a *tabanji*, a hand gun. So it seemed it was not just swords and daggers that we would be depending on.

At Abu Gamul we stayed as guests with Ibrahim wad Salem and his wife *Khalti* Zeinab, Sheikh Annour's niece. *Khalti* Zeinab criticized her uncle for turning me into a smuggler, with all the dangers that surrounded that kind of life. She insisted that I was too young to go deeper into Eritrea. Her arguments prevailed so, after all the trouble of travelling that I went through, I missed the most interesting part of the mission.

Two days later the party returned with loads of coffee beans, sugar, calico and jute sacks. Then, on the way back towards Kireib Assi, travelling in the dark, my camel nearly stepped on a snake. From its sound I knew it was a *washasha*, a rattlesnake, the snake that had nearly killed my father. The camel lurched and threw me onto the terrible thorns of the *kitir* and for a moment I thought I would fall onto the *washasha*'s open jaws. But the camel righted itself. I left half of my *gemiss* fluttering on the thorn trees, but I escaped the bite of the snake.

When we arrived at Khashm el Girba I handed over the camel

and its burden to Sheikh Annour. I heard no more about the idea of accumulating capital, or the need to get married. Had *Khalti* Zeinab changed his mind? Or was it because I had not accompanied them on the final leg of the expedition to Ethiopia? Had he felt that I was not wholehearted about the project? I did not know myself. Should I raise a flock? And might I then get married to one of Sheikh Annour's five daughters, beautiful and well-tempered as they were?

In fact, many years later, that is what I did, but that is beyond the scope of this narrative.

OUR PRIVATE ZOO

I was on a visit to Khidir and Daw at their home in the village when we had the idea of establishing a zoo. There was plenty of time to find wild animals while we were grazing the sheep. I began with hares. I took no dogs with me. The hares had to be caught alive in their burrows. If the tracks were fresh that would mean that the hare was in all probability inside. Sometimes I would find the track of a snake and move on. Using my robe as a protective glove I pulled the hare, squealing, from its den. That summer I caught six hares, some of which we ate.

Next I turned to catching monkeys on the banks of the river gorge just below Mr Paul's old rest-house. Close to the rest-house among the tamarind trees I found a family of baboons with their young holding on to the bellies of their mothers, upside-down. To hunt baboons I needed dogs. When I brought dogs the baboons took off to the rocky banks and tamarind forests. The dogs harassed the biggest of them. They put up a fight, but I was not worried about that; my dogs were well-trained. As the baboons fell back towards the river in disarray, I kept an eye on the movements of the baby-carrying mothers. When I found an isolated one, I called the attention of the dogs to her and when they converged on her, she dropped her young so it could hide. The mother decoyed the dogs away from her young. But I sneaked stealthily towards the hiding place of the young monkey and grasped it by the neck. I put a soft cotton rope around its waist and took it to the village. Now our home zoo had a monkey too.

Next came the turn of the crocodiles – baby crocodiles, of course. I knew I would find them in the same area as the baboons, along the waterline of the deep pond of Um Aswad. For days I patrolled the shoreline for these reptiles. The steep rocky banks of this stretch of the gorge were dangerous. If I ventured into the water, or slipped, the adult crocodiles could take me. I would rest on a rocky bluff on the edge of the water, called Hajar El Magass, Scale Rock. The British had cut it into the shape of an obelisk and made measurement scales on it to monitor the water level. From here I could watch the crocodiles in the pool converging on their prey. There was no way for me to catch an adult crocodile, though, and if I could it was sure to be taken from our zoo and eaten at the camp. I'd eaten delicious crocodile meat back at Shehateib once.

Finally I found a litter of newly-hatched crocodiles by the waterline in a small inlet hidden by rocks and overarching tree branches that touched the water. I took off my *gemiss* and made a bag of it, then carefully approached the unsuspecting little ones. Holding each by the tail, I picked a few of them one by one and threw them into the improvised bag. In the village Daw and Khidir prepared a trough full of water for the new members of the zoo.

To try and catch jackals, I moved to Kireib Assi with my sheep and my three dogs, Shibbilu, Sabra and Gadirin. The first four jackals we caught were injured by the dogs and I had to slaughter them for meat. With just one dog, Gadirin, I caught another. After a long struggle, though, Gadirin and I fell exhausted to the ground and watched the animal walk away. I was never able to catch a jackal for the zoo, though I supplied a fox with a broken leg, which I snared in its burrow, and a kite which I found caught in the undergrowth of a *sidir* forest. The kite had been chasing a rat when its wings got entangled in the thorny branches.

I made a study of the habits of the *rewina* gazelle. I agreed that the other boys could come with me to hunt them, with their dogs. I thought I could make use of Khidir, the oldest and fastest of us, to catch up with the dogs before they killed the gazelle if they caught one. We spotted the *rewina* and the leader buck stared at us. The whole herd now stampeded off and our six dogs followed. Our battleground, Kireib Assi, was all knolls and creeks, Khidir was leading the chase; I followed him closely, but Daw was way behind. I was carrying my throwing stick and sporting an arm knife.

Shortly after, the dogs came back on their tracks chasing a *jedi* fawn. That made things much easier for us. As the animal saw us it veered left followed by the dogs. We followed this time at a shorter distance. The fawn came to a high bank where the watercourse made a turn. Having no other choice, it jumped over the bank and onto the sands of the empty bed of the creek where its legs became stuck. Before it could free itself the dogs were on its back and so were we a moment later.

Khidir scared the dogs away and took the fawn in his hands. When I arrived I found him turning the long neck of the gazelle from side to side as if trying to wake it up from a swoon. The neck, I noticed, was limp. Clearly the fawn was going to die soon and unless we slaughtered it immediately we would lose the meat, as Muslims could not eat the meat of animals that were not properly slaughtered.

I grabbed the animal from the hands of Khidir, unsheathed my arm knife, and turned the animal's neck towards Mecca. I said *Allah u-Akbar*, and slaughtered it.

Khidir jumped up to his feet, completely shocked by what I had just done.

"You horrible nomad! What have you done?" he shouted at me, bracing himself to fight. He held his stick firmly but I was ready for him, with a knife in my hand dripping blood.

At first I did not grasp the cause of Khidir's anger. When I realized that he was protesting against my slaughtering the fawn, I said:

"Khidir, you are nothing but another village sissy! The animal was going to die on your hands and be lost to us. We don't always catch a gazelle, you know!" I said.

"You dumb fool!" Khidir screamed at me. "All you think of is meat."

"Yes, of course, I do. Don't you think a properly slaughtered animal is better than one that just dies anyway?" I said.

"The gazelle was not going to die. You killed the poor little thing. You killed it," Khidir almost cried.

"Poor thing? What are you talking about?"

I was astonished. It was the first time I had a direct clash with a village-dweller. It was the collision between two different cultures. I thought I did what any realistic nomad would have done. Khidir thought I was just being cruel. Yet I knew that being cruel was not one of my traits.

Daw was there now and seeing us locking eyes, he calmed

us down. I slung the trophy on my shoulder and at the village I skinned it and Um Ashawish, the boys' grandmother, roasted the meat for us. Khidir did not eat it. The incident marked the end of the zoo project.

HUNTING BY MOONLIGHT

A full moon loomed large and orange on the eastern horizon. It was a few moments after dusk. *Khali* Ali and I had decided on moonlight hunting that night. I milked the flock early in the evening and we ate as usual out in the open space close to the *zariba*. In less than two hours after sunset all the camp was asleep, old and young. I corralled the animals and fed the dogs a little milk in preparation for the outing. But only a little. They had to be hungry if they were to excel.

Hunting was both a necessity and a means of passing the sultry summer nights. It was one of my favourite activities – perhaps I got this from my father. *Khali* Ali knew that. He was a natural hunter. Night hunting relied on the intelligence of the hunter and the discipline of his dogs. Since the preceding day had been exceptionally hot, *Khali* Ali said, wild animals from the distant clay plain waaras should be now heading for the river to drink. By the time they reached the river they would find us waiting for them there.

At the river we took a hiding place on the high bank overlooking the water, in the night shadows of the forest trees. Our dogs, now unleashed, lay there with cocked ears to detect the slightest move. The surface of the river glinted steel-grey in the moonlight. The water murmured as it slid away towards Pigeon Rock. Water had receded from the most of the riverbed leaving only expanses of closely packed grey stones worn flat by water. We waited there. Nothing happened. The dogs stayed as still as Nubian statues, panting faintly, their long tongues falling limp outside their jaws. Now and then I would pet them to keep them quiet and alert.

Suddenly, all at once, they pulled in their hanging tongues, raised their heads, pricked their ears in the same direction and dashed like arrows towards some mark invisible to us. We grabbed our sticks and raced after them. We could see neither hunters nor prey. We had no idea what the quarry was. It was unlikely to be a gazelle or a hare, which were not usually encountered at night in these parts. And a wild cat would not take that long to pursue before it climbed up a tree. Experience said that the animal we were chasing was a jackal. The sound of the chase grew louder, which meant that the prey had turned back on its tracks and was heading towards us. We could hear the small dry twigs snapping, and a sharp agonized whine. I recognized our dog Gadirin's voice, and wondered what could have happened. A porcupine? A moment later the whining stopped.

It was indeed a jackal. By the time we reached the *khor* the dogs had caught it. We pried them away from the prey and slaughtered it. Our big golden-furred dog, Gadirin, carried a deep gash as if he had been stabbed with a knife. *Khali* Ali slung the trophy on his shoulder. We decided to return through Kireib Assi, to see if our luck would hold there. It was dangerous, but we knew the camp could use more meat. We had three dogs and knives and sticks, enough to deal with hyenas, unless we were conforted by a hungry pack.

Close to the river forest the *khor* was rocky – huge boulders overgrown with the tall rush-like *tumam* and *merikh* plants and *sayal* and *sidir* trees. Now the dogs were chasing another jackal.

There was a crash close by my left shoulder and *Khali* Ali tugged at the robe I was wearing and pulled me violently away from a growling hyena. With a barrage of stones we scared the hyena away. Now we had two jackal carcasses. Finally the dogs cornered a wild cat, a *git*, and chased it up a tree. *Khali* Ali threw a stone at the cat as it stood silhouetted against the moon. As it jumped down the dogs were on it. We freed it from the teeth of the dogs and slaughtered it.

We arrived back at the camp that night carrying plenty of game. We woke up the camp. Women immediately set to cooking the meat. By dawn everyone, including half-awake children, had regaled themselves on the flesh of the jackal and the cat. I gave the dogs some milk. The dogs never ate cats – or jackals, their canid relatives. Only humans ate them.

BACK TO SCHOOL ONCE MORE

I asked my friend Abdallah wad Misslih to take care of my flock so I could make a journey to the railway station at Khashm el Girba. I was hoping to find a schoolmate who could give me information about the result of the examination we had sat half a year before. I did not look like a school student anymore. In my dirty shepherd's attire, with sun-baked skin and unkempt hair, a heavy stick in my hand and a knife round my arm and a sheep-skin sling over on my left shoulder, there was a good chance none of my schoolmates would recognize me. I searched the six o'clock train carriage by carriage. Students would be in third class if they had official travel warrants, and in fourth class if they had to buy their own tickets.

I had finished searching fourth class without any luck when

I heard someone call my name from behind. I looked over my shoulder to see Sheikh Ali Umara Abu Sin and a group of nomads from Asubri. The sheikh and his entourage were waiting for the ten o'clock train to take them to Gedaref for a tribal court meeting.

"Wad Dirar," said Sheikh Ali Umara Abu Sin, addressing me as the son of my father, "how come you are still here? Haven't you heard? You have been admitted to Port Sudan Government Secondary School; your name was on the radio two months ago."

"But now," he added, "I wonder if they will still take you."

The news fell on me like a thunderbolt. Two months and I had not heard. And now I discovered the fact by chance, I turned on my heels and took off running towards the camp. Who could help me? My father? Only Allah and Sheikh Annour knew his whereabouts. My mother was most likely in Andala with her children and husband. Ibrahim, my brother, was married now. He had left his wife with her grandmother at Asubri and joined the national army in Gedaref and been dispatched with his regiment to the south of the country to quell the rebellion which had broken out there the year before.

The only solution Sheikh Annour could think of was to send me to my relatives the Dirars at Asubri to ask for the money needed to go to Port Sudan. The school, I learned, demanded that students buy khaki shorts, a white shirt and brown sandals as school uniform. I needed money for that too. Nomads were never quick to sell one of their animals. They did that only after exhausting all other possibilities. Selling a goat or a sheep at Khashm el Girba would take time. Besides, the proceeds would be insufficient.

Sheikh Annour saw me off on a lorry, paying the fare and leaving me in the care of another sheikh who was travelling the same direction, accompanied by his son, an ex-schoolmate of mine who had dropped out of school. He told the sheikh to take care of me and not to lose sight of me until he had handed me over to my relatives at Asubri. At the Blue Bridge Cafés we disembarked and waited for the Khartoum lorries, which normally arrived in the afternoon. When it was lunchtime, the sheikh and his son ordered food for two and began eating. They did not invite me. This was not proper behaviour among nomads, especially when I had been consigned to their care by Sheikh Annour, but I had other things to worry about. I sat on the bank of the river with a view of Shehateib on the eastern bank, the place where I had passed so much of my life. I could see across the river the tall proud *dom* palms towering over the thick warthog-haunted forest. When I went back to the Cafés, I found a lorry had just arrived from Kassala and a number of nomads were climbing in. The sheikh and his son had already seated themselves on the cargo. I climbed up on one of the back tyres and found a seat at the centre. Moments later, a Hausa man came shouting that I should leave that place because it was his. Two sword-toting nomad ruffians told him to keep quiet. The Hausa man knew that he would be outnumbered in any quarrel with Arabs, so he kept his cool and sat beside me. I was grateful. I did not want a police case to delay my going to school. When we got to Asubri I knocked on the door of my paternal cousin Khalid Dirar. He was shrewd and quick and had always concerned himself with solving the problems of the whole Dirar clan. When I explained to him the reason of my coming he showed great sympathy. He told me my father was at Suwayil, with the Hadendowa. He said I should seek help from him first as it would be more seemly. So I went there the next day.

I saw my father only at intervals of years, but he never seemed to grow older. Here he was: the same broad-shouldered, powerfully built man. He drew my head towards him and kissed it on the crown. He introduced me to his young Hadendowa wife. Then we went to visit Fatima, my step-sister who had mothered me when I was a toddler. From the distance Fatima saw us approaching. I was wearing a white jellabiya, unlike a nomad, and from a distance she mistook me for one of the Tekruri peddlers who wandered among the nomad camps touting beads and trinkets. She wondered what business her father could have with such a person.

Even up close Fatima did not recognize me. How could she? She had not seen me for over a decade. When my father told her who I was, she gasped and collapsed on the ground. Then she threw herself on me, crying and sobbing and showering me with kisses. Fatima had given up hope of seeing me again, but she had followed the news of my feats at school with pride. She had named one of her own sons after me. And here he was – my namesake, Hamid – looking at me with his fingers in his mouth. The reality of me being there with her that moment was too much for Fatima. I was moved too, but my upbringing meant I could show no outward emotion. It confirmed what I knew: that women were more human than men.

I explained to my father the urgency which brought me to him. We were sitting inside his tent close to the entrance. His new wife, eighteen years of age, her breasts bare, was at the *murhaka* milling. She was deaf and mute. (Later, my father would marry a young woman who was blind. Later still he would marry a woman afflicted by madness who was brought to him in order for her to be exorcised. Such was my father's taste in wives.) My father showed me the goats in his corral. He explained that, as I could see from the brands on their ears – the Arabic letter *kha* – they were almost all *gatifa*s, that is to say, they were pledged to the saint in Khatmiya village, Sidi al Hassan al Mirghani, who had appointed my father his *khalifa*. Selling a *gatifa* goat, my father indicated, would be an act of sacrilege. He was trying to tell me that he hardly had any money for me.

He introduced me to the father of his new wife, "This is my son," he said.

The old man replied, "Yes, I recognize the nose!"

My father and I both had noses flatter than did the average Arab or Hadendowa. As an acne-ridden boy of sixteen, I was sensitive to this. The old man's comment lingered on in my mind. For the first time I could see the wings of my nose.

Reirit, my father's wife, brought lunch, a bowl of stiff porridge. The old man moved with his food to sit behind my father, and propped his back against father's back, facing in the exact opposite direction. I had forgotten that, in nomad custom, when a man had married the daughter of another man it was shameful for either to watch the other in the act of eating.

Just then, a girl my age appeared in the tent. A beautiful girl who was related to my father's wife, Rierit. I was mesmerised as I watched them. I felt that I had never seen someone so attractive.

My father was watching.

"Son," he said, "why don't you take that young fawn for a wife and settle down here with your father?" He told me he could go immediately to her parents and ask for her and that he was sure they would be pleased to give her to me. The mother, he said, would rather give her daughter to a man like me than to a warrior because I would provide a better living and treat them with greater respect. Indeed, he said, her mother must have thought highly of me to send her daughter here.

"And the girl herself," he concluded, "has taken to you too, as you may have noticed."

But I remembered school. And the thought of school

overwhelmed that of sex. At that moment, I recollected, my school mates were learning, acquiring new knowledge, and had been doing so for two months while I was in those forgotten backwaters.

I immediately jumped up and told my father that I had to leave right away so I could spend the night at Asubri and leave for Kassala the following morning. He showed me some emaciated sheep and an old ewe and said they were the only sheep he had.

"As you can see for yourself," he said, "none of them is marketable."

I believed him, as a son should. He was my father, after all, and a man of religion. I never asked myself how come it was that he had a new bride if he were so poor. Later I discovered that he had a large flock of sheep on better grazing ground on the west bank.

When I said goodbye to my father he gave me exactly fifty piastres, a half-pound banknote. The Sudanese pound at the time was stronger than the sterling pound. It was worth more than three US dollars. Back at Asubri Khalid gave me one hundred and eighty piastres and his father, Uncle Muhammad, sent me one more pound from his tent down the creek. I was able to glean a total of three pounds and thirty piastres. In the morning I took Wad Mahjoub's lorry to Kassala.

IV

A Wider World

A LORRY JOURNEY TO KASSALA

I prayed inwardly that Wad Mahjoub's lorry would reach Kassala in one piece. His ramshackle machine was the only vehicle serving the string of small villages and nomad camps along the Atbara River, taking passengers to and from Kassala town. It moved with agonising slowness. When would I ever arrive at Kassala in this tortoise called a lorry? Would the sum of three pounds and thirty piastres be enough to ensure all my travel and school needs? When would I get my travel warrant to Port Sudan, considering the bureaucracy of government departments? Would it be too late for me to qualify for a warrant? Would my seat at school still be vacant or had a reserve student already taken it? And how would I return home from Port Sudan if I lost the chance to enroll in school?

Wad Mahjoub's lorry, while it had gathered more than its capacity of passengers, had as yet gathered no speed. We were still on the outskirts of Asubri. The lorry seemed to be a living creature. Once we finally got moving it asked for water every few minutes, it bellowed and coughed, and, through its exhaust pipe, it excreted gouts of carbon. Wad Mahjoub insisted that it was a

Bedford. In Sudan, in those days, a Bedford lorry was called a *sifinja*, a sponge, because it rode smoothly on bumpy roads. But Wad Mahjoub's lorry bucked and kicked even on mirror-smooth trodden ground. It couldn't be a Bedford. Perhaps some kind of mutation.

We reached a desolate area where Wad Mahjoub knew that the terrain would not encourage passengers to quit the lorry. Here he stopped the car to collect our fares. He loomed over us, in his oil-stained *jellabiya*. Everything went quiet. There was no fixed rate; the trip could cost anything from nothing to half a pound. When I discovered that he had to bargain separately with every passenger, I felt my hopes of getting to school in time evaporate.

Half the passengers responded to Wad Mahjoub's call to pay the fare with variations on the lines of "Allah be my witness, I don't have even a chicken!", a chicken being the lowest denomination of currency a nomad was acquainted with. And Wad Mahjoub would reply in this manner, "Allah be my witness, you may not have a chicken but you have camels, sheep and goats. Now get that money out of your leather bags!"

Finally Wad Mahjoub returned to the driver's cabin and pulled out a long steel rod with a crooked handle and thrust it into the throat of his great mechanical beast. Again and again. But the lorry was reluctant to move. I began to think I would never make it to school that year – or the year after. Then, finally, the vehicle began to crawl. *Assayga, wassla*, said Wad Mahjoub – what keeps on walking will reach its destination.

At the tail-gate of the car, the goats and the sheep were floundering in their own excrement. The chickens were hung up along the top railing of the body frame of the car and dangled there with their beaks pointing earthwards, their cloacae skywards. Jireiwa, the chicken merchant, continually inspected and watered his money-makers. He had an *ibrig* full of water, which he used to put a drop into the tiny craters of the cloacae, to stop the birds drying up and dying. Once in a while they would come alive and spray acrid liquid into Jireiwa's face. I looked down from my high perch on the top of the cabin at the ruck of people in the car. Some were leaning against the railing, others squatting on their leather bags, some lying down. Most looked happy enough, but a few, new to the experience, looked tense and sick.

On the road ahead three women were standing by the roadside clearly waiting for transportation. When we reached them, Wad Mahjoub stopped the lorry, killed the engine and opened the hood, shoring it up with a stout stick and opening the radiator, which sent out a whale-spray of steam. It was only then that he turned to the women. The older one, about fifty years old, climbed up like a leopard. She was clearly the kind that could look a man in the eye with defiance. Wad Mahjoub looked worried. He had thought he was going to take all three women or at least two of them. But he wound up taking one single woman. She was the only woman in the car. One woman in the car would certainly mean trouble; the car would run into problems. That was what people believed. I saw Wad Mahjoub look around for a rock. When he found it he put the rock, as unobtrusively as he could, inside the car close to the goats. That was intended to balance and nullify the ill effect of a lone woman passenger. This practice, Wad Mahjoub told me quietly, had been successful throughout the Sudan.

Besides its appetite for water and fuel Wad Mahjoub's lorry also took snuff, though some might say this was to stop a leak. I watched as he took a big wad of tobacco from his cylindrical canister, the *hugga*, and instead of tucking it in his own mouth stuffed it into the radiator. As we proceeded some of the men shouted out lines of poetry that had been composed to urge camels to travel faster. Descending the rough road towards the Blue Bridge Wad Mahjoub's lorry brought forth its whole complement of cries: howling, barking, shrieking, crowing, creaking and squealing like a bag of mice.

Finally we arrived at the Blue Bridge Cafes, but few of us could eat. The lorry duly crossed the Blue Bridge, but when we came to the Timber Bridge a driveshaft snapped. Now we were stuck. The car had come to halt on a rising slope. And it had no handbrake. Wad Mahjoub engaged the gears but they kept slipping. He asked a front-seat passenger to apply his foot to the brakes while he looked for a rock to place behind the tire.

At this point the only woman passenger picked up the rock that Wad Mahjoub had put on board to ward off the trouble she might bring.

"Wad Mahjoub, here! You can put this rock to better use now that it failed to do its original job," she said.

Wad Mahjoub took an axe from behind the driver's seat and cut a green *sayal* pole from the forest. He spliced it to the broken shaft with wire rope and the beast rolled on again. Night fell when we were still ten miles short of Kassala. Wad Mahjoub turned on the headlights by manually connecting two bare wires, after chasing the spiders away. The headlights did not always point forwards. They swivelled independently like a chameleon's eyes, chasing each other across the dark like searchlights. But Wad Mahjoub persevered, narrowly avoiding collisions with a number of trees along the road.

And we arrived. I couldn't believe that I was finally at Kassala again. I fumbled in my pocket to check for my money, Now, after paying the fare, it had dwindled to less than three pounds. But I was heartened to find the money was still there. Suppose it had been stolen or otherwise lost! That would have been a disaster and would have certainly put an end to my schooling. Everything about my education always seemed so fragile and precarious.

I clutched my money in my hand, tucked it in my pocket and quickly made my way to the mosque. This lay close to the hospital, not far from the market place where the lorry had dropped us. I thought I would spend the night there, as I had nowhere else to go. Then, in the morning I could go see *Khali* Umhummad. I found the mosque locked which meant that no one was allowed to sleep inside. I lay down to sleep on the door steps on the western side, away from the market and streets. I cleaned my sleeping place, like any nomad, and stretched myself out there on the ground with my head resting on the step.

But before I had gone to sleep a man in ragged clothes, perhaps a beggar, came and took his sleeping place about two metres away from me. I was worried about my money now and jumped up. But the man said "Don't be alarmed, my son; I mean you no harm, Allah be my witness." It turned out he was one of the dervishes who shunned material life and devoted themselves to the service of Allah.

When I woke up in the early morning I was grey with dust lying among beggars. While I saw little shame in it, being raised in a poor nomadic community, I knew that townfolk would disapprove. I could have stayed with one of the families of my schoolmates but I was too wild, too unsociable and too proud to demean myself by asking such favours.

The first thing I did that morning in Kassala was to speak to *Khali* Umhummad over the wall of the hospital where he was a patient. After the usual salutation, I told him about my intention to go to Port Sudan to continue my education. Then I left him to go seek my travel warrants. At the Bureau of Education in the Kara quarter of the city I got my travel warrants and descended to the market place where I bought my school uniform. By the time I received my tailored new clothes I discovered that I had run completely out of money. Late in the afternoon I went to see *Khali* Umhummad again to bid him farewell before I left to the railway station. I told him I had to move now as the distance to walk was very long. Thus he discovered that I did not have money even for the bus. As I turned to leave, he said, "Wait!" He then undid a small knot at the corner of his *tob* and took out a hexagonal piece of coin, a *freeny*, worth two piastres, and gave it to me. It was all the money he had.

I took the two piastres and ran to the market place where I bought a cup of tea with milk and half a loaf. I never thought that that would be the last time I saw *Khali* Umhummad. But he passed away just a few weeks later, "expectorating bits and pieces of his lungs", as Zeena described it to me later.

I set out on the four-kilometre walk carrying a small tinplate trunk containing a few pieces of clothes and a large, new notebook. But when I had walked for half an hour and had crossed the bridge on the Gash River, I was drained of all energy. I began to shake and my knees gave way. I felt I was going to pass out and sat down lest I should fall. People walked by along the road, unaware of my ordeal. A thought crossed my mind then: why not ask these people for a little food? But I did not know them; they were all townfolk, wearing loose trousers and shirts or white *jellabiya*s. I could not ask them for food as nomads did.

A Zibeidi man walked past me. I greeted him. The man walked on without even deigning to look at me.

When I arrived at the railway station, it was already past sunset. I passed by the station canteen, a robust, solitary red brick room where a dangling shaded electric light cast oscillating shadows on the ground close to me. I sat on a concrete bench in the station yard and busied myself watching a freight train which had just arrived from Port Sudan on its way to Gedaref and Khartoum. The train from Gedaref was late, hindered by heavy rains. I was sitting alone on that concrete bench away from the crowds of passengers. The freight train pulled out of the station.

A tall, well-dressed young man approached me. But I was on the brink of collapse and in no condition to converse with others.

"May I share your seat," he asked politely.

"Oh sure," I said, making a gesture to make more room for him.

He had silky hair, as thick as horsehair. His complexion was blue-black, like a Dinka from the South. But he was a Hadendowa.

He looked at me and said "You are very hungry." Those were his words, in Arabic.

Before I had the chance to answer he headed for the canteen. When he came back he was loaded with food – enough for four.

When we finished eating, I opened my iron trunk and withdrew the large ledger-like notebook that I had cherished for the last three years and offered it to the young man in recognition of his hospitality. The notebook was so beautiful that for three years I had barely had the courage to write in it. He told me he was going to a teacher's training institute, Bakht el Rudah, on the White Nile, beyond Khartoum. Soon his train came and he left. And I was left alone with my gratitude and a full belly, watching the locomotive that had just pulled in.

Steam jetted out of slender piping, heavy black smoke billowed from the colossal engine. Lines of rivets and piping ran the length of the long boiler. At the front was a red, wedge-shaped, cow-catcher. As I watched, a gaunt mechanic in dark-blue overalls moved around the train. Sometimes he ran along a ledge the length of the boiler, sometimes he entered the cabin to shovel coal and stoke the furnace. Or he took a long-spouted grease-gun to lubricate key places. Once in a while he would wipe his forehead with the back of his hand or mop sweat from under his chin with an oil-soaked piece of cloth that he tucked in his side pocket or draped on his shoulder. After a while he came and offered me a cup of tea.

"Where are you heading?" he asked.

"To Port Sudan," I said.

"But this train is going in the opposite direction,"

"I am waiting for the other train," I said. "We were told it would be late."

"But you won't find a seat on it," he said. "That train is a pilgrim's train. I doubt it if it'll have room for a pin."

This was a new problem. I had to reach Port Sudan. Could I climb on top of the train if there were no seats? It started to rain. I wondered if I was ever going to make it to school. I wondered why they placed me in that particular school. At the time, the Sudan had three well-established secondary schools of great fame: Hantoub, Wadi Seidna and Khor Taggat. I had expected to be admitted to Hantoub Secondary School, the nearest of the three to Khashm el Girba. But the Port Sudan Government Secondary School was where I was bound. It had been established only a year before, in 1955.

BY TRAIN TO PORT SUDAN

The train finally arrived, two hours shy of midnight. An impenetrable cluster of human beings choked the entrances to each carriage. The mechanic had been right to warn me; the train seemed impossible to board. When I tried to clamber up the steps of a third class carriage, I was thrown down.

"Get back," said someone. "Where do you think you're going?"

"Don't you have eyes in your head?" said another, "If there is room inside, would we be here? You think we like it?"

I kept pushing and shoving, trying to wedge my thin body between the passengers on the steps.

I finally wound up perched with one leg on the middle rung, holding with one hand to the short rail, the other hand holding my metal trunk in mid-air. In that position I hoped to reach Port Sudan. Even there I had to keep jostling and pushing, listening to the cascade of complaints directed at me. The train started moving. There was no change in my position. The leg I stood on had lost all feeling. When I moved the man on the top rung of the ladder, clearly an intellectual, said loudly.

"So – I see. Imperialism on a ladder! You were given a foothold and now you want to enlarge your domain!" But I did not really understand what he meant.

The conductor appeared from inside the train

"Are you going to kill yourself," he said, "hanging like a bat on this death machine?"

He dragged me up, my tinplate trunk taking toll among the others on the ladder. Then, incredibly, he found me a seat. A fellow-passenger opposite broke the ice.

"What is your name, son?"

"Hamid wad Ahmed wad Dirar," I said, in formal nomad style.

"Did you say you were the son of Ahmed wad Dirar?"

"Yes, sir," I replied.

"And you said your name is Ibrahim?"

"Hamid, sir," I said.

"Where are you heading, son?" he asked.

"To Port Sudan, to the secondary school there," I answered.

"Unbelievable! Which of Ahmed Dirar's boys are you, the younger or the older?"

"The younger, sir; my brother Ibrahim is the older one," I replied.

"Unbelievable! How is your father?"

"My father, sir? He is okay, thank you,"

"You don't remember me?"

"No sir, I am sorry."

"Was Al Hajiz station not where you used to live with Fatima, your sister, and brother and father during the rainy season?"

"Yes, sir, it was," I replied.

"Do you remember that sometimes you and your brother went to a merchant at the station to buy *ajwa* – soft dates?"

"Yes, sir, I remember that," I said.

I realised then that he was the man with the lantern who had walked with me and Ibrahim to his shop when our father gave us money to buy goods.

"I live with my maternal grandfathers now," I said.

"Oh, Omar Duman and Sheikh Annour?"

At the mention of the name Duman, an old man in the group of passengers sharing the bench with me leant forward and asked: "Did you say wad Duman, son?"

"Yes, sir, Omar and Annour are my grandfathers," I said.

"Son, we come from Um Khanjar, near Gedaref. Do you know you have relatives there?" the old man said.

"Yes I do," I said. "Sheikh Adlan and his brothers, sons of El Tom."

My cabin-mates were all pilgrims on their way to Mecca. The amount and variety of food they displayed for supper I had never seen before in my life – and I was their guest. How had the conductor happened to choose a carriage where there were people who knew me? Was it providence? Or coincidence? Or was it, once more, the Spirit of Feki Umhummad wad Beshir at work?

At a station called Salloun all the pilgrims left the train and left by road to the port of Suakin in order to cross the Red Sea to Saudi Arabia. In those days before the oil boom the Saudis were poor and lived on the money of pilgrims. So I resumed my journey to Port Sudan in an almost empty train. On arrival a Hadendowa man met me at the station and took me to the school, a set of grand limestone buildings that had been a British barracks until a few years before. The face of my friend from Kassala, Hamid Khidir, appeared through a window. No one asked why I was late for term. I settled in to the school fast. And that year in the final exam I came second of 175 boys.

But this last was not the doing of the Spirit of Feki Beshir, whatever my mother might say; it was my own hard work.

THE SMELL OF THE SEA

At Port Sudan I smelled the breeze of the sea, saw seagulls, huge ships, tug-boats and towering cranes. At the market, I saw apples for the first time. The seawater was astonishingly salty. But its pureness and limpidity was even more astonishing. In spite of the rolling ships, the water was so clear the seabed was perfectly visible. In the school swimming pool – an enclosure connected to the bay – I saw a fish with wings. "*Absot! Absot!* The whip fish!" the boys shouted. It was a giant skate, gliding in and out of the pool. And there were crabs, animals that walked sideways. I never liked them.

The streets of Port Sudan were neat and clean and the homes were beautiful and whitewashed. One of the most beautiful quarters was called Deim Medina. Then there was Deim Ramla, built of wood, the part of town that housed the brothels. For the first time I found myself living in a place where rains came in winter. There were no mosquitoes and people did not know malaria.

At the school we met African-Americans. They were sailors from the US Navy who came to play basketball. I was stunned by their height and could not understand their English. But I was keen on basketball. They talked to us about racial discrimination. Up to that point, it had never occurred to most of us that we were black. One of the poems we used to recite at that time was an insult poem about a black slave, Kafour, who freed himself from slavery and ruled over Egypt in the tenth century. He had summoned to his court Mutanabbi, the most celebrated poet in the Arab world. Mutanabbi was expecting great rewards, but Kafour gave him nothing. Mutanabbi's revenge, once he had left the country, was a poem reviling Kafour as a slave and a eunuch. It was just as well the visiting Americans could not understand it.

The school's extra-mural seminars were a great source of knowledge. We listened to talks delivered by our own teachers and by invited guest speakers. Muhammad Ali, a spirited art teacher, gave us an evening talk on the music of Tchaikovsky. He put all his talent into that talk, whistling us the tunes from

Tchaikovsky's symphonies. Our other art teacher, Giritli, had worked as a Muslim missionary in the Nuba Mountains. He gave a lecture on the art of flying flags on ships, a dull topic that he made mesmerizing.

The great poet of Port Sudan, Bazaraa, gave us readings from his poetry, some of which we knew from songs on Radio Omdurman. The selections he read for us seemed permeated with sensuality, dwelling on the breasts of young girls. Perhaps he chose them mischievously because he knew we were susceptible teenagers. The British teacher, Mr Macbeth, and the Indian teacher, Mr Salohan, debated the respective values of science and the spirit.

"How can you deny the usefulness of electricity, the telephone and the car?" asked Mr Macbeth.

"But what use are they in the hands of men with no hearts?" countered Mr Salohan.

In spite of all the good things at Port Sudan Government Secondary School, I had moments of misery. I experienced an overwhelming sense of loneliness and claustrophobia. To me the school, enclosed within a high fence of steel bars and cement structures, felt as crowded as a sardine can. Accustomed as I was to a wandering life and open expanses of land, I hated the sense of confinement. The feeling was not mitigated by the fact that the school was almost next door to the notorious Port Sudan prison.

I found solace in the school library. Here I discovered an apparently untouched collection of American novels by an author I had never heard of, Zane Grey. I was attracted by the cover pictures: mountains, open land, creeks, cattle and cowboys on horseback. It looked something like the life of a nomad in Sudan. I loved Zane Grey. It was not until more than forty years later that I discovered, to my great surprise, that he was a New York dentist, whose knowledge of the old west came mostly from books.

I was introduced to student politics and participated in strikes aimed at improving our food. Because I was punctual in doing my prayers and washing myself even in the coldest winter nights the Muslim Brothers tried to recruit me. But within a month I left them. I did not want to be controlled or indoctrinated by anyone. I wanted to be free. I excelled at military training and was selected as a cadet to go to Khartoum to get special training. I returned as lance-corporal and was assigned a platoon of students to train.

During that first year I received two letters from Daw. In the first he told me of the death of my uncle *Khali* Umhummad who had given me his last two piasters, and in the second of the death of Grandma Diya.

THE LOCUST CONTROL CAMPAIGN

I needed to defray some of the costs of my education. The long vacation fell in the months of July, August and September, the hottest and most humid months of the year at Port Sudan. Luckily those were the rainy season months back at Khashm el Girba, when work could be found.

The rainy season brought the locusts. They laid their eggs in the wet sand and soon these would hatch out as hoppers, *attab*, the wingless juvenile stage, then bands of the black and yellow insects would march across the plains, devouring every green thing in their path. If you could catch the adults before they laid their eggs, they could be roasted and eaten, a welcome protein addition to the meagre diet of the nomads. These were Desert

Locusts. They migrated the breadth of the Sahara Desert, north to ravage the irrigated croplands of the Nile valley or south to East Africa and the agricultural regions of Uganda and Kenya. For this reason there was an international organisation to coordinate their control in the countries, such as Sudan, where they bred.

The Locust Control Campaign established its seasonal headquarters at Khashm el Girba and posted notices saying it needed workers to launch its campaign in the areas along the Atbara River. I signed up and took a job as a porter, hauling large jute sacks full of locust bait from the store and loading them on a camel caravan. The bait consisted of crushed groundnut shells and beans mixed with a generous dose of the insecticide DDT, which was later subject to a global ban on account of its residual toxicity for humans and other higher forms of life.

Early in the morning the cavalcade would start moving towards the intended sites of work, as reported by scouts and nomad sheikhs or by farmers. That year our superintendent was called Sheikh Osman. He had a white Rifawi donkey and a permanent job with the Locust Campaign. He was from a more enlightened region of the country, somewhere along the Nile. The sites we worked on were in the region surrounding the village, in the sandy *khor*s and the *karab* land where the locusts usually laid their eggs. Under normal conditions we would be at the site of work after two hours' walk. Once there, we set the bait across the path of the moving insects when they were at the hopper stage. We worked for hours and hours, poisoning the whole landscape, strewing the DDT-impregnated peanut meal everywhere. And, everywhere, swarms of voracious *attab* crept over the land, devouring anything green on their way down to the bare brown soil underneath. The green creeping mass of insects gave off a sizzling sound as it swept across the ground, a green sheet that heaved like a sea, and cut the grass like a mowing machine, leaving not a touch of greenness behind.

During those years in the Atbara area, swarms of creeping locusts and caterpillars with glinting bristles were a common sight in the rainy season. Sometimes the train coming up from the Blue Bridge towards the high tableland would be stopped completely as the wheels of the locomotive slipped and turned in the slime of insects on the tracks.

At the end of the working day, on our way back to Khashm el Girba, the nomads might invite us to ride their camels. The porters did not know how to handle a camel and the camel owners were often amused as they made a spectacle of themselves. Tayeb, a young man from Jedid, a village near Khartoum, once tried to control a camel by beating it with a stick on its neck, as though it were a donkey, instead of pulling the reins. It bucked and flung him off like a sack of wool. I knew that the nomads could not be happy with strangers riding their camels. I had always loved walking, just like my father. As a shepherd and hunter, walking was part of my daily life, so I walked. But one day, returning from Andala, the camel owners insisted that I ride a camel. Perhaps they wanted to see if I could, and anticipated a comic scene.

I took the reins of the best camel. "*Ikh!*" I said, ordering the animal to sit down. Pulling the bridle down, I hopped up onto the saddle. I clucked the camel up and urged it with a "*hod*" and a rub with the leg on the neck and presently it galloped smoothly away. The group galloped to catch up with me. The owner of the camel said, "Forgive me, but by God, for an instant I thought you were a camel thief and you were running away with my camel!"

The camel men could see now that I was of nomad upbringing. They asked me who I was and where I came from. It turned out they all knew the Dirars and the Dumans, particularly my uncle Hassan Dirar, who was known widely as a saddle maker.

I was selected to man a new truck delivering bait to villages along the bank. We loaded the truck with bait at daybreak and travelled along the riverbank delivering quotas to the villages of Sharafa, Ghurashi, Tayalla, Khor Allaban, Kurraj, Gafala, Asubri, Shelakai, Gireigis, and Um Rahaw. By the time we returned it would be dark. Because I carried DDT sacks on my back for so long, my only garment was worn out and had gaping holes in the back. So I opened my brother Ibrahim's trunk containing his wedding clothes and took out a *sideiriya* to wear. I hauled sacks of DDT until Ibrahim's *sideiriya* became threadbare too.

There was a girl I liked in Asubri. I wanted to be introduced to her. But Zeinab Berberi, Ibrahim's wife, told me I looked like a ragamuffin. Zeinab had lived in Kassala for years. She had probably been boasting to her neighbours that she was married to an army soldier and that his younger brother was a high school student. It had never occurred to me that there was something wrong with my appearance. It was true that my clothes were all worn out and torn and my hair was shaggy and my body run down by labour. But I told myself that I was doing honourable work, earning my living by the sweat of my brow. I was proud of myself, working so hard to finance my education. Yet I never managed to meet the girl.

The season of 1958 was better. The Locust Control people took me on to do the books. I was to be stationed at their headquarters in Khashm el Girba. That meant many things. My work, although involving more responsibilities, was not as tough as it had been the previous year. I had time to study, and I had the social status of a white-collar job. I would not be drenched in sweat and DDT all the time. Soon I was promoted to the next rung, *mentaga*, or area officer, with a salary of twelve pounds, the highest for a seasonal employee. It was an occasion to celebrate. I bought dates, groundnuts, coffee beans and sugar for the older people in the camp. I bought a bottle of orange juice for my dogs, Shibbilu, Gadirin and Sabra. But Sheikh Annour did not approve of spoiling the dogs with such precious human food.

THE LOCUSTS' REVENGE

In the season of 1959 there was no Locust Control activity in the region of Khashm el Girba, and I lost the job the campaign had offered me the year before. So that rainy season I started growing sorghum. We had rain-fed farms at Jummeiza; and there were ample rains, so Sheikh Annour, Grandfather Omar and I went there to cultivate. The women at the camp made coarse sorghum flakes for us to take with us as work food. We each took a donkey. At Jummeiza we stayed with Aunt Nofal and her husband Tayalla. The family had a tent for the women and children and a small grass *tukul* for men and male guests.

Then at the end of the season I travelled back from the farm to Khashm el Girba to prepare to return to school in Port Sudan. I had been travelling all day and the sun was setting. When I reached Rigeig, the spot where years before I had nearly been eaten by a hyena, I noticed a strange phenomenon – a bright line on the eastern horizon towards the border with Ethiopia. It looked like sunrise but the sun had just set. As it grew closer, I took it for a dust storm coming down from the Ethiopian highlands. Yet that didn't make sense. It was late in the rainy season and not the time for a dust storm, especially from Ethiopia. I was puzzled.

In Sudan there is a genre of children's stories known as *huja*. In one of these the heroine, Fatima, known as the Red Cane, is tricked by her peers into throwing her jewellery into the river. A dust storm comes, black as night. She screams: "Wa-i!" The dust storm replies: "Huh! You say *Wa-i* in fear of me? What will you say when you see the thing that is coming behind me?" Then the dark dust storm is followed by a red dust storm. Fatima screams again: "Wa-i!" The red storm replies: "If you are saying *Wa-i* because you fear me, you should see what's coming behind." Then, after the red storm, comes a yellow storm and Fatima the Red Cane says, "Wa-i!" And the yellow storm, in its turn, says: "Don't *Wa-i* for me! Keep your *Wa-i* for who is behind me!"

Then, after the three storms, lastly comes the Ghoul, a horrendous, hideous beast feared by all beings. In my case, there in Reigeig, at the end of rains, the Ghoul seemed to be the line on the horizon, the storm of storms.

But it turned out not to be a storm at all, rather a huge swarm of locusts. It was the largest I had ever seen in all my years of locust control. The first of them slapped me on the nose and exploded. More came at speed. As they hit me they choked my ears and plastered my cheeks until I was covered from head to toe with a slimy layer of locust innards. It felt like revenge for the millions of locusts killed by the Locust Control Campaign. I can smell them now. I never ate a locust after that.

CHANGE COMES TO KHASHM EL GIRBA

Back in Port Sudan, the English teacher, Ali Khamiss, told me that the government had decided to build a dam on the Atbara at Khashm el Girba, and establish an agricultural scheme there.

It was a result of support given to the Egyptian government by General Abboud, who had come to power in a military coup in Sudan in 1958. The Aswan high dam in Egypt had created a huge lake that was displacing the town of Wadi Halfa in Sudanese Nubia, just north of the home of my ancestors. The military government decided to move the inhabitants of Wadi Halfa from there to the new agricultural project at Khashm el Girba.

The once serene settlement of Khashm el Girba began to change. Men and women from all walks of life converged on it hoping to strike it rich. The nomadic flavour of the area was destroyed. Arrivals from Khartoum, Wad Medani, Nile Province, Gedaref and Kassala came daily. New buildings were erected overnight to accommodate them – concrete buildings of more than one floor. Italians, almost naked, filled the place. Bars selling beer, whisky, brandy, gin, martini, appeared for the first time in the history of our village.

New types of crime appeared. A nomad worker was at prayer when his Italian boss kicked him in the buttocks as he kneeled. The nomad unsheathed the knife he carried on his arm, turned on his boss and cut open his belly. A woman called Hawa Lambo killed her husband with an axe and buried his corpse underneath their bed. There were crimes we never knew of before. Most shocking of all were the illegitimate babies abandoned in the rubbish dumps of the town. Such things, I had thought, were the crimes of civilization.

The ecology of the region was changed by the influx. The trees along the river were cut down to provide wood and charcoal for the newcomers, leaving the land bare. My childhood Khireissab *waara* and Shehateib *ghaba* all disappeared, and so did the warthogs. Nomadic life receded to the tree line. And the rains dwindled too. In the evenings, the town turned into a brothel. Prostitutes from a neighbouring country dominated the business. But they would not go with the Southerners – the Dinka labourers who were also, increasingly, congregating in Khashm el Girba. These tall men would tower over a prostitute's hut demanding entrance but its occupant would refuse, perhaps from racism, perhaps just because the Southerners were too poor.

Meanwhile I graduated from school. And in 1960 I was admitted to the Faculty of Science at the University of Khartoum, specializing in agriculture, to be trained to work on the new agricultural scheme at Khashm el Girba. My student days in Khartoum formed the last phase of my life before I became an adult; and it is here that the story of my childhood and youth comes to an end.

KHARTOUM IN A TIME OF REVOLUTION

The University of Khartoum, formerly Gordon Memorial College, was a hotbed of revolution. The student union, controlled alternately by the Communists and the Muslim Brothers, considered itself the guardian of freedom and democracy. From the day the military took over power from the elected government the students had taken it on themselves to topple them. The first anti-government demonstration I participated in was on 25 October 1960, three months after I enrolled. It was ostensibly in support of the Nubians who had been displaced by the rising waters of the Aswan Dam. They did not want to leave their forefathers' land in order to be resettled at Khashm el Girba as the government had ordained. I was probably the only person in the huge riot who actually came from Khashm el Girba – and before that, by ancestry, from Nubia. It was in that demonstration that

I had my first experience with tear gas. It was a lot worse than a storm of locusts.

After two years at the Faculty of Science, in 1962, I moved to Shambat, a suburb of Khartoum, to the Faculty of Agriculture. By then, despite the protests, the agricultural scheme and the displacement of the Nubians and their rehabilitation were well underway. I was home on vacation when I witnessed the arrival of the first train carrying the Nubian settlers to Khashm el Girba. The *nazir* of the Shukriya tribe amassed a huge crowd of men, many on camelback, brandishing swords and beating kettle drums, to greet the new guests of the Butana: the Halfawiyin. They were Nubians from Wadi Halfa, just north of my ancestral home.

Bottles of Coca-Cola were distributed to the displaced Halfawiyin while they were still in the train that was to take them to New Halfa (as their new home had been named). I took a look at the newcomers, as I went from car to car along the train. The women were dressed in long black dresses called *jarjar*. Their faces looked strange, though, more like Egyptians. And most of them had no eyelashes. They had lost them from rubbing their eyes to relieve the irritation caused by a tiny insect called *nimitti*. But the girls were beautiful. Although they were the people of my ancestors in Nubia, it never occurred to me that we must be related. My nomad upbringing among the Shukriya meant that I felt completely Shukri: I thought like a Shukri and acted as one.

Within minutes after the Coca-Cola was distributed – and as if well planned – the bottles came flying back to us, whistling through the air. It seemed the Halfawiyin were throwing them to express their displeasure at being removed from their land against their will. As for their hosts, the Shukriya, most of them did not support giving away part of their land to these newcomers. The great poets of the tribe composed lengthy poems lamenting the loss of the Butana to strangers.

A NEW KIND OF DEATH

Returning to the university, newly politicised, I joined enthusiastically in the student struggle against the military government. 1964 was to be our year of action. The students knew that in the South of the country the government was involved in something that we later learned to call genocide. This caused a stir in the university. The bulk of the students were from the North, only a few were from the South. And on the central campus, Southerners virtually never mixed with Northerners. In my first two years on the central campus I did not talk to a single person from the South. They never participated in student demonstrations or other communal activities. Nor, it seemed, were they interested in enlightening us on the problems in the South.

When I moved to Shambat, though, to the Faculty of Agriculture, I found things were quite different. There, the Southerners mixed with everyone else. They were sociable and vocal. Some were individualistic to the point of eccentricity. I remember them all: Alfonse, Monawah, Rubena, Bennet, Peter Tingwa, David Bassiouni, Joseph Awad Morgan and Hilary Sabit Wongo. They were popular. And we debated matters of race and ethnicity with frankness and transparency. We discussed the war in the South that was then intensifying and how it could be resolved. At Shambat Northerners and Southerners created the kind of student community that should have been the norm in the university as a whole.

On October 21, 1964, a fateful event took place. It was to be fateful for the country, and fateful for me personally. Buses were dispatched by the union to take the students from the campus at Shambat to the Central Campus for a meeting to discuss the Southern Problem, as it was then called. I did not attend the meeting myself: I was a member of the Services Committee at Shambat and the chairman, Abdallah Abu Sin – a grandson of the Sheikh who had been my great-grandfather's patron and whose family still held sway in the Butana – asked us to stay on campus to discuss some urgent issues. But the events of that day were a turning point in my political education.

Late in the evening, after my meeting with Abdallah Abu Sin had ended, I took a chair and my guitar to the bank of the Nile, which was close by my room. Everything was quiet under the tall palm trees but for the lapping of waves against the riverbank. An hour or two later, the students who went to the union meeting at Khartoum began to turn up, one by one. It struck me as odd that they should come back in that manner, one by one or in small groups. Normally, they would have arrived together by bus. As I played my guitar, one of the students came up to me.

"You don't know what's happened, do you?" he said.

I put the guitar aside.

"What is it?" I asked.

"Someone was killed at the union meeting," he said,

"What!" I said. "How did that happen?"

He told me that the government's security forces had entered the Barracks – the name, ironically, of the hostel where the meeting was held – and used live ammunition to disperse the students. The students fought back using stones, bricks and steel bars. At least one student was killed; many were wounded. As the fighting continued the women students had begun ululate. They climbed up to the second and third floors of the hostels and threw jugfuls of water down on the heads of the police. University staff members came to the Barracks to help evacuate it, but the police prevented ambulances from entering the university.

Back then such an event was new and shocking. In the days that followed professors and doctors condemned the brutality of the police and described what happened as a crime. It was the first time such a thing had happened at the University. The name of the dead student was Ahmad al Quarashi. On the morning following his death thousands of students and their professors were joined by citizens from Khartoum in a demonstration around the hospital where his corpse had been kept for autopsy. Later Quarashi was to become a symbol of martyrdom, commemorated by a statue on the path leading to the university's main library. In the immediate aftermath of his death he became the focus for the rising discontent of the population. A great number of people came to his funeral. I made notes on it privately for my diary and, publicly, for the student wall newspaper. After his funeral, I wrote, the mourners went on the rampage in Khartoum, looting, burning and distributing leaflets. In the following days a coalition of political parties and trade union leaders was formed with the intention of toppling the government. The government's response was to crush what they saw as the head of the snake – the University of Khartoum. The university was closed indefinitely. The students were ordered out of their hostels and given tickets home.

I went with a group of them in a university bus on their way to Khartoum railway station to catch the Kassala train. At the gate of the station we found a platoon of armed soldiers. They ordered us off the car and frisked us. Then they began searching through the luggage. They found a wad of leaflets instigating people to rise against the government. The owner of the suitcase did not talk. And we all kept silent. So we were all arrested. At the time I was, privately, of the view that the owner of the suitcase should have owned up to save the rest of us. Later I came to realise that this was naive, a countryman's way of thinking. City people, I found out, more politically astute, did not think that way.

After our arrest we were driven to the police headquarters at the Ministry of the Interior on the bank of the Blue Nile. Here we were kept in a barbed wire enclosure with the only shade a single, emaciated *neem* tree. In in our barbed-wire *zariba* we were hit by a late season October rain. The miasma issuing from the sun-baked ground made me sick. I spent days retching and vomiting. But a fellow-prisoner of ours, Abdallahi al Amir, an army officer who had been imprisoned because of his opposition to military rule, had a radio. So we were able to hear the welcome news when General Abboud, in a speech on Radio Omdurman, declared that he was relinquishing power to the people. Following his announcement we were released together with all other political detainees.

But the leaders of the popular uprising did not trust General Abboud. They felt that the government was stalling in its declared intent of handing power back to the people. After a meeting at the University Staff Club they organised a procession to protest the delay and put further pressure on the military authorities, starting from the university and aiming to march along Jama'a Avenue westwards towards the Presidential Palace. It was Wednesday 3 November, 1964. On this day the true nature of the Abboud regime was to be revealed. It was the day I lost any political innocence I had possessed.

I marched at the centre of the procession. I was wearing my smartest clothes: a pair of white twill trousers, a cream-coloured nylon shirt and a new pair of shoes, a gift from some friends in Port Sudan. The procession, carrying banners and shouting slogans demanding freedom and democracy, proceeded along Jama'a Avenue to the Presidential Palace. On our right was the big brown-stone cathedral; on our left the last building on the street before the square – then called Palace Gardens. As we reached Palace Gardens, suddenly there was a burst of machine-gun fire, echoed and amplified by the buildings around. Volleys of bullets ripped into the heart of the mass of unarmed people. There was no warning, no tear gas, no beating with clubs or batons, just bullets. The shouting of slogans gave way to the sound of feet as the crowd fled, running for their lives. True to my nomadic upbringing I did not flee, but took cover, lying low on the steaming tarmac under the noontime sun. When the shooting stopped I raised my head slightly. I saw red stains on the tarmac. And bodies and fallen banners. Shoes lay scattered across the road. I began to stand, but heard a curt warning from a short distance behind me:

"Stay where you are!"

I turned my face towards the source of the command, with my cheek pressed to the tarmac, and saw soldiers taking cover behind the parapet surrounding the new Ministry of Commerce. I was staring directly into the snouts of their machine guns, straight down the barrels. I realised with shock that the government troops had fired on us from behind.

They are criminals, I kept telling myself. Lying on the hot asphalt, I counted the dead and dying around me. There were twelve that I could see. One was touching my feet. There was dirt on his shirt and his black sandals. He groaned and settled on his face. A rumbling sound came from his chest. Then nothing. I stood up and realised that I was bare-footed. Fleeing feet had knocked off my new shoes. I spotted one of the shoes and was looking for the other when I heard a voice whisper "Please help me". A young man was lying near me. He could not walk. His thigh bone had been crushed. His trousers were soaked in blood. He asked me to take off his shirt and tie it on the thigh above the wound. As I passed the shirt underneath his leg I felt heat coming from the tarmac and saw a pool of blood spreading beneath him. I put the tourniquet round the young man's thigh, but nothing could staunch the flow. His blood lay clotting on the tarmac.

I found my missing shoe and walked up to an army officer. He was standing in his neat khaki costume with glittering pips on his shoulders.

"Are you okay?," he said, with an odd air.

"Yes sir," I said.

Startled, he looked me over and then asked, "Are you sure? You are drenched in blood like that and you are okay?" he said.

I saw that my white clothes were no longer white. I looked like a slaughtered ram.

I thought he would arrest me, but instead the officer bade me go. I have no idea why. I walked away like a man in trance, back along the sidewalk of Gamaa Avenue. A platoon of army soldiers was blocking the avenue, unaware of my presence. I sauntered past them as if I were window shopping.

The sergeant saw me.

On his cheeks he bore the horizontal triple scars of the Shaygiya, the marks of the people who live on the Nile south of Nubia, where my ancestors had passed on their way to the Jaaliyin lands.

"You're not running?" said the sergeant with a sneer.

I looked at him in disdain and continued walking.

I heard the sergeant give an order.

"Shoot him!" he said.

I looked back over my shoulder and saw the nearest soldier raise his gun to aim. I looked into the muzzle of his gun, then I turned away.

Then I heard the sergeant say "Oh, let him go."

As I walked on towards the staff club, taking my life in my hands, I was seized by the knowledge that, civilians as we were, we had fallen into an ambush. We had been attacked from behind by the forces of the state. Twelve innocent men cut down by army gunfire. Back home in Shehateib the death of a single man by the sword was an event that might be discussed for a lifetime. His killer would be known. There, death always had a reason. But here, for the first time in my life, I saw men dying *en masse*, defenceless, for no reason at all. I had my first taste of what the military mentality, armed with a wealth of weapons, is capable of when it decides to bare its teeth. My limbs were stained with the blood of those I would never know.

The people of Sudan, I knew from my study of the past – and from my knowledge of my own family history – had been subject to generations of violence, both from within and from without. Turks and Europeans introduced the weapons that had killed my student colleagues. And the colonists had been as violent as any Sudanese. But even Lord Kitchener gave warning before he applied his death machine. Now Sudanese soldiers acting at the behest of an unelected leader, a military figure who had seized control of the state, who had come to power on the back of a tank, against the popular will, had not hesitated to shoot down their fellow-citizens. Morally speaking, what was the difference between General Abboud and a colonizer like Kitchener? There was none. I knew then, more certainly than ever, that it would only be when the men and women of my country were able to choose for themselves who should rule them that we would achieve true independence. Only then would Sudanese really be free.

Glossary, gazetteer & biographical notes

'Ard-el-Hajar	"Land of rocks", ancestral home in Nubia of Hamid Dirar's paternal ancestors
ab-koo-koo	*Tockus erythrorhynchus*, the red-billed hornbill
Abboud	General Ibrahim Abboud, head of state of the Republic of Sudan from 1958 to 1964
Abdallah wad Saad	tribal leader of the Jaaliyin people in the late nineteenth century
abdaraga	cobra ("shielded creature")
abid (*abeed*)	slave(s)
absot	giant skate (fish)
abouy	father
abu-dulleil	clouds that cast a shadow
aghlaf	uncircumcised
ahlan	Welcome (greeting)
Ahmed Dirar	a *feki*, carpenter and nomadic livestock keeper of Nubian (Mahas) and Jaali descent (d.1983), father of Hamid Dirar

GLOSSARY, GAZETTEER & BIOGRAPHICAL NOTES

Ahmed el Mirghani	Sayed Ahmed el Mirghani, leader of the Khatmiya, Islamic order to which most Shukriya belong
Aishab	section of the Shukriya tribe
ajwa	soft dates
Al iriq dassas	"Ancestry (lineage) conceals surprises", proverb invoked by Diya Duman
algarmassis	type of cloth included in bridal trousseau
Ali Dirar	father of Ahmed Dirar; paternal grandfather of Hamid Dirar
alkhumri	type of cloth included in bridal trousseau
Allah u-Akbar	"God is great" – religious exclamation
Alsheett wajaa algananeett	"Alas! Pain in the ass!" – name of a cloth of a particular pattern, worn by women
amar	fermented ink
amab	[Beja / Bedawiyet] *Tamarix aphylla*, the athel tree
Amna Duman	mother of Hamid Dirar and daughter of Ghaniya Duman
Andala	one of the settlements of the Diweihin tribe
angareib	wood-frame bed made with woven strips of hide; also name for the Big Dipper star grouping (or the constellation of which it is part, Ursa Major, the Great Bear)
Annour Duman	sheikh of Khashm el Girba (d. 1995), Hamid Dirar's maternal uncle
Araki (aragi)	distilled alcohol – in Sudan usually made from dates
arrib	to circumcise ("arabise") a male
as-shab	breed of racing camel
Asha Dirar	half-sister of Hamid Dirar, who died after a beating at the hands of their father

GLOSSARY, GAZETTEER & BIOGRAPHICAL NOTES

askari	[Swahili] guard (see also *muhafiz*)
Assayga, wassla	"What keeps walking will reach its destination" (proverb)
Asubri	settlement on the west bank of the Atbara River (meaning, "Be patient, woman"), dwelling place of Sheikh Umara Abu Sin, leader of the Shukriya
Atalmula	maternal kinsman of Hamid Dirar
Atbara River	tributary of the Nile flowing from Ethiopia; in the Kassala area, forms a frontier between Arab communities on the west bank and Hadendowa on the east; joins the Nile at Atbara town
attab	locust at the wingless juvenile "hopper" stage
Awad El Karim Abu Sin	*nazir* of the Shukriya Arabs
Baggara	cattle-keeping Arabs
Bakhrat (bakhra)	ritual purification by smoke from burning slips of paper bearing texts from the Qur'an, generally mixed with ambergris or frankincense
baniga	small triangular, dark coloured cloth pieces sewn into a man's garment at knee level.
barashot	smuggling expedition (from English "parachute")
basinkob	[Beja / Bedawiyet] rebab (Ar. *rababa*), a stringed instrument played with a bow
Bayuda Desert	desert in the bend of the Nile, south of Nubia, north of Shendi
Bedawi (Bedawiyet, Bejawiya)	Beja / Bedawiyet language, as spoken by the Hadendowa
Beshir Dirar	paternal cousin of Hamid Dirar
bilbil	throwing stick
bit	daughter

GLOSSARY, GAZETTEER & BIOGRAPHICAL NOTES

Bit Annour	aunt of Hamid Dirar, mother of Ahmed Dirar's first wife
Bit Burbur	wife of Feki Umhammad wad Beshir
Blue Bridge	old bridge across the Atbara River
bongo	cannabis
bugja	carrying bundle
Butana	region of grassland and woodland savannah bordered by the Nile, the Atbara River and the Blue Nile – including most of Gedaref state and part of Kassala – a seasonal grazing ground for pastoralists
dabalan	fine white cotton cloth
Dahmashi	Feki Dahmashi, a religious teacher in Ghureiba, Nubia, mentor – and later father-in-law – of Dirar, ancestor of Hamid Dirar
dammouriya (*dammoriya, dumuria*)	all-purpose, loosely woven, cotton calico cloth
Daw	son of Shawish Yousif
derissa	railway maintenance crew
dharb-el-sot	dance in which young herdsmen whip each other till they bleed
dharira	perfume used for ritual purposes, made of pulverised sandal wood, cloves and the stones of *Prunus mahaleb*
dhiha	late morning
dhuhur	late afternoon
dibliba	dumpling made with sorghum flour
digniya	"chin-tax" imposed on humans and domestic animals by Turko-Egyptian rulers

GLOSSARY, GAZETTEER & BIOGRAPHICAL NOTES

dilka	mildly abrasive material made from sorghum, imbued with smoke and perfume, used to cleanse bodies of bride and groom before wedding
Diweihin	cattle-keeping people in the Butana, originally from Kordofan
diya	blood money, a payment under customary law to settle disputes over injury or death
Diya	cognomen of Hamid Dirar's great-grandmother, Diya Duman
dom	*Hyphaene thebaica*, species of palm with edible oval fruit
effendi (pl. *effendiya*)	Turko-Egyptian word for school-educated government official, member of local elite in Egypt and colonial and post-independence Sudan
eima	craving for milk
Fashaga	region on the Sudanese-Ethiopian border
Fatima	daughter of Ahmed Dirar, half-sister of Hamid Dirar
feki	religious teacher and healer
ferig	nomad encampment
ferwa	sheepskin sling for carrying load
feterita	sorghum grain
firaya	leather covering for camel's withers
fitga	coarse cotton apparel
gadah	wooden bowl
garaa	half-gourd
gariss	fermented camel's milk
Gash River	seasonal river rising in Eritrea and flowing northwards through Kassala (aka Mareb River)
gatifa	livestock pledged to a religious leader

GLOSSARY, GAZETTEER & BIOGRAPHICAL NOTES

Gedaref (El-Gedaref)	city to the south of Kassala
gemiss	overgarment worn by men
ghaba	gallery forest along a river
Ghaniya Bit el Tom	wife and cousin of Omar Duman, daughter of El Tom Wad Diriss, mother of Amna, and grandmother of Hamid Dirar
ghaniya	woman singer
Ghureiba	village near Korti at the western bend of the Nile
girba	waterskin
git	wild cat
gogai	doves
Gordon, Charles	Major-General Charles Gordon, a British army officer who was Governor-General of Sudan under the Turko-Egyptian regime, killed by Mahdists in Khartoum in 1885
goz	area of sandy soil
guddeim	*Grewia tenax*, a fruit-bearing tree
gurbab	wrap-around cloth worn by women
gutran	extract from wild melon traditionally used to treat skin diseases in sheep and goats
guttiya	hut, small building
habboba-booli	"Grandma, urinate", name of a cloth of a specific pattern
habbobti (haboba, habboba)	("beloved") grandma, grandmother – also term of respect for great-aunt
Hadab	Sheikh Hadab, leader of the Kalolai Hadendowa
Haddafa	a demon, "the Thrower"
Hadendowa	subdivision of the Beja people, large non-Arab group in Eastern Sudan, living on the east bank of the Atbara River

GLOSSARY, GAZETTEER & BIOGRAPHICAL NOTES

hafir	small rain-fed reservoir
Hajiz	location of railway station
Hajwa	maternal relative of Hamid Dirar
hakla	wrestling move in which an opponent is tripped up
Halfawiyin	an Arab tribe
Halima	Halima Bit al Tom, Hamid Dirar's maternal great-aunt
Hanadi Elnour	daughter of Annour Duman, wife of Hamid Dirar and Muhammad Duman, mother of his childen
hanon	cattle taken to distant grazing grounds, while others (*homah*) are kept at the home encampment
hantout	*Ipomoea belpharosepla*, annual fodder shrub of the clay plains
Hardalu (Hardalo, Hardalloo)	Muhammad Ahmad Hardallo (1830–1917) Shukriya poet in the time of the Mahdi
heeb-heeb	sword dance of young warriors
hijab	amulet
hijlij (heglig)	*Balanites aegyptiaca*, thorn tree native to the savanna regions of the Sahel
Hijri	Islamic calendar
hilbateeb	goat-skin bag
hiliss	cotton mattress, part of camel saddle
himar-el-hadid	bicycle ("iron donkey")
hiram	woollen plaid cloth
homah	cattle kept at the home encampment while others (*hanon*) are taken to distant grazing grounds
hosh	household compound
humbuk	*Capparis decidua*

GLOSSARY, GAZETTEER & BIOGRAPHICAL NOTES

hugga	canister for tobacco
humar Rifawi	Rifawi donkey, white Egyptian donkey
Humara	border region between Sudan and Ethiopia
Humran	Arab pastoralist tribe with centre at Seiteet
hur	free-born child
hurrara	sacrifice of livestock following birth of a free-born child
Ibrahim Dirar	brother of Hamid Dirar
ibrig	water jug used for ablutions
igalaba	[Beja/Bedawiyet] hyena
Ismail Pasha	Ismail Kamil Pasha, the third son of Khedive Muhammad Ali Pasha, ruler of Egypt, killed at Shendi by forces of Mek Nimir
istiraha	government rest-house or residence
Jaali-ab-khurtaya	"Jaali wearing a bag", pejorative term for *jellabia*-wearing Jaali man
Jaaliyin, Jaalin (sing. Jaali)	one of the major riverain Arab tribes of Sudan tracing their origin to Ibrahim Ja'al, a descendant of al-Abbas, an uncle of the Prophet Muhammad
Jawamiss	subsection of the Lahawin Arab people
Jellabiya, jellabia	ground-length garment worn by men among riverain people in Sudan
Jummeiza	nomad camp on west bank of Atbara River near Khashm el Girba
jurab	bag or container made of leather
kabbour	drum made of a half-gourd
kafir	pejorative term for non-Muslim
kala-azar	visceral leishmaniasis
karab	eroded, undulating land-forms along the banks of the Atbara River, site of dry season nomad camps

GLOSSARY, GAZETTEER & BIOGRAPHICAL NOTES

Karim	friend of Ahmed Dirar (d.1986)
Kassala	major town in eastern Sudan on banks of seasonal Gash River, centre of the Khatmiyya religious brotherhood
keena	quinine
Ketira	daughter of Bit Burbur, friend of Hamid Dirar's half-sister Fatima
khadim	person of slave ancestry
khali	maternal uncle
Khalid Dirar	paternal relative of Hamid Dirar
khalifa	caliph, religious steward
khalifa	religious leader in an Islamic brotherhood
khalti	maternal aunt
khalwa	school for teaching the Qur'an
Khashm el Girba	town on Atbara River and name of a dam built there in 1964
Khatmiya	*tariqa* (religious brotherhood or sect) with headquarters in Kassala
kherif	rainy season, from July to October
Khidir	son of Shawish Yousif, brother of Daw
khinzeer	pig meat, pork
Khireissab (Wadi el Khireissab)	nomad camp on west bank of Atbara River
khor	seasonal watercourse
Khor el Jurab	"Leather-bag Creek"
khulla	mosquito net protecting new mother and infant
Kibeirizzan	the Timber Bridge, carrying the railway across the Atbara River
Kimaleib	cattle-owning Hadendowa subtribe

315

GLOSSARY, GAZETTEER & BIOGRAPHICAL NOTES

kisra	flat bread, usually made from sorghum or millet
kitir	*Acacia mellifera*, wait-a-bit thorn
Lahawin	Arab camel pastoralists of the Butana
Locust Control Campaign	international organization established to coordinate control of locusts in affected parts of Africa
loh	wooden board used to write verses from the Qur'an
mabruk	expression of congratulation
mahajra	camel thieves
mahaleb	*Prunus mahaleb*, a species of cherry tree cultivated for an almond-like spice from the seeds within its stones
Mahas	one of the peoples of Nubia
Mahdi	Muhammad Ahmad, the Mahdi (religious and political leader, 1844-1885)
Mahmoud wad Ahmed	commander of Mahdist army, late nineteenth century
Maigulu	dog belonging to Hamid Dirar
Majar el Kebish	the Milky Way ("Track of the Dragged Ram")
majlukha	folding razor
malageet	foundlings (non-Shukriya families under the protection of Sheikh Umara Abu Sin)
marafin	hyena
marhab	Welcome (greeting)
mawallad	hybrid, mulato
Mek Nimir	leader of Jaaliyin people in Shendi in mid-nineteenth century
Melka Tajuj	first wife of Ahmed Dirar and daughter of Bit Annour.

GLOSSARY, GAZETTEER & BIOGRAPHICAL NOTES

mentaga	area officer in Locust Control Campaign
merikh	*Leptadaenia pyrotechnica*, a desert herb of the family Asclepiadaceae
Metamma	name of a Jaali town across River Nile from Shendi and of a town in Ethiopia established by Jaaliyin fleeing the Turko-Egyptian invasion
mihajri	camel thief
mihayah	ritual treatment involving drinking water that has been used to wash a slate bearing verses of the Qur'an
Mirmidayeb	Kimeilab Hadendowa camp on east bank of Atbara River
morah	species of gazelle
Muezzin (*muezzin, muazin*)	one who leads the call to prayer
mughrib	sunset
muhafiz (pl. *muhafizin*)	guard, askari, policeman, member of local militia
Muhammad Ali Pasha	Khedive Muhammad Ali Pasha al Masud ibn Aga, Ottoman Albanian military commander and self-declared Khedive of Egypt and Sudan
Muhammad Bey	the Difterdar (Finance Minister of Ottoman Egypt in the early nineteenth century), son-in-law of Khedive Muhammad Ali Pasha and brother-in-law of Ismail Pasha
mulah	stew or porridge
murhaka	millstones
Mushaf	Holy Book (a term for the Qur'an)
Muslim Brotherhood	Islamist movement
nabak	*Ziziphus spina-christi*, Jujube tree, Christ's Thorn, sidir

GLOSSARY, GAZETTEER & BIOGRAPHICAL NOTES

Nasara (*Nasraniya*)	Europeans ("Nazarenes")
Nawayma	branch of the Shukriya tribe
nazir	tribal leader
neem	*Azadirachta indica*, tree of the mahogany family native to India
nihar	noontime
nimitti	*Cladotanytarsus lewisi*, chironomid midges
Nuba Mountains	region in southern Korodfan, homeland of Nuba peoples
Nubia	historical region in what is now northern Sudan and southern Egypt (Hamid Dirar's ancestral home)
Omar Duman (Omar wad Duman)	Diya Duman's elder son (d.1987)
omra	milking pail, made from palm leaves
Omdurman	one of the three cities – Omdurman, Khartoum and Khartoum North – at the confluence of the White Nile and the Blue Nile
Piankhi (Piye)	Kushite king and founder of the 25th dynasty of Egypt; ruled Egypt from Napata in Nubia 744-714 BCE
Port Sudan	major port city on Sudan's Red Sea Coast
rababa	rebab, a stringed instrument
Rahmatat	annual festival to appease the spirits of the dead
Rajab	second husband of Amna Duman, stepfather of Hamid Dirar and father of Hamid's half-brother, Jabir (d. 1998)
rakuba	open-sided, grass-roofed shelter
rewina	species of gazelle
Reirit	one of the wives of Ahmed Dirar, father of Hamid Dirar

GLOSSARY, GAZETTEER & BIOGRAPHICAL NOTES

rushash	early rainy season
sabah	early morning
sagiya	ox-driven wooden water-wheel
sagriya	eagle dance
sakubeiss	thin white muslin cloth
salat	[Beja / Bedawiyet] hot-stone barbequed lamb
samur	*Acacia ehrenbergiana*, a thorny shrub
Sanat el Far	"Year of Rats"
Sanat el Ganabil	"Year of Bombs", 1940, when Italian warplanes dropped bombs in areas of Sudan close to the Ethiopian border
Sanat el Sindica	"Year of the Syndicate" (organisation for food distribution), the famine year 1948
Sanat Sitta	"Year Six", the famine year 1889 (1306 in the Islamic hijri calendar)
sarob	*Capparis decidua*, a thorny shrub
sayal, seyal	*Acacia seyal*, red-bark acacia
seif-assagaa	"Thunderbolt sword", a mythical sword so sharp no scabbard could hold it
Seiteet	region on the border between Sudan and Ethiopia
serba	night-grazing of sheep
serir	sleeping platform
Shabaka	Nubian monarch, pharaoh of the 25th Egyptian dynasty, ruled 705-690 BCE
shambora	penis
shamla	plaid blanket of goat hair
Shangil Bangil	settlement beyond the Blue Bridge, on the east bank of the Atbara River
Sharafa	nomad camp on west bank of Atbara River

GLOSSARY, GAZETTEER & BIOGRAPHICAL NOTES

Shawish Yousif	husband of Halima Bit el Tom, Hamid Dirar's maternal great-aunt (the aunt of Amna Duman), d. 1979
shayom	camel race
sheg el oud	early rainy season
Shehateib	nomad camp on the east bank of the Atbara River, close to the Blue Bridge, near Khashm el Girba
shen-shen	*Camponotus consobrinus*, sugar ant
Shendi	town on Nile, north of Khartoum, heartland of Jaaliyin people
shibriya	superstructure to protect rider on a camel
Shukriya (sing. Shukri)	Arab group, traditionally pastoralist, living in the Butana between the Atbara River and the Blue Nile
sibhat-al-yassur	necklace of black beads
sideiri (pl. *sideriiya*)	waistcoat
sidir	*Ziziphus spina-christi*, Jujube tree, Christ's Thorn, aka *nabak*
simaya	naming ritual for a child
simbria	*Ciconia nigra*, black stork
simoom	seasonal dry wind from the Sahara
sodal	double-twisted throwing dagger
sunut	*Acacia nilotica*, source of timber used to make waterwheels
surwal	loose cotton trousers
Suwayil	nomad camp on the east bank of the Atbara River
tabanji	hand gun
Taharqa	Nubian monarch, successor to Shabaka, conqueror of Egypt, pharaoh of the 25th dynasty 690–664 BCE

GLOSSARY, GAZETTEER & BIOGRAPHICAL NOTES

tahhar	circumciser
Tajuj	tragic heroine of Sudanese folklore
tarrada	twenty-five piastres, a quarter of a Sudanese pound
teb	water pool
tikka	thin belt
tob	as worn by men, a broad white sheet of cloth slung across the shoulders
tob ushari	*tob* of ten forearms length
tohal	kala-azar, visceral leishmaniasis
Toma	wife of Sheikh Annour (d. 1989)
Toshkan	daughter of Hadab, a Hadendowa sheikh
tuggaba	fire to give light for reading the Qur'an
tumam	*Panicum turgidum*, desert bunchgrass
Turkiyya	Turko-Egyptian period, rule of the khedivate of Egypt over northern Sudan from 1820 to 1885
tweili	Persian caracul sheepskin
ujman	pejorative term for non-Arab people
Um Dubban	Islamic studies centre in Khartoum (literally "place of many flies", in reference to the abundance of followers and food, implying generosity of its guardian sheikhs)
Um-simeigha	insect-borne ulcerous infection of the mouth
umajjanna	*Linaria cannabina*, linnet
Umara wad Umhummad wad Hamad wad Abu Sin	sheikh of the Shukriya people during the Mahdist and colonial periods
Umhammad wad Beshir	prominent *feki* (religious leader) from the Humran Arab tribe, betrothed before his death to Amna, future mother of Hamid Dirar

GLOSSARY, GAZETTEER & BIOGRAPHICAL NOTES

Umhummad Zein	poet of the Lahawin ethnic group
usher	Sodom apple, *Calotropis procera*
utfa	superstructure to protect rider on a camel
wad	son of
Wad Zayid	leader of the Dhabanya ethnic group in the Gedaref area
Wadi el Khireissab	settlement on the west bank of the Atbara River
washasha	rattlesnake
wirda um berid	malaria
Yaru	one of Sheikh Yousif's police, of West African descent
Zaghruta (pl. *zagharid*)	cry that proclaims birth of a male child
Zaki	son of Umhammad wad Beshir and Bit Burbur (d.2002)
zariba	fortified enclosure
Zayda bit Faraj	celebrated *ghaniya* (woman singer)
Zeena Duman	maternal cousin of Hamid Dirar
Zeinab Berberi	wife of Hamid Dirar's brother, Ibrahim
Zeinab	niece of Sheikh Annour, maternal relative of Hamid Dirar
Zibeidiya	an Arab tribe
zihba	clothing bought for a bride by her husband-to-be
zumam	nose-stud

Also published by City of Words

Letters from Isohe
Life on the edge in a school in South Sudan
BY ELIZABETH HODGKIN

After the independence of South Sudan Elizabeth Hodgkin, a historian and human rights researcher, taught in a remote village in the Dongotono Mountains. Her letters home – joyful, comic and terrifying by turns – portray a world where rainmakers, grandmothers, gunmen, teachers and priests strive to live from day to day, and young people yearn for education to guide them in world of danger.

ISBN 978-1-9160783-2-1

Also published by City of Words

Out of Our Hands
Encounters with the craftsmen and craftswomen of Hokkaido
BY WILLIE JONES

A personal account of the craftsmen and craftswomen of Japan's wildest island, drawing on years of conversations with swordsmiths, potters, painters, glass-blowers, weavers, dyers, etchers and wood-carvers, and describing with lyrical precision their lifelong dedication to their craft.

ISBN 978-1-9160783-3-8

Printed in Great Britain
by Amazon